NEVER WARS

THE US WAR PLANS TO INVADE THE WORLD

NEVER WARS

THE US WAR PLANS TO INVADE THE WORLD

BLAINE L. PARDOE

FONTHILL

Fonthill Media Language Policy

Fonthill Media publishes in the international English language market. One language edition is published worldwide. As there are minor differences in spelling and presentation, especially with regard to American English and British English, a policy is necessary to define which form of English to use. The Fonthill Policy is to use the form of English native to the author. Blaine Pardoe was born and educated in the United States and currently resides in Amissville, VA, therefore American English has been adopted in this publication.

Fonthill Media Limited
Fonthill Media LLC
www.fonthillmedia.com
office@fonthillmedia.com

First published in the United Kingdom and
the United States of America 2014

British Library Cataloguing in Publication Data:
A catalogue record for this book is available from the British Library

Copyright © Blaine L. Pardoe 2014

ISBN 978-1-78155-293-3

The right of Blaine L. Pardoe to be identified as the author of this work has been asserted by him in accordance with the Copyright, Designs and Patents Act 1988.

Typeset in 10pt on 13pt Sabon LT Std
Printed and bound in England

Contents

Dedication

This book details contemplated wars that the United States might find itself in during the early twentieth century. This is *not* a work of alternate history. These plans were real and, if necessary, would have been dusted off if they needed to be executed.

At the same time it is the works of several authors of the alternate history genre which inspired me to do this research as a piece of military history. This was one of those weird cases where fiction inspired true historical research. You have to remember that some of the better authors of alternate history have degrees or strong backgrounds in history as well. They are simply bold enough to straddle the ground between fiction and nonfiction.

For the record, I love alternate history books. They make you think outside of the box in terms of historical assumptions (and facts). They are stimulating.

To salute the men who gave me inspiration—I dedicate this book to the following:

Harry Turtledove and Robert Conroy

Thank you for many hours of entertainment gentlemen!

Blaine Pardoe

Acknowledgements

The war plans all utilize a color coding scheme to describe the potential opponents. In most of these situations, the United States is assumed to be Blue. There are some variations of this, which I have not covered in this book, for example War Plan White which deals with the US military response to a domestic uprising or riot situations. But for the most part, this book will refer to the US as Blue when documents are directly quoted. The other colors that are applied in this book are as follows:

Color	Nation
Crimson	Canada
Red	The United Kingdom
Gray	The Azores—technically part of Portugal
Green	Mexico
Yellow	Pre-modern day China
Tan	Cuba
Scarlet	Australia
Orange	Japan
Black	Germany

It is important to note that the plans that are presented in this book are not the complete materials that are available.

Spelling of cities, provinces, islands, etc., in the War Plans tends to be inconsistent in the War Plans. Spell-check simply did not exist in typewritten reports, and the nuances of geographic names has evolved over the decades. In War Plan Black, Puerto Rico is often spelled as Porto Rico. In War Plan Green, Veracruz is sometimes listed as Vera Cruz. In War Plan Yellow, Peiping is a reference to Peking, which is also referred to as Nanking, depending on who the author is. When quoted, I have maintained the spelling as it appears in the War Plans.

There are a number of people I need to thank for their assistance on this project. Evelyn Cherpak at the Library of the Naval War College and Ken Schlessinger, at the US National Archives both deserve call-outs for their aide in my search for copies of the War Plans. Thank you for your patience and help.

And finally, thanks to the team at Fonthill Media who understand the historical value and entertainment of this kind of project.

Introduction

Almost a half-decade ago I began work on another book, *The Fires of October* (Fonthill Media 2013), about the planned invasion of Cuba during the Cuban Missile Crisis of 1962. This was my first real in-depth exposure to military planning. It was also my first real deep-dive into evaluating military campaigns that had never taken place.

This missile crisis was such a public event, one filled with tension, terror, and the real threat of the US and the USSR going to war, initially on the tiny Caribbean island, that there was public interest in those plans. People wanted to know what the invasion would have looked like, how it would have unfolded, and what the targets of the military operation were. Oddly enough it was an unexplored aspect to the missile crisis, barely a footnote in many books. Yet, as I learned when I spoke at the US Naval Academy at the 2013 McMullen Symposium, it was as topic of keen interest. It seemed that people were interested in never-implemented war plans.

I began to realize that there was a new genre that was emerging with the release of my book, and the fantastic book by Edward Miller—*War Plan Orange* ... that genre of military planning. In the case of Miller's book, the plans were eventually adopted in the war against Japan in WWII. Still, in reading the book you become entranced with the evolution of the plan over the years and the shift of targets and objectives. For me, what mattered the most was the detail of the plans themselves.

As it turns out the United States had a plethora of military plans, starting around 1903, for waging war all over the globe. These plans were color coded, with a different color for each nation. Many seem almost the work of fantasy—such as the US going to war against Britain and Japan who would somehow become allies. Others were more down to earth, such as the US plans to invade Mexico, a reinvasion of the Philippines, or even China. All were the product of the early twentieth-century thinking, and many never took into account the surges of technology that altered the face of warfare during that period. The idea of mounted cavalry riding into Canada to conduct raids, for example, seems far-fetched by today's military thinking ... even worse in the face of machinegun fire. Yet at the time it was serious and complicated work to plan such attacks around the globe.

Based on the reaction to my book on the planned invasion of Cuba, my publisher was enthusiastic for me to tackle this project—evaluating some of the war plans the US created for attacking the rest of the globe.

Why would people care about old, unused military plans? Those plans, however antiquated, offer a glimpse into US foreign policy and perceived threats/opportunities. Also, no matter how old and seemingly obsolete these plans may be, such planning continues on today. They are fertile study material for understanding both strategy and tactics.

The plans were <u>not</u> used for training purposes with the Naval War College or West Point. The involvement of these two schools was primarily because the staff of these institutions were seen as the best and brightest in US military planning circles. Students were rarely exposed to the war plans except as aides, as was the case in the version of War Plan Black presented in this book. I discovered references to these plans being stored in safes aboard battleships and in specific offices. These were not simulations of war—these were considered to be contingency plans for actual military operations, adding to their historical value.

Readers and historians should not be so quick to disregard these plans. If situations had been different, there is little doubt that these plans could and would have served as the basis for US military operations around the globe. While the plans seem obsolete, they represent a great view into American foreign and military policy and how it regarded other nations and the threats that they posed.

Another motivation for me to undertake this book is personal. I am an old-school wargamer and realized the value of these plans almost instantly. These plans could be utilized by a number of armchair historians to craft boardgames/military simulations to actually play out these wars. This kind of material provides gamers with the ultimate "what if?" scenarios without the burden of rules that dealt with real-life situations.

Understanding how the US military planned for war offers some context into current planning and into why historical events unfolded the way we did. This is a field of study that historians are only now seeking to explore. Most that go down this path now are channeled into the field of "alternate history," where the study of plans like these were a part of history that were simply never executed. Both of these sub-fields offer a wealth of interest and possibilities.

That wasn't to say that this project was easy—because it was far from it. Locating the war plans alone proved difficult. Many were destroyed in a purge of these plans in 1941. Each individual copy that had been typed was supposedly tracked down and supposedly destroyed. Perhaps with the threat of real war looming around the world there was a sense that if any of the old plans were ever disclosed, it might severely limit potential allies.

Thankfully military and government bureaucracies are fallible, and as a result I was able to track down, in part or in full, many of the plans I went looking for. This was in spite of orders, some officers, usually senior (like the Chief of Naval Operations) opted to ignore their own mandates for destruction. In the cases where I was not able to find a complete copy of the plan, I was able to find supporting correspondence about specific parts of the plans which allowed me to reconstruct the essential elements of the plan. This was not an easy task, and does result in some gaps, but overall some of the plans were easy to rebuild in this manner.

Selecting which plans to include in the book was difficult as well. For example, I located three different copies of War Plan Green (the invasion of Mexico), so which one to use—if any? I would like to tell you that there was some complicated and scientific process I used to make these choices. There wasn't. Often times earlier versions of the plans were much more interesting than the alleged "final" editions. I reviewed all of them and picked the ones that I found to be the most interesting and revealing.

Another challenge I faced was in the editing process. These plans were far from static, they were constantly updated, revised, and changed. There was rarely a "final" version of the plans. Handwritten notes in the margins of some plans also proved to be a challenge. So where would I draw the line? If I only documented what I believed to be the final version of the plan, I often missed some of the nuances which made them interesting and worthy of study. I had to determine, on a plan-by-plan basis, what was the best approach for dealing with this. In at least one case, I have addressed multiple versions of the plan to show the shift in strategic thinking that the US underwent. Suffice it to say this approach leaves fertile ground for future historians to crawl through this material and add to it.

Maps proved challenging as well. In those rare cases where I was able to locate the plans, I often discovered that the maps were not included with the archival copies. Where possible, I have included the maps I was able to locate. Locating the appropriate supporting maps provide to be a search exercise all on its own.

The final hurdle I had was that the war plans were not stored in one archives, but were scattered about the country. I had the pleasure of working with the US Navy Historical Command, the Navy War College, and the US National Archives in pursuit of these plans. Everyone had a part of proverbial puzzle which left me to assemble them into something cohesive.

What I did *not* research was the intelligence services of our allies and former enemies to see if any of them ever obtained a copy of these plans or had an awareness of them. While it would be intriguing to see their potential reaction ... or better, counter plans for the invasion of the US; it was simply too much to take on for this book.

The order that these plans have been presented was another challenge. I opted to start with America's closest neighbors and then fan out. Once outside of the United States sphere of influence, I enjoyed a little bit of creative freedom. To me, the last two plans in the book, War Plan Black (Germany) and War Plan Red (Great Britain) were the ones that people would be the most interested and fascinated in.

For now, I offer you a glimpse of America's view of the world in the early twentieth century—a world filled with potential foes, a world that lay poised to go to war with her, and be defeated by her....

Military Planning in the US Undergoes a Metamorphosis

Introduction

The United States has had a long history of joint Navy and Army operations in its history. General George Washington's victory over the British at Yorktown was only made possible with a blockade by the French Navy. During the War of 1812, the naval operations on Lake Champlain were critical to the success of the ground campaigns.

The true emergence of the need for coordinated naval and army coordination took place during the American Civil War. The capture of Forts Henry and Donelson on the Tennessee and Cumberland rivers were the direct result of cooperation and coordination by the army and naval (riverine) forces were instrumental in the Federal forces seizing the forts. The battle of Shiloh was directly influenced by the arrival of naval transports loaded with reinforcements. Likewise, General Ulysses S. Grant's Vicksburg campaign was directly tied to the cooperative leveraging of Admiral David Porter's naval resources ... as was the successful assault on Fort Fisher in South Carolina in 1864-1865.[1] Indeed, the overall Federal Anaconda strategy of blockading the Confederacy to allow for the eventual overall success of the Union armies required an even broader strategic level of coordination which led to eventual victory. Given the string of successes, one might think that the United States had a long standing history of successful planning of joint operations.

While these operations were successful, they were victories borne on the shoulders of the men that led them rather than a military history of true joint operations, cooperation and planning. It was the force of the personalities of the men involved that allowed for the coordination, as opposed to operating under a true joint operational command where one man had direct control of the resources both on the ground and in the water, to ensure victory. More often than not, the Army took the lead in planning the larger operations, asking for the coordination of the Navy. While this informal and undocumented system of command worked, it was fragile and subject to the egos and personalities of the men involved.

That frailty was tested again during the Spanish-American War in 1898. Between 1865 and 1898 the military forces of the United States had slowly withered, the victim of cuts in military spending and an isolationist sentiment on the home front. While the US had introduced stunning innovations in technology, such as the USS *Monitor*'s rotating turret, the use of a balloon for reconnaissance, repeating arms, and rapid fire Gatling-guns; these innovations did not lead to a reformation of the United States military machine—it instead was hamstrung.

After the sinking of the USS *Maine*, alleged to be the result of a Spanish naval mine in Havana Harbor, the United States rushed headlong into a modern military campaign with a military that was far from prepared. Not only did this conflict catch the US unprepared materially, the state of combined operations and war planning was nearly non-existent.

America rushed into the Spanish American War with no true coordination infrastructure of Navy and Army assets in place. The Army had no organized way to logistically coordinate the rapid enlistment of volunteers. The Army had been less than 65,000 men and in a matter of weeks had blossomed to over 267,000 men (regular and militia), all needing weapons, tropical clothing, etc. Lacking the plans needed for such an explosion of personnel, the Army floundered and fumbled.

The Army assumed the Navy would have transports ready and waiting for them to get to battle, but those transports were weeks in coming and even then, they were ill-equipped for the landing forces sent to Cuba and eventually the Philippines. During this almost embarrassing logistical debacle, the Spanish forces dug in and were prepared for a costly and bloody engagement. While the United States defeated the Spanish-led forces in Cuba, there was acknowledgement from all parties that the time it took to move the Army forces from Florida to Cuba would have been impractical in a larger conflict.

Once in Cuba, the Army did not avail itself of Navy support because they had never contemplated needing it. This was best exemplified when General William Shafter neglected to request naval gunfire support before attacking the earthworks at Santiago Cuba. Such softening up might have saved hundreds of lives.

In the Pacific Admiral George Dewey sailed from the west coast of the United States aboard the USS *Olympia* and successfully engaged and decimated the antiquated Spanish squadron there at the Battle of Manila Bay on 1 May 1898. While the press hailed the defeat as a resounding American victory, it did not secure the Philippines for America. Shortly after this victory, Dewey cabled Washington DC to request 5,000 troops for him to secure the city. Such a request was an afterthought, the realization that the Navy alone could not fight and win but required boots on the ground. The necessary ground forces did not arrive until August and even then, the Philippines remained a contested island for years. The lack of joint planning was rarely more evident.

As a practice, the United States did not plan for war outside of defense of its own borders. Military planning was reactive and only done when a crisis presented itself. The Army dabbled in some offensive military planning, contemplating the invasion of Canada as early as 1892, though they did not include the Navy in on their hypothetical invasion. Despite the natural obstacles of the Great Lakes, the Navy also experimented in planning with a hostile Canada as well. In 1890 plans were formulated to contemplate potential war with other belligerent nations—namely Great Britain. Given the size of the Royal Navy, the US Navy planned to concentrate its forces at New York to protect the harbor entrances at Sandy Hook and Montauk. Torpedo boats would be stationed at New London and Narragansett Bay to harass any Royal Navy incursions.[2] As a strategy, it was lacking.

Both plans—Army and Navy—saw Great Britain as a foe but saw their own branches as the key to victory rather than any semblance of a joint effort. Both of these plans were more along the lines of simulations than true plans.

Other plans were drafted as well in preparation for war. In 1891 a number of sailors from the USS *Baltimore* got into a bar fight in Valparaiso, Chile, which resulted in two American deaths and three dozen sailors being imprisoned. While the men eventually escaped imprisonment, the US President Benjamin Harrison pressed for sanctions in the form of compensation and a formal apology from the Chilean government. The entire affair became known as The Baltimore Crisis and went from a simple bar fight to bringing the US to the brink of war. Secretary of the Navy, Benjamin Franklin Tracy, began to formulate plans for an invasion of the South American nation.

The plan called for an attack on Iquique—targeting Chile's most valuable export, nitrates. The intention was not just a raid, but to bring aboard Army and Marine troops. While Secretary Tracy engaged the brilliant strategist Captain Alfred Mahan, he neglected to include the Army in his strategy. President Harrison was contemplating asking Congress for a declaration of war when Chile finally acquiesced and agreed to pay indemnity. The plan to invade Chile never was implemented but it further demonstrated the need for the Army and Navy to coordinate their efforts.[3]

It was painfully clear that as the United States emerged onto the global scene, that the old thinking of separate Army and Navy planning had to be reconsidered and changed. A bar fight in Valparaiso Chile was about to change US military planning.

The Emergence of the Joint Board

In 1903 Secretary of War Elihu Root sought to remedy the inefficiencies that had demonstrated themselves during the Spanish American War. He started with a series of sweeping changes that resonate in some ways even today into the US military planning and organization.

During the conflict with Spain, weaknesses had emerged in the Army command structure. The Commanding General Nelson A. Miles and the bureau chiefs did not get along and often were at loggerheads.[4] This was especially true of the Quartermaster Corps which had eventually become a political battle in Congress known as the Army Beef Scandal.

His first step was to abolish the position of Commanding General entirely. In its place was a new command structure centered around a new position—the Chief of Staff. Rather than be a separate command, as the Commanding General post had been, all army staff departments and all army forces would fall directly under command of the Chief of Staff.

Secretary Root also created a General Staff Corps whose responsibility would include planning for the defense of the United States and preparing plans for troop mobilization and assembly. This was modeled after the Prussian Army's approach to military planning, though the US variant was much more scaled back.[5]

While Root's reforms primarily addressed the Army, he also recognized the need to address joint military planning. The solution was the creation of the Joint Army and Navy Board on 17 July 1903 by a joint order from the Secretary of War Root (General Order No. 107) and the Secretary of the Navy William H. Moody (General Order No. 136).[6] The Joint Army and Navy Board was quickly dubbed, "The J.B." and it represented the United States first attempt to combine military planning of the Army and the Navy.

The creation of the J.B. did not immediately solve the issues that were raised during the Spanish American War, but rather was a first step. The charter of the board called for the members with, "conferring upon, discussing, and reaching common conclusions regarding all matters calling for the cooperation of the two services." Cooperation was a vague word and essentially the Joint Board lacked the authority to actually implement any joint plans. In many respects, it was an advisory group of officers.

This lack of teeth, so to speak, hindered the overall effectiveness. The charter denied the Joint Board the ability to operate independently to address joint planning on its own. Instead it could only create plans that were submitted to it by the Secretary of War and the Secretary of the Navy. This limited the scope and reach of the J.B. from the very start. The group was described as "a planning and deliberative body rather than a center of executive authority."[7] Even those plans there were drafted or recommended required both secretaries to approve them as well as the President of the United States.

The Secretary of the Navy and the Secretary of War each appointed four officers to the Joint Board. Officers were named individually, though there was an underlying approach to the staffing. From the Army, the positions were filled by the Chief of Staff, Assistant Chief of Staff, President of the Army War College, and Chief of Artillery. The latter role was changed to the Chief of Coast Artillery in the years between The Great War and World War II. The naval representatives were members of the General Board of the Navy. This group was staffed by the President of the War College, the Director of Naval Intelligence, and the Chief of the Bureau of Navigation. The General Board of the Navy was chaired by a senior admiral, initially by Admiral George Dewey of the Battle of Manila Bay fame.

The Navy's composition changed during the lifetime of the Joint Board. Eventually the role of the Chief of the Bureau of Navigation was replaced in 1909 with the Aide for Operations. This seat was changed again in 1915 with the role of the Chief of Naval Operations.

Both the Army and Navy were required to provide four officers to the Joint Board—drawn from the groups above. The most senior officer would serve as the presiding officer and the most junior officer would act as the recorder.

The Evolution of the Joint Board

The Joint Board had their first meeting on 30 July 1903. The meeting schedule was inconsistent and irregular, usually two-to-three times a year. Between March 1908 and October 1909 no meetings were held. A similar gap occurred between April 1914 and October 1915 when no requests from the secretaries for the Joint Board to execute any planning.

By 1904 the Army and Navy asked that the Joint Board to consider a potential threat from European powers against the long-standing Monroe Doctrine. The scenarios and target nations were not defined, simply that the J.B. should consider potential incursions by hostile nations in the western hemisphere.

Once formed the Joint Board had to address the complexities of what to plan. Brigadier General Tasker Bliss outlined this for the board members in a detailed memorandum in June of 1904:

> ... To confer upon, discuss, and reach common conclusions regarding all matters calling for the cooperation of the two services, And it being its further duty, according to the same order, to make confidential reports to each Department of its conclusions regarding these matters, it is to be assumed that the plans thus jointly studied and agreed upon by the two General Staffs will be submitted to the Board which, after approving them (with or without modification), will submit them to the Secretary of the Navy and the Secretary of War as being plans in the execution of which the two Departments will cooperate in the event that the contingencies for which the plans were prepared should actually be realized.[8]

But what should the Joint Board plan against? What should their methodology be in approaching possible scenarios of war? This was outlined in the same memorandum:

> For this purpose we have to consider, first of all, the probable causes of war. These being assumed, we may safely infer the theatre of war, our probable enemy or combination of enemies, his essential object and our own, the minimum strength and character of the enemy forces necessary for him as the basis of a reasonable hope to attain his object, those necessary for us as the basis of a reasonable hope to defeat his object, and all other conditions which must be assumed and, as far as possible, provided for.
>
> I assume the following to be the most probable causes of wars in which the United States may be involved:
>
> 1) The necessity of the enforcement of the Monroe Doctrine by the United States;
> 2) Efforts for extension of trade;
> 3) Intervention by the United States in the domestic affairs in some insular or continental country lying south of us on this hemisphere, for the purpose of maintaining an orderly government therein.[9]

The Influence of the Monroe Doctrine on War Planning

The Monroe Doctrine came into existence as cornerstone of US foreign policy on 2 December 1823. This doctrine stated that further efforts on the part of European powers to colonize land or interfere in the affairs of countries in North or South America would be viewed as acts of aggression against the United States. At the same time the doctrine stated that the United States would not interfere with existing colonies or meddle in the internal affairs of the European powers. While dated, the Monroe Doctrine was considered the hallmark of US foreign policy and its principles drove a great deal of the military planning by the joint board.

As outlined by the Army chief of staff in 1904, all Joint Board plans were going to need to factor in the Monroe Doctrine's influences not just on which countries the United States might be facing in future wars, but how that war might unfold. The summation of the planning is as follows:

> As a matter of fact these three causes [of war] may, from the point of view of the United States, but summed up in the first one, i.e. the Monroe Doctrine; from the point of view of any foreign power they may be summed up in the second, i.e. efforts for extension of trade. In the not remote future they may for all practical purposes be summed up in the second one for the United States also, but I do not think that when the United States comes to fight it will be for the *declared* purpose of extension of trade, although that may be the real cause of war and the real object, concealed under an appeal to the Monroe Doctrine. In other words, foreign aggression will probably be for the purpose of the extension of trade; to repel such aggression (which would be essentially a menace to our present or prospective trade) the United States would fight if at all, in the name of Monroe Doctrine.[10]
>
> A nation which, like us, has one foreign policy that thus leads to war may, as a result of such a war, have to adoption additional foreign policy leading, possibly, to other wars. Thus, the spirit of the Monroe Doctrine (our one foreign policy) brought on the war of 1898. That war resulting in the unanticipated acquisition by conquest of an immense empire in the remote waters of the Pacific. That acquisition brings us into new porting of contact with the great nations of the world, imposes new duties, new responsibilities, new relations utterly at variance with our immemorial traditions. The Monroe Doctrine grew out of and was an expression of our policy to remain isolated from the rest of the world. Its application in 1898 left our isolation in one direction untouched while it completely destroyed it in the other. There is no doubt that this will result in due time to the formation of a second line of foreign policy, and we shall then have one policy based on contact with another based on isolation from the rest of the world. We may yet find ourselves fighting for our Monroe Doctrine on one side of the world and against somebody else's Monroe Doctrine on the other side of the world. However, that time has not yet come.[11]
>
> The time may come when the relations of the Philippines to our Oriental trade may involve us in a war of which that trade may be admitted cause or object. For the present although the Philippines will undoubtedly and immediately become involved in a war between ourselves and a European power growing out of the Monroe Doctrine, they are

more likely to be a vulnerable object of the enemy's attack rather than a base for aggressive movements of ours upon the Asiatic mainland.

At first sight, therefore, it would seem that, in the very nature of the case, there is no such relation between them as would make the Philippine Islands a cause of war under the Monroe Doctrine, since they lie entirely outside its declared scope. Unfortunately for us, this is not the case. It is in the power of an adversary to make us fight for that doctrine when *his* object is not aggression on the Western Hemisphere but the Philippine Islands. It is always in the power of some country whose continental territory we cannot successfully attack, which possesses no territory elsewhere which is worth our attack, and which is stronger in Asiatic waters than we are, to take such measures may force us into war in defense of the Monroe Doctrine and to then confine all its efforts to an attempt to wrest the Philippine Islands from us. We may begin a war for some cause originating in Central and South American and yet not have an opportunity to fire a shot at our adversary in that quarter. We would be almost certain to lose the Philippines (provided they waited to strike until they were stronger in that quarter than we) without any chance of our securing from them an equivalent or anything approaching an equivalent. Only in the case of a war with England would we have any chance of reimbursing ourselves by more desirable property nearer home to replace that which we should have lost further away. And this fact alone makes England the least probable of any of our possible enemies.

In the view of its wide application I think I am right, therefore, in saying that the Monroe Doctrine is the most probable cause of our next war. Under that name we will offer to fight when we think something is involved for which that doctrine was first promulgated, and under that name an adversary may force us to fight although he may have not the remotest intention to make an aggression against that doctrine but uses it as a cause for provoking us to a war in which his object is a totally different kind of aggression. Let us see whether the assumption of this probable cause enables us to make a scientific guess as to the probable theaters and the other conditions of war which we should anticipate and provide for.

The United States can be forced to intervene in the domestic affairs of an independent state lying south of us for the purpose of establishing and maintaining an orderly government therein. By the very terms of her own organic law and of our own we are bound to do this in respect to one of these countries. i.e., Cuba. Even if this were not the case the first corollary of the Monroe Doctrine would force us to this step, whenever necessary, both in respect to her and to any other of these countries. In certain cases the necessity grows more and more remote with increasing civilization. In other cases—such as that of San Domingo—the necessity seems to be growing more and more imminent. In the case of that country which, next to ours, has made the greatest advancement in material prosperity and orderly government (I mean Mexico), may well informed persons entertain grave apprehensions for the future. They see reason to believe that this progress has been due to the strong hand and unusual genius for government of one man alone, whose death or disability (which in the course of nature cannot be long postponed) will cause a reversion to former conditions. The seriousness of this case lines in the fact that the world cannot tolerate even a slight reversion to former conditions. The capital invested in Mexico and other Latin-American countries is the capital of the great nations of the world and of which the least part, perhaps, comes from the United States. The moment the conditions, whenever may be the cause, become for a short time those of peace and order of the security of vested rights, this capital pours in in increasing volume. These conditions cause investment in national and state bonds, in railway and other transportation securities, in manufacturing, mining and agricultural ventures, and in a short time the common people of every civilized nation have a direct interest in the maintenance of the condition which make these investments valuable.

Even though the amount of our invested capital or one or another of these countries gives us no such direct interest as would make it worth our while to intervene by force of arms for the preservation of order, we must do it, or we must permit some one [sic] else to do it with all the uncertain and grave consequences to us that might result from such foreign intervention.

The first thing to be noted is that the consequences of such intervention on our part will be a local war with the state whose affairs we intervene and carried on by us within the limits of that state since, under present conditions, none of them (except perhaps Mexico) is able to carry the war into our own territory.

It is probable that this war will remain a local one or will it involve us in one with a European or Asiatic country or with a coalition of such countries? This suggest the further question, "what are the conditions which would make such a widespread complication possible?" Let us first consider the probabilities of intervention in such a war by a single foreign power.

At the time when the Monroe Doctrine was first promulgated it is probable that our forefathers apprehended intervention by Europe in the affairs of Central and South America for political purposes, and that such intervention would be with the object of establishing obnoxious forms of government direction dependent upon European suzerains. For the following reasons this danger has, I think, become remote.[12]

The interest which Europe takes in Latin-America is two-fold. It is the first place the interest of the colonies and of the trader or the investor of capital in local industries. This interest is opposed to a political connection. The colonist has gone there primarily to escape disadvantageous economical conditions at home; but universal experience shows that he associated these conditions with political conditions and looks with no favor upon the re-imposition of the latter in his new home.

The trader and investor of capital have, as such, no country. They care not from whom they import nor to whom they export provided their buying and selling market is the most advantageous. They know that a class political tie with their mother country can have no other object or result than the imposition of regulations in the restraint of trade which would be favorable to that mother country but unfavorable to them. The inhabitants of the South American countries, dependent upon the rest of the world for manufactured articles and finding the rest of the world their only market for articles of extensive home production an at the same time having no political connection with any foreign country, are today buying and selling with probably fewer artificial restraints of trade than is the case of any other country. There is, therefore, no disposition thus far shown on the part of

European immigrants in South America to strengthen political bonds between their new homes and their old ones. The most careful and reliable students of this question have found no reason to believe that the tendency of European colonization and the investment of European capital in Latin-American is to introduce obnoxious (from our point of view) forms of government or to establish obnoxious political relations between one or another of these countries and that from which the colonists and capital come.

Thus, were the Argentina or Brazil to become entirely Germanized or Italianized there is every reason to believe that, if internal conditions become no worse than they are, those countries will still rely on us for aid to protect them from political aggression by the mother land precisely as now they would expect our protection against Spain or Portugal were the latter in a position to seriously threaten such aggression.

But there is one condition that would change all this. Invested capital and labor seeking steady employment demand a stable and orderly government. When the immigrant labor and capital become sufficiently powerful they will demand in no uncertain way a check upon revolutions, upon disorderly and arbitrary government and upon causeless wars between states which have in the past been so great a cure of Latin-America. If the United States does not provide this check they will naturally turn to their mother countries in Europe. They will be more than satisfied if they can get the check from the former but otherwise they will naturally demand it from the latter. The honest and just application of the Monroe Doctrine, which is intended to prevent the intervention of a European country in such a case, requires that we should intervene ourselves.

The danger is—and it amounts to a not improbable cause of war—that while we are making up our minds whether it is worth our while to intervene, some European power may decide that it has allowed us a fair latitude and that the time has come to accede to the demands of its own subjects for the protection of their legitimate interests. Therefore, the principle thing to be noted in this connection is—and it would be well for our people to thoroughly appreciate it—that the more certain, promptly and effectually we intervene in such cases, the less likely it is that this local war of intervention between ourselves and a Latin-American state will ramify into a war with a European power.

The second interest which a European state has in Latin-America is, although a national one, not political but one growing out of trade relations. Long before the great nations of Europe have completed the solidification of their interest in the Continent of Africa and in the Far East, it is to be hoped that the states of Central and South America will have become too powerful, by population and material wealth, to fear political aggression from anything short of a coalition of all Europe. This will very largely depend upon the influence which the United States may exert in maintaining peace and good government and thereby making those countries attractive for immigration and capital. The very accomplishment of this result, however, will make European nations greedy to control the resulting trade. At present these Latin-American countries, with a population of not more than sixty millions of people, have a total trade of about one billion dollars. This is a fraction of what they will have long before their capacity for population and production is fully developed. Here again the United States will find a certain protection against a serious attempt at European intervention in the divergence of European interests. If the situation of South

America were like that of Africa they might all combine in a peaceful partition. This is not possible until the time should come, which some people see in their dreams, for a coalition of Europe against the United States. In the absence of such a coalition the effect of the successful intervention by a single European state could only be to dominate the trade of some South American country to the disadvantage of the rest of European trade.

Therefore, Europe as a whole would doubtless prefer to see the United States play the part of policeman in South America provided conditions for trade were left equal for all.

It would seem, therefore, that existing conditions and those to be anticipated rather make against the chances of intervention by any single old-world power.

Nevertheless such intervention is always possible. It may come:

1) Because the intervening power may think that it is acting in a territory beyond the limit of our effective naval influence and power;

2) A South American state in which we ourselves have intervened may, in its desperation, off a foreign power such advantageous terms as will tempt it to take the risk, especially if it knows that its home territory is safe from our attack;

3) A foreign nation may intervene, not with the idea of fighting us in South America but of carrying the war to the Philippines.

I think that the third contingency is more likely to be realized than either of the other two.

If it be true that the general conditions are, on the whole rather against the probability of a single foreign state intervening in the affairs of Latin-America (except as a cover to its designs upon the Philippines), it is equally true that a coalition of such powers is not likely to intervene?[13]

The Role of Alliances in Joint Board Planning

Coalitions are impossible in the absence of a community of interests. But the converse of the proposition is equally true; coalitions are probable in proportion to the degree of community of interest.

It seems quite certain that a political coalition of Europe for such a purpose is out of the question. It is hard to believe that France can have any alliance with Russia except as to further the former's designs against Germany; that England can have any alliance with Germany except to guarantee her against Russia, or with Russia except to guarantee the isolation of Germany. It is conceivable that any three of them might combine against the fourth, but it is inconceivable that all four would, under present conditions, combine in a deliberately pre-conceived plan for a war of aggression in Latin America. The rival interests which absorb the energies of each one nearer home—in Africa, in Asia Minor, in the Near and Far East—are also too great to allow any of the three of them to tie themselves up in a long and costly war so far from their home bases, leaving one of them to pursue unchecked his designs in the old world. And it is perfectly certain that some one of them may find his old-world interests so great and his interests in Latin-America so slight that he would withhold from such a combination.[14]

The Venezuela Crisis's Influence to Planning

The influence of the 1895 Venezuela Crisis factored into the planning of the United States as well. This crisis dealt with a long-standing dispute between Venezuela and Great Britain over the territories of Essequibo and Guayana Esequiba. Britain refused initially to accept international arbitration over a portion of the landholdings east of a surveyor's line known as the "Schomburgk Line." In the dispute Venezuela dragged the United States into the conflict, pointing out that the British actions constituted a violation of the Monroe Doctrine. America stepped into the crisis and for a period of time, Great Britain misjudged the resolve the United States when it came to the doctrine—to the point where the US contemplated going to war over the issue. Eventually diplomats were able to resolve the issue, but it was a driving influence of General Tasker Bliss's views of the mission of the Joint Board:

> But our danger—which is a real and great one—does not come from a coalition of these powers, deliberately entered into as the result of a carefully worked out plan for aggression in South or Central America. It comes from a coalition entered into with our own consent for the purposes of making a mere demonstration. The events of a moment may solidify a mere paper coalition of that kind into one which only war, possibly very disastrous for us, will dissolve. The recent demonstration in Venezuela is a case exactly in point. It was made with our consent. It was made by powers temporarily allied for that purpose but who by no possibility would have allied to engage in a war, deliberate and preconceived, with the United States. The danger was in the first step. The demonstration soon aroused a dangerous spirit among our people which counted for a good deal in the final adjustment of the matter. It was mere good fortune that nothing had happened which made it impossible for the allies to recede and agree to arbitration without the loss of prestige in their home countries.
>
> Suppose, now, that Venezuela fails to comply with the terms of the Hague judgment. There would then doubtless be another demonstration. Our government, in its disgust at the situation would consent to more readily than before. But our people forget that when they permit the first step they are bound (or will be held by the demonstrating powers to be bound) to permit those which logically follow. An armed demonstration to collect a debt in South America must infallibly (if the debtor nation refuses to be bound by a decision) result in one of these three things:
>
> 1) The creditor nations must ignominiously abandon their case;
>
> 2) Or they must indemnify themselves by the seizure of territory and its partition according to their relative claims;
>
> 3) Or they must seize and hold the agencies for the collection of public revenue.
>
> The allies will fight before they will accept the first condition; we will fight before we permit the second; and the third condition becomes intimately quite as serious. The seizure of custom house and the collection of import duties (which are the sole public revenue of these countries) means intervention in the general fiscal affairs of the state; means the military and civil occupation and control of the ports and their defenses; the seizure of

local navies; the erection of barracks and the establishment of garrisons; and, unless the natives quietly accept all the foregoing, the conducting of military operations against them. All this must be paid for and involves indefinite prolongation of the occupation. Our people will soon see that the third of the above conditions is equivalent to the second and will force action accordingly.[15]

The Asset and Liability of the Panama Canal in American Military Planning

The United States in 1904 was deeply committed in the construction of the Panama Canal which would open up fast waterway passage between the Atlantic and Pacific Oceans. While the canal was to present a massive strategic advantage for the country that owned it, it was also a potential liability. This factored in to the Joint Board's planning as well.

> There is another possible, but for the present more remote, cause of coalition against the United States. The successful completion of the Panama Canal—that is, the construction of a canal under conditions that make it attractive to the world's commerce—will cause the readjustment of a certain part of that commerce on new lines. It will be a part, and for the present only a small part of the commerce directed to and coming from the Asiatic mainland along the Pacific. Within recent years (since the real agitation for a Panama Canal began) the greatest powers of Europe have acquired extensive interests in that quarter. They find there the United States as a vigorous competitor. It is too soon to predict the exact influence that the canal will have on the trade rivalries, to what extent it will make American completion in the East more formidable, to what extent American control of the canal will threaten European trade interest in time of war.
>
> But the military advantages of the canal to whomsoever controls it are obvious. It doubles the military resources of the United States for operations upon the sea in this hemisphere and considerably increases them for operation in the Orient. In the great struggle for supremacy in the Far East which seems to be impending over the great European powers, the ability to use this canal by one or more of them and to close it against the others may be of vital importance.
>
> Unless, therefore, it can be neutralized under the guarantee of the world—close to all war navies, including our own, or open to all—it is certain to become the centre of contention. It may become so, in spite of any guarantee. The point to be here noted is that, other things being anywhere near equal, its control rests with the power that can control the approaches to the Caribbean Sea.[16]

Planning Guidelines

The Army's proposed guidelines for the Joint Board drove much of the planning and thinking of the board in their early years in terms of what countries the US might have to go to war with and why. These were detailed as follows:

1) The most probable cause of our next war is to be found in one of the various applications of the Monroe Doctrine;

2) That a very possible application of this doctrine may bring on a war of intervention by the United States with a country of Latin-America, at the outset with the approval of the world and with no foreign complications;

3) That for any of the reasons above indicated a foreign power my intervene at some stage of the struggle;

4) That the war may be brought on by the prior intervention of a foreign power;

5) That this foreign power may intervene by reason of some direct interest it has or belies it has in Latin-America, or as a mere cloak to its designs in the Philippine Archipelago;

6) That whatever the cause of intervention of the foreign power, it will immediately attempt to secure some advantage which it can hold even if unsuccessful in the war, that therefore the Philippine Islands, whatever point of view we take, being a most valuable and undefended part of our possessions, will be an object of attack; and that for the same reason and for the additional reason of their value in the control of the main land of the Caribbean Sea the intervening power will threaten Puerto Rico, San Domingo and Cuba;

7) That therefore the Philippine Archipelago and the Caribbean can be assured in all probability as theatres in such a war;

8) That the foreign intervention may be by a coalition of powers;

9) That England is the power least likely to enter such a coalition;

10) That the intervention of the United States in Mexico may become necessary, with the least chance of any other foreign complication connected therewith;

I, therefore, suggest a progressive study to be jointly undertaken by the two General Staffs, a problem under the following assumptions;

1) That the United States intervenes in some South American Country (Venezuela, for example).

2) That the theatre of war include the Caribbean Sea and the Philippine Archipelago;

3) After the foregoing studies are completed assume a coalition of two European powers, excluding England;

4) For the purpose of completing a study of the Canadian frontier, assume England as an intervening power under assumption:

a) Alone

b) In coalition

5) Assume intervention by the United States in Mexico, with other foreign complication. The study of each assumption will be made on the basis of existing resources. If the working out of a given assumption indicates probable failure by the United States as a result of lack of ships or other material of war, a careful and conservative statement of the provisions that should be made to ensure probable success will be given.[17]

War Based on Color

In order to address these plans, the Joint Board adopted a color coding scheme for the involved nations. This system was adopted in December of 1904 and remained, with minor additions and modifications until WWII. The service branches did not readily adopt this color scheme and by 1919 the plan colors for some countries were altered. The classifications were as follows:

Table: War Plan Color Coding:[18]

Target Country:	1904 Target Country Designation:	Post 1919 Re-Designations:
Britain	Red	Red. *Note: Variants of Red were devised for each of the UK nations. Crimson for Canada, Garnet for New Zealand, India was Ruby, Australia was Scarlet, Ireland was coded Indigo.*
Germany	Black	Black
France	White	Gold
Spain	Yellow	Olive
Japan	Orange	Orange
Italy	Gray	None
Russia	Green	Purple
Austria	Crimson	None
China	Saffron	Yellow
Cuba	Tan	Tan
Central America and the Caribbean		Gray—Azores
Philippines	Brown	Brown
Red-Orange		A British-Japanese alliance
Mexico	Green	Green
Iceland	Indigo	Indigo
Latin America		Violet
The United States (defense plans)	Blue	Blue
The United States (internal uprisings)	Blue	White
Canada	Crimson (note: This also appears as the same coloring for Austria though the plans for Austria were never drafted)	Crimson

The United States was designated as Blue when fighting other potential countries, and as White when dealing with domestic uprisings and insurrections. Given the communist upheavals and revolutions in the post-Great War period, the Joint Board drafted a set of plans to deal with a similar activity in the US which was color-coded as the White Plans.

Despite its formation the Joint Board played no noticeable role in military planning for the US entry into The Great War. The early years of the Joint Board were seen more as a mental exercise than an integral part of planning. "The early war plans were little more than abstract exercises and bore little relation to actual events."[19] By the time the US entered World War One, most of the officers attached to the Joint Board found themselves attached to other military efforts.

By the end of the war, thoughts turned again to reform the Joint Board. A new joint order was issued on 24 and 25 July, 1919 by the Secretaries of War (General Order No. 94) and Navy (General Order No. 491). Between 1919 and 1941 the Joint Board created three subordinate units: the Joint Planning Committee (1919), the Joint Economy Board (1933), and the Joint Intelligence Committee (1941). The new membership of the Joint Board provided for a permanent secretary and reduced the number of members from eight to six.

Rather than appointments to be on an individual basis, the new board would be based on specific assignments. Naval representation came from the Office of the Chief of Naval Operations, the Assistant Chief of Naval Operations, and the Director of Plans. The last role would evolve over time this would be designed as Planning, then finally War Plans. The Army representation came from the General Staff and included the Director of the Operations Division (later this would be the Operations and Training Division), and the Director of the War Plans Division (in later years this would be replaced by the Assistant Chief of Staff, War Plans Division). As the years went by additional changes to the Army representation would change. The Director of the Operations and Training Division was replaced with the Deputy Chief of Staff in 1923. With the influence of air power emerging as a key component to military planning, an addition was made to the Joint Board to include the Army's Deputy Chief of Staff for Air and the Navy's Chief of the Bureau of Aeronautics. This change came about in July of 1941, on the eve of the United States entry into World War II.

Of the three subordinate units to the Joint Board; the Joint Planning Committee, the Joint Economy Board, and the Joint Intelligence Committee; the Joint Planning Committee was by and large the most active. It was responsible for preparing detailed reports and plans on key issues as assigned by the Joint Board. Other joint organizations, including the Joint Army and Navy Munitions Board, the Aeronautical Board, and the Joint Army and Navy Selective Service Committee, sometimes submitted recommendations to the Joint Board but were not formally subordinate to it.[20]

The War Plans Division was created by War Department General Order 14 on 9 February 1918 as an effort to consolidate the administrative functions of the War Department General Staff. The division took over the functions and records of the former War College Division except for those duties assigned to the newly formed

Military Intelligence Division. General John J. Pershing appointed his deputy, Major General James G. Harbord to come up with the organization structure for the General Staff. General Harbord and his panel adopted the "G" divisions for the General Staff which had been used in the Great War to coordinate with the French and British Armies.

G1   Personnel
G2   Military Intelligence
G3   Operations and Training
G4   Logistics
WPD War Planning Department
This structure remained in place until 1942.[21]

The interwar period was when the Joint Board took on a growing level of importance in the growing military planning community. They established policies for inter-service working relationships and coordination. They published these policies on an ongoing, if not irregular basis. These policies defined the scope of operations that required joint service coordination, as well as defining which branch of the service would have specific responsibilities in such situations. The Joint Board also issued directives for joint exercises and maneuvers which became an increasing activity as World War II loomed.

Updating and modification of the war plans was constant in the interwar years. One would be hard pressed to pull any one of these plans and see exactly what made up the "current" version of the plan. Individual paragraphs or entire sections were under scrutiny always, with both minor and major word editing being commonplace. The number of officers that provided input to the plans that were devised by the Joint Board numbered in the hundreds. It is unknown if this constant modification and tweaking actually added value to the plans overall.

Their most important Joint Board activity overall was the preparation of the war plans themselves. These plans rarely followed a consistent format, but most dealt with not just the war plans themselves but that overall mobilization and logistics required to execute the plans, along with intelligence analysis of the target country and the types of communication infrastructure that was needed to coordinate both service branches.

War Plans Security

While the members of the Joint Board had their own personal copies of the plans, the plans generally were not well circulated given the sensitive nature of their contents. References have been found in the US National Archives of copies being stored in the captain's safe aboard the US flagships of the Navy. Additionally, the Army distributed copies of the plans to the appropriate members of the General Staff where the plans were to be utilized. Thus War Plan Green for operations in Mexico would not be provided to the American Army commander in the Philippines.

The only exception to this concept was if troops were to be drawn from one command to support an operation. If that were the case, the war plans were then shared with both commands.

At most, at any given point in time, no more than thirty-six copies of the colored war plans were ever circulated—and those were tracked carefully—at least at the beginning of their publication.

The Rainbow Plans and the Dissolution of the Joint Board

Starting in 1938 and the rising war tensions in Europe, it became clear that the previous color-coded war plans were not practical. The formation of the Axis powers demonstrated that the next war would be one where alliances would drive the looming war—though some of the individual plans would still serve as building blocks for the more complicated alliance plans—dubbed the Rainbow Plans. The phrase "Rainbow Plans" is often misused as being the same as the colored war plans, when in reality the Rainbow Plans were defined on their own distinctly.

The breakdown of the Rainbow War Plans are as follows:

- Rainbow One: This defined limited action in order to prevent a violation of the Monroe Doctrine as far south as 10 degrees south latitude. By its very nature, Rainbow Plan One was designed to be a defensive operation. This plan was approved by the Secretaries of War and Navy on 14 August 1939 as WPL-42.
- Rainbow Two: In essence this was a broad expansion of Rainbow One. This would be followed by concerted action by the United States, Great Britain, and France against the Fascist powers. U.S. forces would assume sole responsibility for fighting the war in the Pacific.
- Rainbow Three, also known as WPL44: This was the execution of the Rainbow One war plans followed by projecting American forces into the western Pacific.
- Rainbow Four: This plan called for the United States Army to send troops to the southern end of South America and to assume a defensive posture similar to that outlined in Rainbow One. Once the fighting in the Atlantic was stabilized, the United States was to permit the transfer of major naval forces for an offensive against Japan.
- Rainbow 5—also known as WPL46: This called for an execution of Rainbow One to be followed by U.S. armed forces (both Navy and Army being projected into the eastern Atlantic or Europe, and/or Africa in concert with Great Britain and France. This plan was modified through December of 1941 to adjust to the changing situation that was emerging in Europe.[22]

With the arrival World War II the force structure of the military services of the United States changed, as did the need for sweeping strategic planning of hypothetical scenarios. There were ample real-life invasions that needed to be planned and executed.

The newly created Joint Chiefs of Staff superseded the need for the antiquated Joint Board and their responsibilities were absorbed by a half-dozen other service divisions. The need for a separate combined planning group was obsolete by the new Joint Chiefs of Staff who assumed that role.

The final formal meeting of the Joint Board took place on 16 March 1942. When the Joint Chiefs met on 4 May 1942 it was noted that their meeting was, in essence, the members of the Joint Board with "additional officers present." From that point forward the Joint Chiefs of Staff assumed the formal responsibilities of the old Joint Board.[23]

Impacts

The colored war plans themselves at first glimpse seem to be archaic and outdated, of little use in the newly changing face of warfare in World War II. To the casual reader, they almost appear humorous in the face of threats that emerged and the dynamic nature of a changing strategic situation which required more flexible planning than most of the war plans provided. They detailed wars that never occurred, so the study of these plans was limited to scholars who were willing to explore some of their more tantalizing details.

This kind of analysis is harsh and unfair. These plans were important foundations for developing a strategic thinking and joint operations form of warfare which would dominate the looming war. Without the skills earned working in the darkness during the early years of the Joint Board, the US would have struggled to attempt to develop this competency in its general staff.

Not all of the war plans proved worthless. The war plans devised by the United States were utilized during WWII either in part or whole. War Plan Orange, for example, evolved to outline the general strategy that the United States utilized against the Empire of Japan. In fact, with the countless refinements that were applied to the plan, the overall timeline for executing the war against Japan was remarkably accurate in War Plan Orange.

Other plans, such as the plan to invade the Azores (War Plan Gray) were leveraged from a strategic perspective, though the actual invasion was more of an assignment of troops rather than a contested landing. Some like War Plan Tan (dealing with Cuba), were not true invasions but interventions. War Plan Brown, the re-invasion of the Philippines does not share much with General MacArthur's actual invasion to recapture the islands in WWII, though the list of target cities and key installations certainly mirrored those that the US factored into their invasion planning. War Plan Indigo, the planned invasion of Ireland, was under careful consideration as late as 1942, fearing that Germany might attempt to seize the island themselves or support some sort of an Irish uprising against British rule.[24]

Ultimately the activities of the Joint Board were critical to the US military planning and thinking. Thus an understanding of these plans becomes critical to understand the military mindset that emerged and eventually helped lead to Allied victory in World War II.

The 1905 Plan for War with Britain and Canada War Plan Red/Crimson

Introduction

While officially subtitled titled, "Assumption—War has broken out with Great Britain," the 1904–1904 War Plan for the United States attacking Canada reflects some of the earliest documented attempts at US military planning.[1] This is clearly the Crimson War Plan and is referenced in a cover letter as such, though in the plan itself the word "Crimson" never appears. Even during this stage of war planning, the thoughts were not largely strategic but more of how to deal with the immediate threat—in this case the shared border between the United States and Canada.

The intent of taking the war to Great Britain herself was not contemplated in the 1905 plan. In this scenario, the US Navy was to play an incredibly minor role in the Great Lakes and St. Lawrence Seaway. There are vague lines in the plan which indicate that the Navy's role was to be much more strategic and global in nature, striking at British interests around the world. These will be covered in greater detail in the chapter on War Plan Red where they are identified in greater detail. No matter how you evaluate this, it is solely a plan for attacking Canada … and it was to be a US Army operation from start to finish.

In this war plan, the US would not be waging an all-out war against Canada but would be more focused on fighting a limited offensive aimed at securing its borders and protecting its cities. It was expected that this conflict would have limited time for mobilization, "promptness of action and celerity of movement required."[2]

Perhaps the most telling indication of the time period is the US reliance on mounted cavalry to perform many of the activities outlined in the war plan. After the Spanish American War it should have become clear to planners that mounted cavalry charges would not stand the ground against rapid fire infantry weapons and artillery. Like most of her European counterparts, the illusion of cavalry breaking through into the "green fields beyond," in the rear of the enemy and wreaking havoc still was an illusion that the United States cherished. The Great War would alter that perception greatly.

Strategic Objectives

Canada in 1905 was and remains today a vast country, bitter cold in the north, with a relatively small population. It is also a nation that is rich in reserves. War Plan Crimson points out that two of Canada's largest exports, nickel and food, were considered vital for the United Kingdom. Estimates in the plan showed upwards of 27 percent of the British Isles' supply of wheat came from the Canadian prairies—along with considerable amounts of fish. Great Britain imported over 75 percent of her nickel, a strategic war supply element, from Canada as well.[3]

The ultimate strategic goals of any US operation into Canada were to sever these exports to affect a stranglehold on Britain.

Military Objectives of War Plan Crimson

There are a handful of key objectives outlined in this plan these are:

I.   To seize immediately the bridges between Fort Erie and Buffalo
II.   To seize immediately the bridges at Niagara Falls.
III. To seize at once and destroy the locks of the Welland Canal
IV.   To protect the City of Buffalo from bombardment from the Canada Shore.[4]

The bridges were considered to be of paramount importance since holding them blocked Canadian troops from invading south, while allowing the United State the capability of seizing the initiative and driving north into Canada.

Between Port Erie and Buffalo there was only one bridge span—the International Bridge, owned and maintained by the Grand Trunk Railroad. Army engineers had determined that the ties on the bridge were wide enough and close enough together to allow for troops to use this railroad bridge to cross. The International Bridge was a single track bridge over most of the bridge but was double-track-wide on Squaw Island. On the Squaw Island the width of the trusses was twelve feet, which "would afford much protection against oblique fire," which was expected during a forced crossing.[5]

Ferry service between Fort Erie and from Grand Island (below Buffalo) did run as well. This ferry service was going to need to be seized as part of the operation as well.

At Niagara Falls three bridge spans crossed the river. These were detailed a follows:

- An 840 foot steel arch bridge which supported a wagon track which also carried a pair of trolley tracks. This bridge also had two passenger walk-ways. This bridge only had parapets which were the only source of cover for forces attempting to cross the bridge under fire.
- A double-track steel cantilever bridge owned by the Michigan Central Railway. This was 1.5 miles downriver from the first bridge. The ties on this bridge were wide and

the space between the ties was filled two thirds of the way across the bridge allowing for wagon traffic. While the bridge was sturdy, it offered almost no protection from enemy fire.

- A double-track deck arched steel bridge with an 880 foot span owned by the Grand Trunk Railroad which was configured to support wagon traffic. The engineering analysis of the span indicated that this bridge had hand rails which would be useful in moving troops north into Canada. It had sheet iron strips mounted between the ties to act as gutters which made passage on the bridge easy for wagons. As far as protection went, the heavy steel trusses were believed to provide good cover. The real challenge comes from the approaches.

At the extremities of the wagon way are road on each bank parallel to the river, and the sides of these roads away from the river, are abutments of the railroad bed. These require that artillery or infantry firing along the wagon way should occupy the prolongation of the wagon way only, hence their numbers are limited by the width of the latter. An artillery position on the American side, north of the railroad, is available for covering fire with the Canada prolongation of the wagon way.[6]

An additional bridge was located between Queenstown and Lewiston. This suspension bridge supported trolley, wagon, and foot traffic. It was a clear bridge, with little or no cover of its 800 foot span. The bridge had a 65 foot drop to the river below. This bridge was seen as problematic because on both sides of the river the bridge was dominated by natural heights, giving attackers and defenders easy coverage of the bridge by artillery or infantry. The Queenstown Heights were believed to be angled enough to provide oblique fire to anyone attempting to cross the bridge.[7]

The Welland Canal along the St. Lawrence Seaway was seen as an asset for the Canadians in a conflict, but of little value to the American military. The canal extended from Fort Colhoren on Lake Erie to Port Dalhousie on Lake Ontario, twenty-six miles away. Essentially it runs parallel to the Niagara River, without the natural obstruction that Niagara Falls presents. The canal, in 1905, was fourteen feet deep, 100 feet wide. The lock system consisted of twenty-five locks which elevated or lowered barge/boat traffic a total of 327 feet. Control of the canal assured that St. Lawrence seaway was bottled up for shipping.

There was an older cut of the Welland Canal between Thorold and Port Dalhousie which was only eight feet deep. This was seven miles long. Of the twenty-five locks on the canal, twenty-four were at Thorold. The final lock was about a half-mile south of Thorold and was one of the more minor locks—only changing the elevation by one foot.

Support and maintenance for the canal was based at Port Dalhousie. This consisted of a repair shop and supplies for repairs of the gates.

Port Dalhousie was named for George Ramsay, 9th Earl of Dalhousie, Governor General of British North America, had waves on each side of the basin which were about a half-mile in length. At Port Colborne, the wharf on the east side was 750 feet long, on the west side 900 feet in length. Two-hundred feet of this wharf were deemed suitable for disembarking troops but could not be relied upon for sundries or supplies.

At the inner end of the Port Dalhousie basis were twin guard locks and a diversion channel. The Lake Erie end of the two locks is crossed by a road swing bridge; the other end by a railroad swing bridge. The flow through the diversion channel was controlled by five drum wicket of about twenty-foot span, placed obliquely. The swing bridges have their seats of their roller paths about ten-eleven feet above the water level. If they are forced from these seats, the might still admit the passage of boats with funnels.

The canal gates had been covertly inspected by Army engineers who had posed as vacationers sneaking into Canada as spies to gather their information. From what they could tell the gates were designed to be anchored to the lock walls by five iron rods. If the tie rods were broken the leaf of the gate would close, rendering the lock inoperable. The Army speculated that the repair facilities at Port Dalhousie had replacement rods ready, but even if they did not, they could be fabricated with relative ease. Crane barges could be floated down to the site of any damage and repairs could be affected on a single lock in a matter of hours.

Just destroying the rods would only temporarily cripple the lock systems and shut down the canal. If the heavy castings about the gudgeons which supported the gates like hinges could be damaged with high explosives, the lock gates could be crippled for a significant period of time. While the gates themselves are wooden, it was known that spare gates were held at the repair basin.[8]

"Efforts to secure maps showing these road have been attended with no success."[9] As such the Army planners were forced to refer to a Rand, McNally & Company Atlas of Ontario and folders from the Matthews–Northrup Road Map of Erie and Niagara Counties, along with folder maps obtained from the Niagara Falls and Buffalo International Traction Company's Interurban Rail Line.[10] Suffice it to say that this kind of logistical gap, the lack of a topographical cohesive map, would have posed significant issues. The Army's War Planners on the Joint Board relied on tourist maps and visual observations of the terrain to plan this invasion of Canada.

The topography of the terrain was thought to be accommodating to the operation.

> So far as could be seen, the country west of the river is comparatively flat. At Niagara Falls, Ont., west of Bridge No. 1, along the west border of the Park, there was an abrupt rise about 100 yards from the river. West of this, all is quite level in General. Chippewa Creek runs back, I believe, to the canal.[11]

From the planning document it is clear that a true reconnaissance beyond the river and canal had not been conducted. In fact, the entire plan was based on a series of rail and trolley rides on the bridges in question.

> By trolley from Niagara Falls, Ont., to St. Catherines after dark. By day light, from St. Catherines by trolley, to Niagara Falls, Ont.; to Niagara Falls, U.S.A., over Bridge No. 1, and return to St. Catherines. By trolley from St. Catherines to Port Dalhousie and return, examined

at Port Dalhousie, the basin repair ways and basin, locks No's 25 and 24, and waste weir. Then:

By rail from St. Catherines to Thorold and Port Colborne and then, at Port Colborne, examined basin, guard locks and bridges. By trolley from St. Catherines to Niagara Falls, Ont.; by trolley to the Canadian Falls, along the westerly edge of Niagara Falls and return. By trolley along Canadian side to Queenstown and across Suspension bridge, thence to Fort Niagara and return on the American side to the Grand Trunk Bridge (No. 3) and crossing on foot to the Canadian side. Then went out on both railroad bridges, No's 2 and 3.

Then the author of the plan went, "By trolley from Niagara Falls, Ont., across Bridge No. 1, thence to Buffalo near International Railway Bridge. Walked on easterly span."[12] In many respects this level of surveying the potential battlefield for a coming war was more like a honeymoon weekend rather than a true military operation.

Other Fronts

While War Plan Crimson concentrated on an attack on Canada in the east, this did not mean that the entire border of Canada was ignored in the planning. The United States did not contemplate major incursions elsewhere but would assume more of a defensive stance across the rest of the border:

It should be borne in mind that the main theatre of operations being in the East, but few regular troops will be available for the movement into Canadian territory west of Lake Superior. There should, however, be a sufficient nucleus to serve as a model in the instruction of the militia, and to form a small reserve of thoroughly reliable troops.[13]

The belief, in the plan, was that if the Army struck quickly and seized the initiative, Canada would be forced to only a defensive strategy which would serve to protect US interests.

War Plan Crimson Plan of Attack

Invading Canada was not designed to be a war of conquest or subjugation. The American plan for attack called for seizing the bridges between Fort Erie and Buffalo in a single line of action—with the ultimate goal of securing Fort Erie. Fort Erie had been the first British fort constructed on the Canadian border following the Seven Years War in 1764. The fort was captured twice by the Americans during the War of 1812. The British laid siege to the fort in mid-August of 1814 and compelled the Americans to withdraw once they landed forces on the American side of the lake. The Americans sortied from the fort, capturing the British siege batteries. By the time winter approached, the Americans wrecked the fort and fell back to Buffalo. In 1905 the fort remained in ruins and was stripped of stones for local buildings. A brigade of Irish Republicans (Fenians) used the old fort as a base for raids into Ontario. By 1905 the old fort was hardly a threat—it had long been used as a park and picnic area by locals. If, however, artillery were placed there, it *might* pose a threat to Buffalo.

The next set of objectives were the bridges at Niagara Falls. These were seen as a prerequisite to seizing the Welland Canal.[14] Thorold is seven miles from Niagara Falls Ontario, but with its control, the Welland Canal would be effectively negated. Holding both the Niagara River and the Welland Canal made moving along the waterways from the Atlantic to the Great Lakes impossible.

The American First Division was tasked with seizing Fort Erie, and establishing a line of defensive works four miles or more west of the International Bridge. The First Division was to "obtain" two large steamers and load them with iron ore, cement and run them into Port Colborne and have them sunk as close as possible to the upstream lock gates. Further, the First Division was to cover movements up against the canal with a third vessel which was to be outfitted with machineguns, unless the approaches could be covered by artillery.[15]

Destruction of the canal was critical to the American plans.

> If it be desired to greatly damage the locks, without great destruction, then high explosives might be used to destroy the lower sheaves about which the wire traction ropes used to open the gates, change direction; or the castings about the gudgeons should be broken with like means. This should be affected at the downstream gate of the high-lift dock at Thorold, and if time permit, at both gates of the next lock downstream.
>
> If the march to Thorold be impracticable, two freighters laden with pig iron or with broken stone and cement might be sent into Port Colborne basin and sunk there, or better, one against the upper guard gate of each of the twin locks.[16]

Clearly the American plans called for disabling the canal to ensure that any future attacks would still not open up the waterway—at least not quickly.

This task was going to fall to the US Second Division. His orders were to seize Niagara Falls, Ontario, then raid as far as Thorold—at least so far as to damage the canal locks, gates, and/or their machinery and prevent it from operating both the old and new branches of the canal. Once this was done, at his discretion, the Second Division was authorized to retire. One battalion was to be sent to link up with the First Division forces.[17] Once the Welland Canal was secured or obstructed, a detachment was to be placed on the southern path on the canal. Further, Fort Erie was to be secured to prevent its use, and a main body of troops were to be stationed at Niagara Falls Ontario.

A force of militia cavalry and artillery were to operate in the area of Thorold. They were to take and hold the Grand Trunk Railroad station and prepare it for defense should the Canadians attempt to move on the railroad bridges.[18]

Further, "the crossings at Lewiston by suspension bridge or ferry, and by ferries below, should be prevented by forces on the American side."[19]

These would be the initial moves on the part of the Americans, limited in scope and damage. Raids were assumed to be a follow-up action to this plan and will be covered later in this chapter.

The Canadians

American military planning against Canada was drawn primarily on reports from the Canadian Department of Militia and Defense and the Minister of Public Works. The reports ranged from 1901 through 1 March 1904.

Canada was broken into ten Military Districts. The London and Toronto Districts were assumed to be occupied with the American incursion of troops at the outbreak of hostilities—though moves against Toronto were not contemplated in the plan. The planners assumed that troops from the Kingston District may be shifted against the US incursion but it also contemplated that the Canadians, after the loss of the Niagara, would be reinforcing the city of Windsor and along the Detroit and St. Clair Rivers. Since these were a logical choke point to the Great Lakes, the planning was relatively sound strategically.

For all of its vast size, the Canadian military was centered primarily on the London and Toronto districts. Of the permanent militia—there were 982 authorized and 835 actually formed. In the latest analysis by the United States, 31 December 1902, there were 94 Royal Canadian Dragoons at Toronto and 154 R.C.F Artillery at London and Toronto. Of these, roughly one-third had severed less than one year, three eighths had served three years or more.[20]

The size of the Canadian military forces that would be first thrown at the American's were broken down as follows:

Table: Canadian Militia Strength

Location:	Officers:	Enlisted Men:	Horses:	Untrained Officers:	Untrained Enlisted Men:	Additional Horses:
Toronto City	89	872	14	Unknown	None	11
Toronto Rural	290	3,170	461	162	2,236	154
London City	210	2,768	27	43	127	4
London Rural	427	4,680	970	230	3,182	285
Total	1,016	11,490	1,472	443	5,545	454

The forces marked as "rural" had been trained in camp but no service ammunition was used. They were armed with Lee-Enfield .303 rifles. Canadian sources indicated that their armorers reported that many of the rifles were unserviceable through improper handling.

Canada had ample ammunition for a limited conflict with the US. In 1902 they had manufactured 2,065,800 cordite cartridges and imported 4,121,700 from England. Over a million of the ball cartridges had been issued to Toronto and London for practice.[21] Small arms ammunition amounted to 1,630,204 rounds for the entire country—with 398,744 rounds issued to twenty-five local rifle associations in the London District and twenty-one such organizations in and around Toronto.

These local associations were, essentially, another form of *ad hoc* militia that could be thrown into battle if/when they were needed. Of the twenty-five in the London District, six were organized into companies which were tied to three regiments. Of the twenty-one in and around Toronto, five could be organized into four regiments and one into a field artillery battery. The remaining associations were expected to take part in local defense but lacked any practical camp experience.[22]

The rural militia was not seen as a viable threat. Their own Commanding General reported, "Such a force certainly does not provide the trained framework needed to make a civilian army efficient in time of war."[23] Of the city militia, "They cannot in any sense be said to approach a state of readiness to take in the field. They all suffer from want of field training, owning to the fact that they get practically no camp experience."[24]

The general summary of the militia in the US plans was that even if there was a political build-up to the American incursion, the Canadian forces would be remarkably ineffective. The belief was that the US would be able to mobilize along the Atlantic Front quickly and move forces into position before any serious Canadian mobilization could take place.

In terms of Artillery, Canada possessed fifteen batteries of field artillery and two additional batteries of the Royal Canadian Field Artillery. Two of those batteries, Seven and Eight, were both located in the Niagara area. Neither of them had even drilled during 1902, the last bit of intelligence that the United States had on those units. Most of these batteries were twelve pounder and six cwt. pieces. Recent (1902) newspaper reports also showed that the Canadians had been provided with twelve quick firing Maxim machineguns. While the American experts placed no weight on these new weapons, the machineguns most certainly would have wreaked havoc once they were employed. Images of mounted cavalry charging machineguns makes even the most hardened historian cringe.

The Canadian Medical Department consisted of a total of seventy-two officers, twenty-five second Lieutenant supernumerary, "several of whom are qualified and waiting for vacancies. There are certainly six field hospitals and maybe more."[25]

Imperial (British) Forces

American intelligence about the number of British troops in Canada was based more on newspaper articles than tangible intelligence field work. According to a newspaper article from Halifax on 13 February 1904, instructions had been received from the British War Office to see if temporary quarters could be secured in Canada for seven line regiments and a detachment of Royal Engineers. Their purpose was to be in readiness to transport to the east, if considered necessary—presumably to deal with any other threats to Britain or her allies. The article stated that one regiment would be quartered in Toronto, others would be out of the Niagara River District.[26]

Additionally, other articles indicated that the British Army was exploring what it would take to move 60,000 troops across Canada in times of emergency—giving some indication overall of the British fighting force that could be mustered. In the article, railway officials reported that such a mobilization would require two weeks' notice. With such notice, they could undertake such a movement in four days.[27]

When trouble with England, on account of Venezuela, threatened, it was noted that an English engineer officer was ordered out to London, Ont. Considering London's central location with reference to the Niagara and Detroit River frontiers, it is inferred that in the event of possible war, Canada would give special attention to these frontiers and would not divert elsewhere man of the troops above tabulated.[28]

While the majority of troops would be four hours away by rail from Niagara Falls, five hours from Buffalo, the entire force that Canada was anticipated to muster in the event of an American incursion was:

Type:	Number:
Canadian militia, infantry and cavalry:	18,494 men, 1,926 horses
Imperial infantry:	1,000 men
Royal Canadian Dragoons:	94 men
Royal Canadian Field Artillery:	2 batteries
Militia Light Artillery:	8 batteries[29]

American Forces

The assembled forces of the United States for this rather limited war against Canada would be a mix of regular forces and National Guard (militia).

For Headquarters Guard, Niagara Falls, New York
   One troop of cavalry

For operations at Buffalo: "To cross Niagara River from Tonawanda via Grand Island, river current less here than at Buffalo, and occupy the line of Black Creek":

One company Signal Corps
One squadron of cavalry
Six regiments of Infantry, each with three machine guns
Three batteries of field artillery
Two siege batteries."[30]

For operations at Niagara Falls and Welland Canal:

One company of cavalry
Four batteries of field artillery
Four batteries of field artillery, militia
Four regiments of infantry, each with three machine guns
One mounted engineer detachment

For depots at Batavia:

One regiment of militia

To replace regular garrisons by militia:

Fort Niagara, one regiment and one battery of field artillery
Fort Porter, one battalion
Fort McPherson, one battalion
Fort Thomas, one battalion
Columbus Barracks, one battalion

For operations against Welland Canal at Port Colborne:

Two vessels, not exceeding ___ feet draft, loaded[31]

Where the American Troops Would be Drawn From

The peacetime Army of the United States in 1905 was a pale shadow of the forces that fought in the American Civil War or even the Spanish American War. The planned invasion of Canada would leverage a mix of both Regular Army and the National Guard forces to fill the ranks. The projected breakdown of these units is as follows:

Regular Army

Engineer detachment, mounted, Fort Leavenworth
Two companies Signal Corps, Fort Myer
One regiment cavalry (4th), Forts Leavenworth and Riley and Jefferson Barracks
One regiment cavalry (7th), Camp Thomas
Two batteries field artillery (3rd and 4th), Fort Myer
Two batteries field artillery (6th and 7th), For Riley

Two batteries, field artillery (14th and 21st), Fort Sheridan
One battery, field artillery (29th), Fort Leavenworth
One battery, field artillery (siege) (16th), Fort Leavenworth
One battery, field artillery (siege) (11th), Fort Hamilton
One infantry battalion (1st Infantry), Fort Porter
One regiment (2nd Infantry), Fort Logan
One regiment (3rd Infantry), Fort Thomas and Columbus Barracks
One regiment (6th Infantry), Fort Leavenworth
One battalion (8th Infantry—two companies; 9th Infantry, two companies)
Fort Niagara
One regiment (16th Infantry), Forts McPherson and Slocum
One regiment (25th Infantry), Forts Niobrara and Reno
One regiment (26th Infantry), Texas posts
One regiment (27th Infantry), Fort Sheridan and Columbus Barracks
One regiment (29th Infantry), Arizona, Texas, and Utah posts
One regiment (30th Infantry), Arkansas, Nebraska, and Oklahoma Posts

Note: One battalion less than 10 regiments, deducted from the Niagara Falls force.[32]

Militia
One troop cavalry (from New York) 1 troop squadron
Two batteries, field artillery (from New York) 1st and 2nd light batteries
Two batteries, field artillery (from Pennsylvania) Batteries B and C
One battery, field artillery (from New York) 6th light battery from Fort Niagara
One regiment infantry (from New York) 12th infantry from Fort Niagara
One battalion infantry (from New York) 74th infantry, 1st battalion
One regiment infantry (from Pennsylvania), 1st regiment
One battalion infantry (from Georgia, Fort McPherson) 5th infantry, 1st battalion
One battalion infantry (from Kentucky, Fort Thomas) 2nd infantry, 1st battalion
One battalion infantry (from Ohio) 1st infantry, 1st battalion[33]

The militia selected for the operation were chosen for specific reasons:

Militia organization have been chosen for corps headquarters guard, to cover Niagara Falls bridges from [the] American end, and to serve as garrisons in place of regular troops taking the field, and to guard depots of supplies. They have been taken from States in which posts and depot are located, except in the case of Pennsylvania. The numbers taken are approximately in proportion to the populations of the States.

As a rule, it is desirable that the organization be removed from the allurements of near homes; an exception is the 1st Battalion, 74th Infantry, New York, which would be to some extent supervised by the Colonel, who is highly commended.

As regards militia form George, Kentucky and Ohio, battalions are chosen which may have been drilled as such; all available light batteries properly armed, are wanted from New York and Pennsylvania. As two regiments of infantry, which are of full strength, have three battalions, and have drilled as regiments, might be taken from these last two States.[34]

The plan contemplated the issues of pre-positioning of the regular army and militia troops near the Niagara frontier but noted that there was not suitable facilities for such camps. If it was required by Army commanders as a political posturing against Great Britain, the state of Pennsylvania was cited as the most logical place for such staging. This would provide them rapid access to Buffalo via railways as well as the rest of the Niagara region.

New York was designated as a camp location as well—north of the Allegheny River and west of the Genesee. Here two or more lines of railroad were accessible for rapid deployment.

In the event of pre-positioning of troops, the planners suggested that at least one battery of siege artillery be placed at Fort Hamilton and two batteries of field artillery be sent to Fort Niagara.[35]

Supplies and Preparations

At the outset of hostilities, the Commanding Officer of Fort Niagara was to seize all vessels on the lower Niagara and prevent communication by any means between the United States and the Canadian shore—including telegraph stations. Gun emplacements were to be erected for field batteries to cover the wharves on other shore or to prevent travel along the river.

The Commanding Officer of Fort Porter was to interrupt and disrupt communications between the US and the Canadian shore from Buffalo and as far as the North Tonawanda.

Supplies for this operation were to be drawn from local garrisons. The plan called for pulling sixty-days' worth of supplies as part of the overall operation. One field hospital was to be established as well as one ambulance section.[36]

The Raiding Force

With the issuance of the plan, the Commanding Officer of the Atlantic Division had his staff perform their own analysis of the operations. While they do not clearly state their opinions, they did amend the plan to provide for more offensive operations than were detailed in the original plans. While the original 1905 plan indicated that the Americans would move to protect Buffalo and prohibit travel between the Atlantic Ocean and the Great Lakes, it did not strike at Canada or even press an offensive operation to seize control of the nation. These changes, however, alter the strategic concept and press for more of an offensive campaign. The American force took on more of an appearance of an "Expeditionary Force."[37]

The chief impetus for such a raid was any indication that the Canadians were moving troops against the US forces in Niagara.

> As the movement contemplated is a raid, in which promptness of action and celerity of movement are of vital importance, and as the regular force in the other Divisions would almost certainly be needed for operations at other localities, it is suggested that in the solution to the problem only resources available in the Atlantic Division shall be used.[38]

Clearly there were concerns by the Joint Board planners that the British might respond quickly with reinforcements and armaments to prop up Canada.

One of the primary targets was the Canadian Pacific Railroad. The Joint Board issued memorandum to qualify "At what points can the Canadian Pacific Railroad best be broken, having in view prompt action and effective demolition?"[39] As one of the primary means of moving men and material across Canada, the destruction or seizure of this railroad would severely limit Canada's capability to wage war. Severing this rail line cut off the west coast of Canada, meaning any British reinforcement of the west coast would keep those troops limited to operations against the western US.

Composition of the Raiding Force

Cavalry
Two (2) Regiments and one (1) Squadron *(120 officers, 3 chaplains, 5 veterinary surgeons, 2,006 enlisted men and 2,254 horses.)* Drawn from the 12th Cavalry (Kerr's Regiment, Fort Oglethorpe Georgia); 15th Cavalry (Wallace's Regiment, Fort Ethan Allen, Vermont); 13th Cavalry (Hatfield's Regiment, Headquarters, Band, and Second Squadron, Fort Myer Virginia.)

Field Artillery
Two (2) field officers
Five (5) Batteries: *(22 officers, 2 veterinary surgeons, 692 enlisted men, 590 horses)* (Drawn from the 3rd and 4th Field Batteries, Fort Myer, Virginia); 11th Field Battery (Siege), Port Adams, Rhode Island); 23rd and 27th Field Batteries (Fort Ethan Allan, Vermont)

Infantry
Four (4) Regiments and two (2) companies. *(209 officers, 4 chaplains, 3,395 enlisted men, 70 horses.)* Drawn from: 5th Infantry (Cowles' Regiment, Plattsburg Barracks, New York); 8th Infantry (Smith's Regiment, 10 companies, Headquarters and four companies, Fort Jay, New York, four companies from Fort Niagara New York, two companies from Fort Slocum, New York); 17th Infantry (Van Orsdale's Regiment,

Fort McPherson, Georgia); 23rd Infantry (Reade's Regiment, Headquarters and 8 companies, Madison Barracks, New York and 4 companies from Fort Ontario, New York); 1st Infantry (Duggan's Regiment, 3 companies, Fort Porter, New York); 9th Infantry (Regan's Regiment, 1 company at Allegheny Arsenal, Pennsylvania).

Engineers
One (1) Battalion, four (4) companies. *(17 officers, 418 enlisted men, 104 horses).* Drawn from Washington DC Barracks.

Signal Corps
One (1) company. *(4 officers, 144 enlisted men, and 25 horses)* Drawn from Company G, Fort Wood, New York.

<u>*Hospital Corps*</u>
57 Officers and 403 enlisted men.[40]

The bulk of this division-sized force was to be assembled and encamped at the outbreak of hostilities in a tract of land on Gill Creek, east of Sugar Street and north of Packard road adjoining the town of Niagara New York. The cavalry force (identified in the War Plan as "Wade's Division") was to be assembled and caped near Batavia New York. The site was five miles east and north east of Batavia. The camp was bounded by the New York Central Railroad and connected via a good road network, the Black Creek and Old State Road. There was an ample water supply (Godfrey's Pond). If additional forces were called upon, there was an auxiliary camp site located further sough between Horse Shoe Lake and the Morganville Road.[41]

The Mission of the Raiding Force?

While American planners had placed a sizable and relatively mobile raiding force in the theatre of operations, their exact plans and targets were not identified. From the sparse references to the force in the plans, it is assumed that it was designated to disrupt communications, specifically telegraph communications, in Canada as well as engage and harass any Canadian or Imperial (British) units being sent to counterattack the Americans. In short, these raids would be *ad hoc* in nature and at the discretion of the local commander. Suggested targets included railroad junctions, key railroad bridges, telegraph stations, and Royal Canadian Mounted Police garrisons.

Auxiliary Force (Reserves)

The Commanding Officer of the Atlantic Division recognized that the 1905 plan did not address the needs for a reserve force.

The details of the organization and supply of the auxiliary force and of the various corps of volunteers which it would be evidently be necessary to call into service, in case of hostilities with Great Britain, are not given as they are not required by the terms of Problems and Instructions concerning the solution. Attention however is requested to the strategic location of the City of Albany, New York, for the organization and encampment of volunteers. Troops could be readily forwarded by rail from Albany to both the Niagara and Lake Champlain frontiers. By occupying this point, the city of New York and the vicinity would be guarded against overland invasion form the two frontiers above mentioned, and the forces held in a favorable position for offensive movements along the frontiers of New York and Vermont.[42]

As such establishment of an auxiliary force, drawn primarily from National Guard Units, was deemed "appropriate and necessary."[43]

Auxiliary Force Composition

Cavalry
Tennessee:
Two (2) Troops Tennessee Cavalry—Troop A, Nashville, Troop B, Chattanooga

Massachusetts:
One (1) troop Massachusetts Cavalry, Troop F, Clemsford

New York:
Squadron A three (3) troops, Troops 1, 2, and 3 New York City

Rhode Island:
One (1) Troop Rhode Island Cavalry, Troop A, Pawtucket

Pennsylvania:
One (1) Troop Pennsylvania Cavalry, 1st Troop, Philadelphia
Field Artillery
Alabama:
Three (3) Batteries, Light Artillery Battery B—Montgomery, Battery C, Selma

Connecticut:
One (1) Battery Connecticut Light Artillery, Battery A, Branford

Georgia:
One (1) Battery, Chatham Artillery, Savannah

Massachusetts:
One (1) Battery, Massachusetts Light Artillery, Battery B, Worcester

Mississippi:
Two (2) Batteries, Light Artillery, Battery E, Vicksburg, Battery I, Meridian

New Hampshire: One (1) Battery, 1st New Hampshire Light Battery, Manchester

New Jersey: Two (2) Batteries Light Artillery, Battery A, Orange, Battery B, Camden

New York:
Three (3) Batteries Light Artillery. 1st Battery, New York, 3rd Battery, Brooklyn, 6th Battery, Binghamton

North Carolina:
One (1) Battery Light Artillery, Battery A, Charlotte

Pennsylvania:
Two (2) Batteries Light Artillery. Battery B, East Pittsburg, Battery C, Phoenixville

Rhode Island:
One (1) Battery Light Artillery, Battery A, Providence

South Carolina:
One (1) Battery Light Artillery, (German Artillery), Charleston

Virginia:
Three (3) Batteries Light Artillery. Battery A, Richmond, Battery B, Norfolk, Battery C, Portsmouth.

Infantry
Tennessee:
3rd Infantry to assemble at Knoxville.

Georgia:
4th Infantry to assemble at Albany
5th Infantry to assemble in Atlanta

Alabama:
2nd Infantry to assemble at Eufaula
1st Infantry to assemble at Mobile

New Jersey:
2nd Infantry to assemble at Trenton

Pennsylvania:
Five (5) regiments (1st, 2nd, 6th, and 18th) and the 1st Pennsylvania Infantry to assemble at Philadelphia
6th Pennsylvania Infantry to assemble in Philadelphia
9th Pennsylvania Infantry to assemble in Wilkes Barre
18th Pennsylvania Infantry to assemble at Pittsburg

Maryland:
1st Infantry to rendezvous at Hagerstown

Massachusetts:
5th Massachusetts Infantry (assembly point to be determined)
2nd Infantry to assemble at Springfield
6th Infantry to assemble at Boston

New York:
1st Infantry to rendezvous at Albany
2nd Infantry to rendezvous at Troy
14th Infantry to rendezvous at Brooklyn

Connecticut:
1st Infantry to rendezvous at Hartford

Virginia:
70th Infantry to rendezvous at Richmond

North Carolina:
1st North Carolina Infantry to rendezvous at Charlotte
3rd North Carolina Infantry to rendezvous at Reidsville

South Carolina:
1st and 2nd Infantry to assemble at Charleston [4]

Summary Evaluation of the War Plan

As one of the earlier war plans crafted by the Joint Board, this plan still lacks the in-depth coordination sought out between the Army and Navy. There is a broad assumption in the Army's plan that the Navy would be dealing with Britain's Royal Navy while the Army would deal with the immediate threat of Canada. A strategic decision fought at sea, however, would have potentially dramatic impacts on War Plan Crimson—but these are not addressed at all in the documents. It would have been immeasurably better to have the Navy be involved with securing ships for the blocking of the Port Colborne end of the Welland Canal rather than the Army—yet no planning for Navy involvement was made. Considering that this campaign was part of a broader operation against Great Britain and the Navy would be carrying much of that burden, it still shows the earmarks of rivalry between the two branches.

The plan is not audacious in nature but primarily a limited offensive, attempting to prohibit the British from moving naval forces in the Great Lakes to wreak havoc on shipping there. By attacking in a limited manner, the US was able to protect its own interests while putting pressures on the Canadians to capitulate. In essence, this plan negated the British from enabling a theater of operations that had proved useful in previous wars.

In the 1904–1905 period when the plans were created, it is clear that both Canada and the United States had relatively limited means to wage an all-out total war against each other. Canadian defense relied heavily on militia groups that had no formal training nor had they trained using live ammunition. The United States, while committing a sizable force of the Regular Army, still relied a great deal on militia in the form of National Guard units.

The technology proposed in the war is fascinating because of its influence on proposed tactics and units. While machineguns are clearly defined, their overall impact on infantry and cavalry formations seems to be glossed over. The US still believed in an era of cavalry penetrating the enemies' rear generating chaos. Rapid fire weapons would put an end to this illusion. The thinking of the United States mirrored that of her European counterparts prior to the start of the Great War. It would take several years of massive losses for military planners to realize the folly in horse-mounted cavalry carrying the day.

Key strategic port facilities were not on the targets at all in this early draft of War Plan Crimson. This means that the British, if they could successfully secure the oceans, would be free to move troops into Canada. The war against the United States could be allowed to escalate quickly out of control.

In reviewing these invasion plans there is clearly no intention on the United States occupying Canada. Avoidance of major cities like Toronto and London does not completely negate the strategic value of Canada to Great Britain. For the most part, the planners would be leaving Canada still free without tying down tens of thousands of American troops to occupy and control their neighbor to the north. The invasion, very limited in nature, forces Canada to concentrate its small military forces on moving against a relatively small target (the Niagara frontier) to dislodge the US forces. This prevents them from being used for offensive military operations elsewhere. This level of strategic sophistication in the planning is clearly shown, if not documented in the thinking of the Joint Board.

The 1928/1929 Plans for War with Mexico
War Plan Green Variants #1, #2, and #3

The Disturbing Neighbor to the South

Next to Canada, Mexico shares the largest border with the United States. While modern relations between the governments are amiable, that has not always been the case. During the tenure of the Joint Board, there were two incidents with Mexico that led to conflict. The most notable of these was Pancho Villa's private war against America—1915–1917 and the Tampico Affair of 1914.

The so-called "Tampico Affair" had all of the trappings of a teenager throwing a party when his/her parents are out of town and that party getting quickly out of hand. Nine drunken and armed American sailors were arrested in the port city of Tampico when they entered a fuel loading station. The sailors were released but the naval commander demanded an apology and a twenty-one gun salute. The apology was delivered but not the salute. President Woodrow Wilson asked Congress for permission to occupy the port of Veracruz for the slight to the US.

In the middle of this a German steamer filled with imported arms and munitions arrived in port with its cargo intended for one of Mexico's civil war factions. Fearing that foreign interests were funding (and arming) the civil war, President Wilson ordered the US Marine Corps to seize Veracruz. This was to be the second time that the city was to be invaded by the United States, the first being in 1847.

On 21 April 1914 Marines and sailors landed in the port from the USS *Florida* and the USS *Utah*. At first the Mexican army fell back. The local citizenry was armed as were prisoners in the jails. Veracruz quickly became an urban battlefield. While the fighting was fierce for a short time, the sheer skill, training, and arms of the US forces prevailed. Veracruz remained under American "protection" until November of 1914 when the matter was finally resolved at the Niagara Peace Conference.

The civil war in Mexico continued to be a thorn in America's rump however. In 1915, President Woodrow Wilson officially endorsed the Mexican national government of Venustiano Carranza. This act infuriated one of the rebel leaders, Pancho Villa. Initially Villa waged his war against the United States behind the Mexican borders. He attacked American citizens living in Northern Mexico—waging a private war on terror intended to change the mind of the US leadership. When his minor attacks did not generate the results he wanted, Villa attacked a train carrying American citizens working for the American Smelting and Refining Company on 11 January 1916. Sixteen Americans were taken from the train outside of Santa Isabel, Chihuahua, stripped and publicly executed. The massacre took place in Mexico and despite the agitated press and cries for justice, the US refused to do much more than deploy additional forces along the Mexican border. Given the response two years earlier in the Tampico Affair, it demonstrated remarkable restraint and inconsistency on the part of the US Government.

Apparently dissatisfied with his attempt at stirring American ire, Villa upped the ante in his deadly game with the United States by crossing the US border on 9 March 1916 on a deliberate raid. He attacked the American town of Columbus, New Mexico, which was garrisoned by the 13th Cavalry Regiment. Villa's men burned the town, stole horses and mules, seized the garrison's machineguns and ammunition and fought an irregular series of battles with the military and local civilians. When they were done with the raid, ten civilians and eight soldiers were dead and a number of others were wounded. It was an attack that demonstrated audacity and to a certain extent, stupidity on the part of Villa.

This attack, the first on US soil since the War of 1812, could not go unanswered. President Wilson authorized General John "Blackjack" Pershing to lead an expeditionary force into Mexico with the expressed aim of capturing Pancho Villa. The American force consisted of 4,800 men and included a lone airplane (A Curtis JN-3) of the First Aero Squadron. This expeditionary force did not leverage any plans devised or developed by the Joint Board.

The Expeditionary Force lumbered across the border in March of 1916, waging one of the United States' first war on terror—seeking a single man who had orchestrated an attack on American civilians. Pancho Villa had become the Osama Bin-Laden of his era. It was in stark contrast to the Great War across the Atlantic where Europe was fighting its second year of vicious fighting. On 29 March the US force engaged the Villistas at San Geronimo Ranch, near the town of Guerrero. The battle raged for five hours and left over seventy-five of Villa's men killed or wounded and only five of the Americans were wounded. Pancho Villa was forced to retreat into the mountains to escape. Little did General Pershing realize that this would be the most successful battle his tiny invasion force was to fight, and was the only one that came even close to capturing Villa.

The Americans pursued the Mexican rebels, fighting a string of small skirmishes across Mexico for the next few years. For the most part the rebels managed to avoid a large-scale engagement with the superior US force. Many American officers that took part in the Expeditionary forces would go onto greatness in the Great War and WWII. Lieutenant George S. Patton led a contingent of three Dodge cars against rebel leader Julio Cárdenas at San Miguelito Ranch, near Rubio, Chihuahua on 14 May 1916. Patton personally shot and killed Cárdenas in the first US armored vehicle attack.

The fighting was not all one-sided. The Villistas struck back on 25 May in a tiny ambush which left one American killed and two others wounded. This tiny ambush really exemplified most of the fighting that took place—quick hit and run attacks with limited results other than to prove to Pershing that his foe was still potent and dangerous.

The last battle of the expeditionary forces took place on 21 June 1916 when the US force clashed with Carrancista soldiers at the Battle of Carrizal. At best the battle was a draw, with less than twenty-four Mexican soldiers killed in the fight—though the Americans had the same number of men captured. The US expeditionary force withdrew in January of 1917—having never captured Pancho Villa.

Relations in the Great War and Post-War Era

Mexico was brought the forefront of American war fears again in 1917 when it was revealed that the German Kaiser had been floating the concept of Mexico attacking the United States. This ploy was uncovered by the British who had cracked the German codes and had decoded a message from German Foreign Secretary Arthur Zimmerman to the German Ambassador to Mexico. If Mexico attacked America, it would keep the United States from sending troops into Europe against Germany and her allies (the Central Powers). In exchange for this effort, Germany would back Mexico reclaiming Texas, New Mexico, and Arizona. The message, dubbed the Zimmerman Telegram, had an explosive effect almost the opposite of what the Germans had hoped for. Americans were outraged at this violation of the Monroe Doctrine and the possibility of war on their own soil being orchestrated out of Europe. Combined with the lifting of restrictions on submarine warfare, it compelled the United States to declare war on Germany.

Mexico, for its part, actually explored the concept but came to the conclusion that the Mexicans lacked the military strength to even contemplate such a venture. Even if Mexico could have taken the territory, there was the issue of what to do with the large number of Americans that would be living in the recaptured territory. Ultimately Mexico remained quiet on the matter. The United States entered the war in Europe, driven there by a threat to her southern border. The Joint Board began to create plans, at a high level, for the invasion of Mexico. These were dubbed Plan Green.[1]

Mexico's tensions with the United States did not calm with the eventual petering out of their civil war. Relations between the two nations broke down in 1920 but President Coolidge had been able to restore them in 1923 after negotiating property claims and the rights of Americans in Mexico. Mexico seethed with anti-American sentiments and the United States had been imposing an embargo against the country for years—which President Coolidge lifted in 1924.

There was hope that relations would return to a more positive stance but that fizzled away in 1925 with Mexico restricted American oil operations. The Mexican government, to shore up their economy, nationalized privately held oil and mining interests in the country. The problem was that many of these were owned by American corporations. The Americans were willing to accept compensation for their interests, but the myriad maze of the Mexican court system did not offer much in the way of financial relief.

At the time, President Coolidge instructed his ambassador, Dwight Morrow, to go to Mexico and "keep us out of a war with Mexico." At the same time, while attempting to negotiate for peace, the Joint Board updated their war plan for Mexico—dubbed War Plan Green. Morrow was able to negotiate the US out of war with Mexico.

The Basis for the Plan

Plan Green underwent several modifications during its shelf-life as a war plan. The first version of the plan from 1919:

> War is assumed to have broken out between the United States and Mexico. The main army operates on the line Vera Cruz—City of Mexico. An army based on the Rio Grande operates against Monterey, as a division assists the main army, and with a view, should events permit, to pushing south to the San Luis Potosi or the City of Mexico.[2]

To cope with this the planning was quite loose and vague in nature. "The Commanding General of the Southwestern Division will—

1. Select the point of concentration and base of supplies and determine the line or lines of operations to the designated objective, and state in full the reasons influencing the selection.
2. Prepare orders necessary for the mobilization and concentration of the troops (Regulars and organized militia) in the Southwestern Division, designating the organization and their commanders by names as they now stand, it being understood that these designations will be subject to change in future as stations and personnel of organizations change.
3. Prepare the necessary orders for organizing the command into brigades and higher units.
4. Prepare all orders necessary for the movement up to, and including, the crossing of the Rio Grande and the first encampment on Mexican soil.
5. Prepare a complete list of the supplies of every kind needed of the invading force, and state where the supplies can most readily be obtained. The supplies should be sufficient to last the command nine months.
6. If more troops are need for this operation than are now in the Southwestern Division, state where and how these additional troops can most readily be obtained, bearing in mind that the troops now available in other departments will probably be needed elsewhere.
7. State how soon after the receipt of orders from the Chief of Staff of the Army the necessary force can be assembled, fully equipped, and placed across the Rio Grande to begin its march on Monterey.[3]

As one can see, the initial planning for war with Mexico was barely conceived—even in light of the incursions by Pancho Villa and the 1914 invasion of Veracruz. As such it was deemed best to concentrate on a later version of the plans which reflects the true joint nature of Army and Navy maneuvers with specific targets identified as mission objectives.

The version outlined in this chapter is the most comprehensive of these—the 1929 revised plan. This plan is broken down into three plans components, each of which will be explored.

Complete copies of the plan exist in a variety of forms, some replete with penciled in edits, others missing entire sections. So this plan, as presented, is compiled from various copies of plans and addendums dealing with enemy troop forces, topography, etc.

Throughout the plan Mexico is referred to by its color designation, "Green."

Like many of the War Plans, Plan Green outlines the general situational assumptions that would trigger the United States to engage the nation in war. In the case of Mexico, these assumptions are as follows:

It is the general arrangement of the *Joint Army and Navy Basic War Plan—Green*, envisages the growth and spread of disturbed conditions in Green to that extent where intervention becomes necessary, and, initially, a preparatory plan is put into effect, which provides for reinforcement of the border and the organization of expeditionary forces for a limited occupation of Green territory without a declaration of war. As later developments of the situation may require, the basic plan facilitates the orderly transition from it to either one or two other plans which call for greater efforts under conditions of actual war. This plan does not prevent, however, in an emergency, a direct transition from peace to war and the immediate initiation of one of the foregoing plans applicable to conditions of actual war, without first putting into execution the preparatory plan mentioned.[4]

As a condition precedent to intervention, it is assumed that internal disturbances in Green have brought about such conditions as to threaten to jeopardize the interest of the United States, or the lives and property of its citizens, and the United States Government, while alerting or reinforcing its border forces as a protective measure to the extent the situation may require, will, initially, at least, follow its recognized policy of non-interference in the internal affairs of Latin-American countries. It may be expected, however, to follow its policy of withholding recognition to any government that may be established by other than constitutional means, and, if the existing recognized Green Government is friendly, the United States may be expected to give it moral support, and, following precedents, may endeavor to prevent the shipment of arms and munitions of war to factions hostile to the recognized government, or if that government is unfriendly, may declare a strict embargo on arms and munitions applicable to all of Green.[5]

The Three Green War Plans

The Joint Board devised three variations of War Plan Green in the 1928 edition. This variation was an addition from the 1917 War Plan Green which simply dealt with an invasion of Mexico with no criteria or varying objectives. This change reflects some of the post-WWI evolution in American military planning as well as experience. The three plans had clear delineations and criteria for implementation.

Basic Plan Green #1 was based on the assumption that there were widespread disturbances in Mexico. These would lead to "chaotic conditions," where the Mexican government would be:

> ...unable or unwilling to protect the lives and property of American citizens and other foreign nationals, and the United States seeks to afford such protection by establishing order and a stable, responsible government, throughout Green.[6]

War Plan Green #2 was different in that the assumption was that there was not widespread chaos in Mexico at all. Instead, it was envisioned that a government were to come into power in Mexico that would be hostile to the interests of the United States. Under this scenario:

> ... the United States seeks to force the establishment in Green of a Federal Government which will be in harmony with the interests and foreign obligations of the United States, by prompt action directed against the hostile government, avoiding, unless forced to it by later developments, any general occupation of Green territory.[7]

Under this variant's criteria, the United States would topple the hostile government and implement a new government that was more to its liking.

War Plan #3 was slightly vaguer in its nature:

> Conditions in Green are such that, due to insurrection or other internal disturbances, the lives and property of American citizens and other foreign nationals are endangered and the United States seeks to furnish protection without a declaration of war.[8]

The US would facilitate action under War Plan Green #1 or #2. In essence, War Plan #3 was envisioned as a defensive situation while preparing to initiate an invasion, if necessary.

War Plan Green #1

War Plan Green #1 opened initially with a focus on the defense of the US border, they outlined a series of assaults for an all-out invasion of Mexico. The combined Army and Navy objectives were:

> ...to gain control of and establish order and stable government throughout Green, with as little interference with the peaceful pursuits of the native population as may be consistent with the necessary military operations.[9]

The defense of the US border was seen as critical before any other offensive operations were contemplated. War Plan Green #1 envisioned that the area of greatest threat was "mainly from the direction of the Brownsville—Laredo area."[10] It was in this border region that the Americans felt Mexico might be able to actually cause problems or even counterattack any American aggression.

Defense of the border was not enough to achieve the plan objectives. To gain control of Mexico, an invasion was required. This was a plan that leveraged the US Navy on both coasts to blockade Mexico and essentially bottle it up from foreign arms or intervention. The Navy would be landing troops in the form of the US Marine Corps, to seize key oil fields and port facilities. Meanwhile the Army would drive south from the US border. Overall it was a complicated operation that required a great deal of coordination between the services.

The Army was in charge of protecting the border with the anticipation of invading and pacifying Mexico. The Army also was going to be preparing for the establishment of an American backed military government once Mexico became stable. To accomplish this, the Army had three specific tasks to be executed—which were applicable to all three of the Green War Plans:

1. Protection of the southern border of the United States.
2. Interception, if order by the President, of munitions of war destined for Mexico.
3. Transportation by sea of Army forces and their supplies to overseas destinations. In this capacity the Army Transport Service would be assigned under a Naval convoy commander unless otherwise requested by the Army.[11]
   Additionally the Army had responsibilities, once the border defense was secure it to make an incursion into Mexico-proper. The specific objectives for the Army in this latter phase, the invasion were as follows:

1. Invasion of Green and the occupation and the exercise of control over such territory as may be necessary for a general pacification of the country.
2. Establishment of a Military Government throughout the occupied territory.
3. Organization and ultimate establishment of a stable and responsible Green Government which would be willing and able to maintain order, and to insure protection of American rights and interests.
4. Relief of Naval forces in the Tampico Tuxpan area and in the Mazatlan—Mazatlan Junction area as soon as practical, estimated time two weeks.[12]

The Army forces would be broken into three Army Expeditionary Forces (AEF's). The first (AEF "A") would be based in Texas, Arizona and New Mexico. The second, AEF "B", would be designated the Tampico Expedition and would be aimed at driving to the Tampico area and relieving the US Marine forces which were going to seize control of the oil fields there. The third force, AEF "C" (the Mazatlan Expedition) would work towards the Mexican west coast city to secure its port facilities there and relieve the US Navy/US Marine Corps troops.[13]

The Navy had a very complicated role under Green War Plan #1. They were responsible for controlling sea communications and to assist the Army as needed.[14] To accomplish this, the Navy was responsible for the:

1. Containment, capture, or destruction of hostile Green Naval Forces.
2. Removal of United States citizens, if circumstances warrant, from Green ports on both coasts.
3. Provision of security for the sea communications.15

While on the surface this seems like a minor role, the Joint Board planners envisioned a much broader role for the US Navy and, subsequently, the US Marine Corps.

In order to accomplish the naval mission, the US Navy was given specific tasks to accomplish. These are outlined as follows:

1. Blockade of both coasts of Green until the President directs otherwise, either with respect to blockade as a whole or as to the blockade of particular ports in the actual possession of the land or naval forces of the United States.
2. Seizure and holding of the Tampico and the Tampico-Tuxpan oil field region until relieved by the Army.
3. Prevention of importation of enemy supplies into Green from Guatemala via the Pan-American Railroad.
4. Seizure and holding of Mazatlan and prevention of transportation of enemy troops and supplies through Mazatlan Junction until relieved by the Army.
5. Cooperation with the Army in ferrying Army aircraft from Brownsville to Tampico. Note: In the case of forced landings, the aircraft pilots will have been previously instructed by the Army to land on the beach or in the water near a naval vessel.
6. Preparation of a landing field and provision of supplies of fuel and oil at Tampico for Army aircraft.
7. Provision of hospital ship service for the Army forces based on Tampico and Mazatlan.
8. Full cooperation with the Army in the execution of its mission.
9. Seizure of the lighthouses and organization and administration of the Lighthouse Service on the Green coasts.[16]

Of all of these operations there were two where fighting was most likely—the Tampico/Tuxpan oil fields and Mazatlan. In both of these objectives, the US Marine Corps, strongly supported by the Navy, were to attack and seize the facilities and await the Army forces marching via land south. There was an open option that the Army could have the Navy transport the vessels, but the assumption, given the placement of the Army troops along the Texas, Arizona, and New Mexico borders—were that they would march to the south to link up with their comrades in arms.

The details of the seizure of the Tampico region are covered later in this chapter.

The Forces to be Used

The pacification of Mexico was not something that was to be taken lightly. The Army's needs would easily outstrip the Regular Army forces and require a massive influx from the state National Guards to provide the numbers of troops required to secure Mexico. The Army's needs were defined in War Plan Green #1 as the following:

> For the execution of this plan, the War Department shall make available Regular Army and National Guard units to a strength of approximately 210,000, to include forces for the protection of the border, for the main expeditionary force for invasion of Green from the border, and for the two main expeditionary forces, initially consisting of one Infantry Division for the Tampico–Tuxpan Area and one reinforced brigade for the Mazatlan–Mazatlan Junction Area. Units will be deployed initially at strength and will be raised to authorized peace strength by increased enlistment.[17]

For the Army, the "M-Day" or day of mobilization would be defined when the National guard was called into Federal Service—not when they were actually in place and ready to fight. The Marine Corps Reserves and the Naval Reserve Force would not coordinate their mobilization efforts. Their mobilization was left to the discretion of the Department of the Navy but it was generally assumed they would coordinate with the War Department.[18]

Naval forces were less in terms of manpower but more in terms of material resources (ships):

> For the execution of this Plan, the Navy Department shall make available such Naval forces as are required to carry out the Navy Mission and Tasks thereunder, including two expeditionary forces of Marine Corps troops of approximate strengths of 5,500 and 2,000 respectively. All units will be of the regular Navy, Marine Corps, and Coast Guard, raised to authorized strengths by increased enlistments, plus such units of the Naval and Marine Corps Reserves as it is found to be necessary to call to active duty.[19]

Earlier planning by the Joint Board, specifically in 1919, had explored the Marine contingent needs to take the Tampico oil fields. These early estimates, would be modified in the final plans, but would serve as a basis for the overall plan in 1929.

"To the first brigades is assigned (1) the occupation of the city of Tampico and the adjacent oil terminals, water supply, etc., (b) the occupation and protection of the oil fields around Panuco, Topila, and Abano [sic]; and (c) the occupation of Vera Cruz. IT is probable that about on regiment would be assigned to each of these tasks as indicated.

"The second brigade, somewhat smaller than the first, is to be used in the occupation of necessary localities and protection of property in the following areas—(a) From San Geronimo to Cerro Azul and Tierra Amarilla; (b) from La Pena to Potrero; and (c) from Tamishua to Alamo.

1st Brigade
Tampico and Western Fields Vera Cruz

	Enlisted
Tampico City, terminals, water supply etc. one regiment	1,250
Topilia—Panuco (with possible detachment to Abano vicinity) one regiment	1,250
Vera Cruz detachment one regiment	1,250
1 MG Co. From brigade	125

For general duty

Brigade Headquarters	110
Brigade Signal Co.	125

Brigade reserve

One infantry BN (from 2nd Brigade)	250
Brigade MG Bn (less one company)	150
One battery 30 guns (four guns)	150

Total enlisted 1st Brigade	4,660

2nd Brigade
Southern Fields

San Geronimo to Cerro Azul

One regiment	1,250
One MG Co (From Brigade Bn)	125

Tamishua to Potrero

One regiment, less One Bn	1,000

Tuxpam [sic] to Alamo

One regiment, less One Bn	1,000

For general duties

Brigade Headquarters	110
Brigade Signal Co.	125

Brigade reserve

One infantry Bn	250
Brigade MG Bn less One Co.	150
One battery 30 guns (four guns)	150

Total enlisted 2nd Brigade	4,160[20]

These initial plans would be greatly modified but would serve as the basis for the overall invasion force. Later in this chapter the final planning invasion force is detailed.

The Strike on Mazatlan

While the 1928/1929 War Plan Green does not specify how Mazatlan was to be taken, the Joint Board had drawn up a preliminary plan in 1905 for such an operation and this plan most likely would have been the basis for any attack—if not serving as the attack plan itself. The plan for the invasion of Mazatlan was devised to minimize losses to the American landing force. The ship's batteries used in the supporting gunfire would effectively clear away resistance to the landing forces as they came ashore. Communications and coordination was going to be crucial as the force landed.

Once the US Marines secured Mazatlan, they would be relieved by a US Army expeditionary force which would be marching south overland. This meant that the Marines would be holding onto the city for several weeks even under the best circumstances.

The keys to taking Mazatlan depended on securing the high ground—in this case Felton Hill and Hill 15. Prior to the Marines landing, there would be a preliminary bombardment of these two hills with naval gunfire. While directed at military targets presumed to be on those hills, it was recognized that the bombardment would have an effect on the civilian population. The Joint Board anticipated there would be panic on their part, making navigating the streets of the city more difficult. Those that didn't panic would aid the local garrison to attempt to repulse the American landings.

The 1905 assessment of the city indicated that Mazatlan had a military garrison of approximately 600. It was believed that they had possession of at least one-to-two pieces of artillery. These forces were not believed to be elite Mexican troops. In fact they were anticipated to be armed with a variety of weapons.

Perhaps the greatest threat came from snipers. The male citizens of Mazatlan were known to be armed and those that did not flee or hide from the bombardment, might be compelled by patriotic fervor to attempt to defend the city. Snipers in the city itself were expected to add to confusion and rack up American casualties. The American response to the sniping issue was one of blunt force—directing naval gunfire barrages on those buildings that might house such snipers. Little thought was given in the planning to the damage that such bombardments might cause, or the risk of resulting fires.

The US attack force was to be divided into three groups. These were defined as the following:

Force A
One gunboat—This gunboat would anchor inside Black Rock with a view of the radio station and Felton Hill opening between Cardones Chivas Islands [sic]. This force would then land a party with field pieces and machineguns. This attack force would

consist of two hundred men. Force A's Mission: (a) Land, retraining force on Piedra Island. (b) Utilizing their artillery battery, keep East slope of Felton Hill and Hill No. 15 clear of the enemy.

Force B
One gunboat—placed to provide cover southwest of Felton Hill. This gunboat would land two hundred men and five machineguns. The mission of Force B was to be as follows: (a) Clear west slope of Felton Hill and Hill No. 15 of enemy forces through naval gunfire if practicable. (b) Land the infantry force. This force was to form on the road at the base of the cliff, on the west side of Felton Hill, using the slope of the hillside for cover. This force was to later take Felton Hill, going up the northwest slope, under cover of the ship's batteries.

Force C
This force was to consist of navy transports and the main body of infantry forces. The mission of Force C was to initially anchor at Viejo Bay, close in-shore, about west of Tiburon Point. They would then (a) Heavily bombard Hills 15, 16, 17, and 18 and north slope of Felton Hill. (b) Land main expedition on beach in lee of Tiburon Point. This force would consist of 300 to 500 troops, five machineguns, and possibly one piece of field artillery.

    The time schedule that the attacks were to unfold is as follows:

Time: Zero hour (daylight assault is recommended)
Ships A, B, and C take up bombardment of east, west and north slopes, respectively, of Felton Hill and Hill No. 15—to clean them of all enemy resistance.

Ship A—Land part on the beach east of Opuesto Point, which will then establish itself on Piedra Island overlooking Mazatlan and Estero del Astillero. This force would then establish visual signal station.

Ship B—Land party on the beach under west slope of Pelton Hill. This party will form on the road under protection of the cliff, then take the summit going up the northwest slope.

Time: When the party from Force B is ready to move up the slope of Felton Hill.
Force C will move its barrage to concentrate on Hills 15, 16, 17 and 18. They will leave the northwest slope of Felton Hill clear for the attacking party from Force B.

Time: About two hours, when reports are received from Piedra Island and Felton Hill parties established there.
Force C—This force will land the main body of troops in the lee of Tiburon Point, forming a line from west to east. This line will take, in succession, Hills 15, 16, 18, and 17. They will then form a defense on each of these facing north and south. The barrage

from this main body will cover the advance of the main landing party toward the east.

Force A—will send two motor launches with sand bag protection and machineguns to patrol Estero del Astillero.

Force B—will patrol off Felton Hill to aid retraining force as necessary to hold Felton Hill.

Time: When the main body of the landing force complete its move across the peninsula. The Main Expeditionary Force will advance slowly under direction of the expedition commander; a column of one hundred men per street on the parallel streets.

Two additional forces would be formed/utilized in this assault:

Special Force—This force will form on Hill 18 once it is secured and advance to take Hill 19. The objectives of this Special Force is to secure the water tanks there and remaining as a reserve/retaining force for the east flank of the invasion. The composition of the Special Force was to be defined on an ad hoc basis by the invasion commander at his discretion, using the forces on Hill 18.

Reserve Force—The invasion reserves, consisting of upwards of several hundred men, were to move into Mazatlan proper. These were to be spread out for security purposes, forming on each third street to advance and follow the main body.[21]

Command and Coordination

War Plan Green #1 was to be a complex operation for the Army. There were three theaters of war that were contemplated for the AEF (Army Expeditionary Force); the principle theater, a secondary theater (in the west) and the Zone of the Interior which was primarily the continental United States for defense purposes.

> The Principle Theater of Operations under command of the Commanding General, A.E.F., will include Mexico (less lower California), and that part of the Eighth Crops Area lying between the border and the main lines (inclusive) of the Southern Pacific Railroad from Yuma Arizona, to San Antonio, Texas, and the San Antonio and Arkansas Pass Railroad from San Antonio, Texas, to Corpus Christi, including San Antonio, Fort Sam Houston (less section occupied by Hq., VIII Corps Area), El Paso and Fort Bliss.[22]

For the primary invasion of Mexico, this was to be the key theater that the American forces would operate from.

> The Secondary Theater of Operations, under command of the Commanding General, Western Frontier Command, will include Lower California and that part of the Ninth Corps Area south of 33 degrees North Latitude.[23]

The rest of the United States fell into the third, Zone of the Interior.

The reason that these lines of demarcation were drawn was the Army assigned Army Corps to geographic areas of the United States and this maintaining a separate command structure for the west simply mirrored that geographic breakdown of continental army commands.

The Navy breakdown was governed by the oceans.

> The Principle Theater of Operations, under command of the Commander-in-Chief, United States Fleet, will include both coasts of Green, and all sea areas adjacent thereto, including such extensions of these sea areas along both coasts of Central America as may be necessary to carry out the operations required. The Principal Theater of Operations will be divided into two sub-theaters as follows: The Gulf and Caribbean Sub-Theater, under command of the Commander, Scouting, will include the Gulf and Caribbean coasts of Green and all sea areas adjacent thereto, with such extension of these sea areas along the Caribbean Cost of Central America as may be necessary to carry out the operations involved. The Pacific Sub-Theater, under the command of the Commander Battle, will include the Pacific Coast of Green and all sea areas adjacent thereto, with such extension of these sea areas along the Pacific Coast of Central American as may be necessary to carry out the operations required.[24]

The heaviest burden would fall in the Gulf and Caribbean Sub-Theater since it was here that the Navy's largest role would be played out, the attack, seizure and securing of the Tampico-Tuxpan oil fields.

How would the Army and the Navy coordinate once hostilities had commenced? The plan called for a coordination between in terms of mere communications, with no consideration for the complexities which were destined to arise as battles began to be fought. The Commanding General of the AEF (who was destined to be the Commanding General of the VIII Corps Area) and the Commander-in-Chief, United States Fleet were anticipated to maintain direct contact throughout the campaign, though they would not share a common command facility.[25] During the actual invasion of Mexico, Norfolk Virginia would have been the most likely place for the Navy to run operations out of. The Army would most likely be out of Fort Sam Houston in Texas. The distances in the 1920s meant that any communications (usually by telegraph) between these command centers would take considerable time. This meant that tactical decisions were going to have to be handled locally.

The AEF—Force "B" (designated as the Tampico Expedition) would coordinate directly with the Navy Commander, Scouting in the Atlantic/Caribbean. The Army Expeditionary Force "C" (The Mazatlan Expedition) would have direct communications with the Navy Commander, Battle in the Pacific. Finally the Commanding General, Western Front Command (which would be led by the Commanding General, IX Corps Area) would have direct communications lines opened with the Commandant of the Eleventh Naval District.

The biggest areas of command coordination were envisioned to take place at Tampico—Tuxpan and Mazatlan. At Tampico, the US Marine Corps was to secure those oil fields, essentially striking along Mexico's east coast but far from the US border. AEF "B" (The Tampico Expedition) was the march south from the US boarder to relieve the Marines. The practicalities of when command was to pass between the Navy (Marines) and the Army was determined to be when the one infantry brigade was ashore or in the area of Marine operations.

At Mazatlan it was anticipated that the Marines would secure the city and then await AEF "C" (The Mazatlan Expedition) to march south and west to the city. Likewise a change of command authority over the city would take place once the Army arrived with at least one infantry regiment.[26]

No matter what, coordinating three expeditions across a country as large as Mexico was going to be a complicated and slow task.

War Plan Green #2

War Plan Green #2 assumed that a government had come to power in Mexico which was either a threat to the United States or outwardly hostile. As such its objectives were different than those of War Plan Green #1 since this would involve ending one government and installing another.

> The Joint Mission under this plan is expeditiously to gain control of Mexico City and Green communications, by military operations limited general to those against Green Federal Forces.[27]

The Army was tasked with protecting the US border and an "active defense," then to move to capture Mexico City, "and gain control of the Green Federal Government at the earliest possible date."[28] The Army was also tasked with the protection of the US Mexican border. The Navy's role was to, "assist the Army in controlling the Green Federal Government."[29] They were also expected to contain, capture or destroy any hostile Mexican naval forces and to assist in the removal of US citizens if the circumstances warranted. While this sounds minor, the US Marines were going to play a critical role and the Navy was expected to provide transport capabilities.

The political purpose of the plan was an application of military force to drive a change of government.

> The political purpose sought by this Plan is to force the establishment of a Federal Government which the United States will recognize, and the foreign policies of which will be in harmony with the interests and foreign policies of the United States. ... based on the foregoing political purpose, the military purpose of this Plan is the use of the armed forces of the United States to overthrow the present existing Federal Government of Mexico and to control Mexico City until a government satisfactory to the United States has been set up. Under existing political conditions in Mexico, it appears that the foregoing purpose can best be initiated by driving from Mexico City the existing Federal Government,

meanwhile depriving it of munitions of war from outside sources, and interrupting the receipt of its revenues. Occupation of the country should be the minimum required by the land operations which should be directed primarily toward guarding the border defensively and invading Mexico through Vera Cruz. Wide publicity as to the object of military operations may reduce Mexican resistance by influencing the Mexican people to give allegiance to a new Federal Government.[30]

This invasion of Mexico was as ambitious as War Plan Green #1. The Navy would strike first, providing the Army with a launching-off point for striking at Mexico City. The US Navy was to initiate:

...the expeditious seizure of Vera Cruz and, weather permitting, the immediate occupation of the Antigua Vera Cruz—San Francisco Area from the sea. Support of the Army until, in the opinion of the Army Senior Commander present, Army forces are securely established on shore.[31]

The Navy was expected to blockade the Mexican ports from receiving munitions of war and likewise was to interrupt railway communications to Guatemala. The Navy was to provide a much broader role in terms of ensuring that air support was available. "Employment with the Army in its march on Mexico City of such air units and other naval elements are desired by the Army and considered available by the navy." The Navy was anticipated to provide the transportation of the Army Air Corps components from Galveston to Vera Cruz as soon as an airplane carrier became available.[32]

Other seaports that the US Navy was to concentrate on included Tampico, Mazatlan, and Acapulco.[33] The plan did not call for the seizure of these ports but for them to be secured. This could best be interpreted as a limited naval blockade.

The assault and capture of Veracruz was not just seen as a demonstration of the strength of the US Marine Corps. The US Army would be landing at least one infantry regiment along with the Marines.[34] Veracruz had recently been invaded in 1914 by President Wilson, so it was familiar ground for the Marine Corps and the Army. It was a city that had long been viewed by the United States as the proverbial back door into Mexico City.

As with War Plan Green #1, the Navy, "will prepare to seize and to occupy the Tampico—Tuxpan area, when Army Operations in the Vera Cruz area make naval forces available."[35]

The Army's role in the invasion of Mexico was seen as much more broad and political in nature than in War Plan Green #1:

While supporting, where practicable, Green factions hostile to the existing Federal Government, and while restricting, as far as practicable, the employment of military forces against any but Green Federal Forces, the Army tasks are:

1. In protecting the border by an active defense, the occupation of Green territory will be the minimum consistent with the necessities of the situation.

2. Expeditious relief of the Navy in the beachhead at Vera Cruz. Expeditious seizure of the Antigua Vera Cruz—San Francisco area, or the relief of the Navy therein.
3. Invasion of Green <u>via</u> Vera Cruz, with the objectives of capturing Mexico City and controlling the Federal Government of Green.
4. Should the Marine Corps troops indicated … be not available in the United States in sufficient strength to accomplish the task of (seizing Vera Cruz), the Army will embark at Galveston, Texas, for initial operations at Vera Cruz, the necessary units to make up the deficiency in Marine Corps Troops.[36]

The Army would execute these objectives in three distinct phases of operations. These were:

Phase No. 1. Protection of the southern border of the United States and United States interests at important Green seaports. Concentration at the ports of embarkation of the expeditionary forces required in phase two for occupation of seaports.

Phase No. 2. Border protection and occupation of Green seaports, if and when directed by the President, together with troop concentrations at the border and ports of embarkation preparatory to further operations in Green as contemplated in Phase No. 3.

Phase No. 3. Further operations in Green, if and when each action becomes necessary for the purpose of:

1. Occupying Mexico City, and if necessary other parts of Green territory as may be required to enforce United State policies.
2. Establishing a military government throughout the occupied territory.[37]

How, exactly the occupation force was to go about establishing a new government, is not included as part of the plan.

The Army forces for this invasion were to debark as follows:

First Army (embark from New York City)—allocated for Tampico and for Vera Cruz
Third Army (advance from Loredo [sic]-Brownsville for potential operations at Monterrey, San Luis Potosi, Aguascalientes, Irapuato, and Queretaro.
Fourth Army (embark form El Paso via San Francisco) for use in Mazatlan.[38]

The Importance of Veracruz

The Joint Board planners as early as 1919 had been envisioning an end-run to Mexico City via Veracruz based on their experience in 1914 when the city was seized:

> The first rule for conquering a nation is to defeat its army. The Mexican Army, if it accepts battle at all, will certainly do so in defense of the heart of its country. And the heart of the country is the Mexico City locality. To one-twelfth of her area, lie one-third of her

population, all of her arsenals and sources of military supplies, and her most important industrial centers, namely, Mexico City and Pueblo. An attack upon Mexico City will not only bring the Mexican Army to a decisive battle, but will, if successful, afford to the United States the facilities it will need to reorganize and reestablish government.

Assuming an attack upon Mexico City to be desirable, the question of the route then arises. While a complete discussion of the subject is beyond the scope of this study, it may be said that the conclusion reached by almost all who have made a study of the Mexico problem is that the campaign against Mexico City should be made via Vera Cruz. The decision against a northern route, via the border, is based largely upon he enormous lines of communication that must be maintained and guarded against bandits. In addition to the great length, there are hundreds of miles of waterless, traceless desert, with many strong defensive positions for the use of the Mexican Army. The railroads themselves are practically without rolling stock and are so worn out that a hundred thousand men might be required to rebuild, repair, and guard one line from the border to Mexico City.

The distance from Vera Cruz to Mexico City is small as compared to that from the border, there are two lines of railroad Vera Cruz has the many advantages of a water-base, the more healthful highland are within easy striking distance and there is every prospect that a campaign via this route could be brought to the conclusion in from one-third to one-half the time that it could be by a northern route. It is not to be inferred that the Very Cruz route is without serious difficulties; on the contrary, there are many exceedingly serious problems for an invader, but they are perhaps fewer than on other routes and can be solved in less time. If it is desired to bring the major operations to a speedy terminus and so return promptly to civil life the greater part of the Army, the Very Cruz route should be followed.[39]

Planners assumed that there was still a need for a southern-march, but felt that Vera Cruz was more critical to the overall success of the operation:

The advance from the north will be ultimately have to be made, but it can and should wait until the demands of the Vera Cruz campaign for troops have been met. It is conceded that all American forces along the border man, however, advance southward from the earliest moment, but only such distances as will permit not only the safe guarding of their communications; but the holding in hand a fore sufficient to meet all local demands for action against Mexican troops or bandits.

There will be immediate clamor, both from civilians and military men along the border for an immediate advance, but if any priority at all is to be maintained, action must be at first confined to that necessary to protect American interests immediately adjacent to the border.[40]

The Forces to be Used

Despite the fact that Green War Plan #2 centered on the toppling of the Mexican Federal Government, the Joint Board war planners felt that it would require less Army troops than the invasion planned in Green War Plan #1. The plan did not call for a widespread occupation of Mexico, but felt that taking Mexico City out of the equation would decapitate the Mexican Government.

Army estimates were still high for the campaign:

> For the execution of this plan, The War Department shall make available Regular Army units to the strength of approximately 140,000 to include forces for the protection of the border and an expeditionary force for the Very Cruz Area consisting of two corps of two Infantry Divisions each, plus one Cavalry Division, General Headquarters Air Force, and auxiliary troops. Units will be employed initially at existing strength and will be raised without delay to authorized peace strength by increased enlistment.[41]

The Navy would also be using somewhat less forces than anticipated in War Plan Green #1:

> For the execution of this Plan, the Navy Department shall make available such Naval forces as are required to carry out the Navy Mission and Tasks thereunder, including two expeditionary forces of Marine Corps Troops of approximate strengths of 5,000 and 1,500 respectively. All units will be of the regular Navy, Marine Corps and Coast Guard, raise to authorize strengths by increased enlistments.[42]

The timing of the planned invasion would be governed heavily by the US Navy since they would determine the actual date of the landings at Veracruz:

> For purposes of planning, M-Day (mobilization) will be taken as the day on which the President orders intervention. To insure the necessary cooperation between Army and Naval forces in the seizure of Vera Cruz and the occupation of the Antigua Vera Cruz— San Francisco Area, the date of such seizure (Navy D-Day), will be determined by the Navy Department after consultation with the War Department. Such a date will be contingent upon: First; readiness of Naval Forces to undertake the landing, and, second; the availability of at least one infantry regiment of the Army to land on the day following. For planning purposes it will be assumed that Navy D-Day coincides with M-plus-10 days.[43]

Along the rest of the US border, War Plan Green #2 called for a limited invasion into Mexico, only to protect US citizens and political interests. These were to be "shallow invasion corridors," aimed at protecting utilities and centers of American population.[44] Likewise there was a nervousness that the Mexicans may use the few aircraft that they had to bomb American border towns and facilities. American aircraft were under orders to engage and destroy any aircraft attempting such a bombing operation and "effective steps are to be taken to ensure that such attacks are minimized."[45] What those steps were, however, remains unclear.

Command and Coordination

The Joint Board anticipated two initial Army theaters of operations—with the creation of others on an *ad hoc* basis as the plan came to fruition:

> The Theater of Operations ,under command of the Commanding General, First Army, will include Southern and Central Mexico as far north as the line Tuxpam [sic] (exclusive), San Luis Potosi, Aguascalientes, Guadalajara, Colima, (all inclusive). Theaters of Operations will be created on the border only if and when the progress of events shows such actions as advisable.[46]

There was no difference whatsoever in the planned US Navy theaters of operations from War Plan Green #1:

> The Principle Theater of Operations, under command of the Commander-in-Chief, United States Fleet, will include both coasts of Green, and all sea areas adjacent thereto, including such extensions of these sea areas along both coasts of Central America as may be necessary to carry out the operations required. The Principal Theater of Operations will be divided into two sub-theaters as follows: The Gulf and Caribbean Sub-Theater, under command of the Commander, Scouting, will include the Gulf and Caribbean coasts of Green and all sea areas adjacent thereto, with such extension of these sea areas along the Caribbean Cost of Central America as may be necessary to carry out the operations involved. The Pacific Sub-Theater, under the command of the Commander Battle, will include the Pacific Coast of Green and all sea areas adjacent thereto, with such extension of these sea areas along the Pacific Coast of Central American as may be necessary to carry out the operations required.[47]

Veracruz was destined to be the crux of any joint operations between the Army and Navy since it was the springboard for driving towards Mexico City. The Joint Board had to try and define how cooperation between the two services would be handled:

> In general, by direct communication between Commanding General, First Army, upon designation, and Commander-in-Chief United States Fleet. After embarkation of Divisions and during movement to Vera Cruz; by direct communications between Army Division Commanders and Commander-in-Chief United States Fleet or Commander Scouting. At Vera Cruz, between Senior Army Commander present and Commander-in-Chief, United States Fleet or Commander, Scouting Fleet.[48]

Once the US began to land forces, command and control had a relatively simple manner for passing on command:

> Command in the Vera Cruz area shall pass from the Navy to the Army when on reinforced infantry brigade is ashore. Command in the Antigua Vera Cruz—San Francisco area shall pass from the Navy to the Army when one infantry regiment is in the area.[49]

How, exactly, the Army and Navy would implement a new government was never addressed in War Plan Green #2, despite the fact that this was the overall aim of the invasion. The plans seem to present a scenario that the authority of the Mexican Federal Government was directly linked to the control of Mexico City. If Mexico City was taken, the Government would cease to be. Mexico City was the administrative center of the Mexican Government. Removing the existing administration may have been done with relative ease, but to put a new government in place would significantly extend the military mission in Mexico. Where elections were known to be rigged and political corruption had led to recent rebellions, for a fair and democratic election— the US military was going to need significant numbers of troops in a full occupation of much of the country. This was seemingly overlooked in Variant #2 of War Plan Green.

War Plan Green #3

Chaos south of the US border presenting a threat to American citizens was the basis for War Plan Green #3. In these circumstances the United States would direct the Army and Navy to act in the defense and protection of American citizens. In some respects, the disturbances in Mexico presented a more complicated political situation than a military one—though both would be challenging:

It is assumed that, during such state of insurrection or civil disturbance, the UNITED STATES will, initially at least, follow its well-recognized policy of non-interference in the internal affairs of its LATIN AMERICAN neighbors; but, that it will, without taking sides in such disputes, refuse to recognize any government established by other than constitutional means, and to this end will afford moral support to the existing recognized government, and may, in pursuance of the president's endeavor to prevent the shipment of arms and munitions of war to the factions hostile to the recognized government.

Under the above conditions, danger to lives and property of American and other foreign nations in Green will depend upon the leaders of such insurgent factions will endeavor, so long as it appears advantageous to them, to suppress open anti-American and anti-foreign agitation. In areas, however, where the authority of the recognized government is opening disputed or nullified, it is to be assumed that Americans or other foreign nationals and their property are likely to suffer by reason of military operations or through violent acts of the contending parties.[50]

War Plan Green #3 also recognizes that instability in the government may require initiation of one of the other Green War Plans:

A widespread and long continued series of violent attacks directed against American citizens and their property may eventually require that the United State proceed under either the No. 1 or No. 2 Green Plan, the former a condition of chaos throughout Green requiring occupation and pacification of the country, and the latter an operation against a recognized federal government hostile to the interests of the United States. This plan contemplated by this estimate should therefore provide for an orderly transition to either Green No. 1 or Green No.2, as conditions warrant.[51]

The US Navy was similar to that in War Plan Green #1. The Navy was to:

1. Close observation of the seaports of Green, for the purpose of guarding American consulates, tendering good offices where American interests are in dispute, and remonstrating against violence to American interests.
2. Extension of the preceding measures to cover foreign interests when necessary and when requested.
3. Interception, if ordered, by the President, of arms and munitions of war designated for factions hostile to the recognized Government of Green.
4. If necessary, seizure and occupation of areas adjacent to the seacoast of green where violence to American interests may be threatened, primarily the Tampico–Tuxpan oil region. Such seizure and occupation may be in the nature of a joint expedition.
5. Assistance and support of the Army in its occupation of Green territory.[52]

The Army was not just to secure the border, but to be prepared to seize and occupy:

…such area adjacent to the seacoast of Green as may be necessary as protective measures by join operations with the Navy, or support or relieve the Navy in such areas.[53]

As with War Plan Green #1, the Tampico–Tuxpan area and the precious oil fields there were considered strategic targets that could help compel the Mexican officials to regain control. The criteria for the creation of the War Plan details the importance of this region:

The area adjacent to the seacoast of Green, of greatest importance to American and foreign interests, is the Tampico–Tuxpan oil region. It is this region which may demand the greatest protection to the lives and property of American citizens and other foreign nationals residing in Green. Any plans directed toward coping with a condition of insurrection in Green should contain a plan for the seizure and occupation of this region. Such seizure and occupation may be necessary without preliminary warning and speedy action will be necessary to prevent grave damage to the oil well and oil properties; the plan must therefore contemplate the initiation of such seizure and occupation by the Navy. On account, however, of the unknown strength of the hostile forces that may be encountered, the area involved, and the intermediate duration of the occupation, the plan should contemplate the early support and relief of the Navy by the Army. As an alternative, the plan should also contemplate a joint expedition for the seizure of this area, and occupation by the Army. For early relief of the Navy in this area, one infantry division at peace strength is considered the minimum Army force required.[54]

The plan called for the creation of upwards of three Army Expeditionary Forces. One could be used for potential operations near the oil fields. The other two were designated for addressing the seacoasts of Mexico, securing them as needed.

In essence, this war plan would be one where the United States defended itself and took action only to protect American interests—and those of corporate America in the case of the Tampico oil fields.

The Forces to be Used

War Plan Green #3 was not as audacious as her predecessors in terms of manpower requirements. The Army requirements were defined as follows:

> For the execution of this plan, the War Department shall make available initially the Regular Army at existing strength, to include forces for the protection of the border and three expeditionary forces. The expeditionary forces will consist of one Infantry Division for the Tampico–Tuxpan Area and two reinforced brigades for other area.[55]

Likewise the Navy's commitment is seen as reduced as well:

> For the execution of this plan, the Navy Department shall make available such Naval forces are as required to carry out the Navy Mission an Tasks thereunder, including an expeditionary force of Marine Corps troops of approximate strength of 5,500. All units will be regular Navy and Marine Corps at existing appropriation strengths. The Coast Guard will not be employed under this plan.[56]

Command and Coordination

The very nature of this plan negates some of the coordination that the larger, more aggressive Green War Plans present:

> No common time origin for the initiation of separate Army and Navy operations is contemplated, since the Army and the Navy may be require to initiate any one or more of the assigned tasks independently. Orders initiation operations may authorize any or all of the Tasks assigned to the Army and Navy, or may direct the omission of certain features thereof.[57]

For those operations of a joint nature arranged by the War and Navy Departments as part of securing the sea coasts or protecting American citizens, the two departments would appoint a commanding officer for joint operations:

For operations of Army forces in support of or relief of Naval landings, the Navy Department will notify the War Department of the nature and date of the Naval landing, and the War Department will arrange for the support or relief of the Navy.[58]

Clearly in the case of this War Plan, the US Navy would be the driving force in command structures and points of coordination.

As with the other two Green War Plans, the definition of the theaters of operations was the same:

The Principle Theater of Operations, under command of the Commander-in-Chief, United States Fleet, will include both coasts of Green, and all sea areas adjacent thereto, including such extensions of these sea areas along both coasts of Central America as may be necessary to carry out the operations required. The Principal Theater of Operations will be divided into two sub-theaters as follows: The Gulf and Caribbean Sub-Theater, under command of the Commander, Scouting, will include the Gulf and Caribbean coasts of Green and all sea areas adjacent thereto, with such extension of these sea areas along the Caribbean Cost of Central America as may be necessary to carry out the operations involved. The Pacific Sub-Theater, under the command of the Commander Battle, will include the Pacific Coast of Green and all sea areas adjacent thereto, with such extension of these sea areas along the Pacific Coast of Central American as may be necessary to carry out the operations required.[59]

The wild card in War Plan Green #3 was the possibility of landings at Tampico—Tuxpan. While not specifically ordered, it was planned for in this plan which indicates that it was considered highly likely. If that were to take place, a higher degree of coordination, locally, between the Army and Navy was contemplated:

In the event of Navy landings in Green seaports requiring the support or relief of the Navy by Army forces, command ashore in the Tampico–Tuxpan area shall pass to the Army when one infantry brigade is ashore. In the event of a joint expedition, command of the Army forces shall remain vested in the Army.[60]

A Common Element in Planning War Plan Green— the US/Mexican Border

All three plans, in some capacity or another, attempt to wrestle with the issue of the long shared border between Mexico and the United States. In 1916 the Joint Board performed some preliminary analysis of how such a campaign might be mounted. These plans would serve as starting points in future Green War Plans dealing with Mexico:

On account of the immense area of the States of Northern Mexico … the lack of good communications except along the railroads and the impoverished state of the country, all operations of large bodies of troops must be confined to the railroads. It follows, therefore, that each of the various columns may be designated for operations in Mexico, must secure the lines of railway in the area to be pacified.

An examination of a railway map of Mexico shows that the railways enter Northern Mexico at Brownsville, Laredo and Eagle Pass, converging on Monterrey; also, that a railway enters the State of Chihuahua at El Paso and runs via the City of Chihuahua to Torreon. A branch of this latter road runs from Juarez via Casas Grandes to Chihuahua with a spur from La Junta to Las Tascates. Other branches of the main line reach Paraje Seco, El Oro and Sierra Mojada from Jimenez. Torreon and Monterrey are connected by two lines—one via Gomez Palacio and Saucedo and the other via Saltillo. From Torreon and Monterrey, lines of railway radiate to Durango, Zacatecas, Aguas Calientes, City of Mexico, San Luis Potosi, Celaya, City of Mexico and Tampico. Torreon and Monterrey, therefore, constitute strategic centers and the control of the line Torreon–Monterrey becomes an object of the first importance to an invading force.[61]

Clearly the railroads held sway on American invasion planning. In the 1918 plans these route governed any incursions into Northern Mexico:

To accomplish the principal objective of the campaign—the control of the strategic line Monterrey—Torreon—the following are the possible lines of advance:

    (a) Matamoras—Camargo—Monterrey—Torreon;

    (b) Nuevo Laredo—Monterrey;

    (c) Piedras Negras—Paredon—Monterrey;

    (d) Juarez—Chihuahua—Torreon.

Of these, the line Matamoras–Monterrey–Torreon is by far the shortest and best.

The Nuevo Laredo–Monterrey line is important only because its control would give an additional line of supply and because it would enable the military to extend control and protection of the country through which the railway passes.

The line Piedras Negras–Paredon–Monterrey derives its greatest importance from the fact that its passion gives us control of the extensive coal fields in northeastern Coahuila. The importance of these coal fields was well understood by the contending revolutionary factions in the recent campaigns.

An advance along this line, however, would be difficult and slow. It is believed that as strong column could reach Monterrey from Matamoras and then extend to Reata (thus cutting off the coal supply) in less time than a separate force could reach the coal fields from Piedras Negras; the former plan would obviate the necessity of keeping up two lines of communications.

The Line Juarez–Chihuahua–Torreon is of primary importance in any campaign for the control of Northern Mexico because of the great extent of the territory which its possession will enable us to control.[62]

No matter what, any drive, even in a limited nature into the Northern Mexico, was going to be a significant strain on manpower—this was something that the 1929 planners still were reeling from in their estimates. On top of simply securing territory, there was expected to be an influx of Mexican citizens fleeing north across the US border—and the risk of arms being smuggled from the United States back into Mexico to aid the opposition to American forces.[63]

A Common Element in Planning in War Plan Green— the Tampico Oil Fields

Part of the foundation for the Green War Plans was work done for the Joint Board by the Army War College. Their analysis of the Tampico–Tuxpan region became the basis for this region being a focus for the plans. Other analysis done by the Joint Board outlined the criticality of this region to Mexico's capability to wage war:

> Approximately 80 percent of the GREEN locomotives are oil-burning and GREEN has no extensive storage of fuel oil outside of this area. As played in the war game extensive GREEN troop movements were made which could not have been possible with this source of fuel oil denied to them.[64]

Controlling the oil not only paralyzed troop movements for Mexico, it also denied the government the vital revenues from these resources. Even more so, the region of the oil fields was the largest concentration of foreign nationals and US citizens in the country (outside of the US border.) Seizing Tampico was seen as a strategic necessity for the US in almost every possible contingency.

Tampico also offered other strategic value:

> ... it affords a base for a comparatively short line of advance inland on San Luis Potosi and north-central Mexico. It is the principal city of the State of Tamaulipas and is located on the banks of the navigable Panuco River some seven miles inland from the Gulf Coast.[65]

Tampico had a population of 27,000, of which, over 3,000 were American workers and their families. Most worked in the oil fields but others worked for the railroads or engaged in ranching and growing fruit to support the local population.[66] For the most part the Americans in Tampico were concentrated in two communities:

> Another almost entirely American colonel is Ebano, near Ebano Station on the National Railway about 30 miles west of Tampico. At one time there were over 300 American males and several families in Ebano. Another small American settlement is near Panuco, on the Panuco River, 50 miles from Tampico by water and about half that distance by road. Here are less than 100 Americans at the East Coast Oil Company's plant. This is an American corporation, owned mainly by the Southern Pacific Railroad. At the mouth of the Panuco River, on the north bank is La Barra, a small town and seaside resort. It is reached by the National Railway and is connected by electric line with Tampico, about six miles away.

Here are the quarantine station, the pilot station, and oil refinery of the Mexican Aguila Petroleum Company, a British corporation.[67]

In any effort to protect Americans, these settlements would be early objectives for any landing Marines.

The geography was going to play a critical role in any battle fought there:

Tampico is built on a peninsula lying between Laguna Carpintero and the Panuco River, and on ground rising gradually from the river to a height of nearly 70 feet. The main part of the city parallels the Panuco River and is separated from the Custom House and wharves, along the river front, by the Cascajal Canal. The waters of the Tamesi River, first emptying into Laguna Chairel to the west of the City, thence in parts pass by this canal to confluence with the Panuco River just below the city. This canal, some 100 feet in width and 6 feet in depth, is usually called the Tamesi Canal, or Tamesi River, and is spanned by an iron bridge, abreast of the main part of the city, connecting Calle de Muelle and the main plaza with the Custom House Wharves and the railroad terminals of the National Railways of Mexico, which are located upon an island called Isla de Zapote, between the canal, Laguna Chairel and the Panuco River.

There are three plazas and one garden, or square, all with band stands in the center. The principal one is just opposite the Custom House wharves and railway terminals. It is called Plaza de la Libertad and has around it the main business section of the city, many of the buildings being three or four stories high. Just off the southwest corner of this Plaza, is a good market. Another plaza, called the Jardin de la Constitution, is about three blocks to the north and west of the Plaza de la Libertad, and has the Cathedral on its northwest side. To the right of the Cathedral are the Municipal Offices, the Police Station and the Jail.

Still further to the northwest, is the Plaza de los Arrieros, on the east side of which is situated the Military Hospital.[68]

From a military perspective, the surrounding terrain outside of Tampico would be both useful and challenging:

A long low range of hills begins 1½ miles northeast of the city, near the Panuco River, and extends in a crescent shape to the north and west. On the crest of these hills, northwest of Tampico, is the reservoir of the city water supply, about 100 feet above the river level. These hills command the city and the approaches thereto. To the east of the city and across the Panuco River, there is a north and south range of hills which also commands the city and the vicinity; at the foot of these hills there is thick brush, but it becomes scant at the top. With the exception of these two ranges of hills, the country immediately surrounding the city is generally impassable for troops in force. To the west and south is an extensive network of waterways formed by the Rivers Panuco and Tamesi and the Lagunas Chairel and the Pueblo Viejo, while to the northwest there are found extensive marshes. As one travels west the country is general low and marshy. During the rainy season, one expansive sheet of water follows another, though in dry season much of the country thus covered is passable in almost any direction.

About two miles from the mouth of the Panuco River is the entrance to the Chijel Canal, depth 3 feet, width 60 feet, which connects Tampico via the Panuco River with Laguna Tamishua, an inland lake located about ten miles south of the Panuco River. There has been projected an extension of this inland waterway, under the name of the Tampico–Tuxpan Canal, from the Laguna Tamishua by estuaries and the Tuxpan River to the city of Tuxpan, 88 miles south of Tampico, this proposed route would open up a very fertile country at its southern extremity.[69]

For the landing Marines who were designated to land at Tampico, one of the key aspects of the city would be the port facilities since most Marine landings were not amphibious operations but rather landings via ships at port facilities:

There are five wharves for sea going vessels along the north bank of the Panuco River in and below the city and all are in use, via: Fiscal Wharf (Custom House, Tampico), New Bullion Wharf (Golfo), Coal Wharf (Arbol Grande), Export Wharf (Dona Cecilia), and Railroad Coal Wharf (Telleres). Cargoes are handled from steamer to wharf. General cargoes and passengers are handled at the Fiscal Wharf which is operated by the National Railways Company. At all of the other wharves, owned by the same company, full cargoes of different kinds are handled.

The Fiscal Wharf, a steel and concrete structure, is 2,860 feet long, 55 feet wide and can accommodate seven vessels at one time. It is owned by the Government. This wharf is equipped with one three-ton travelling crane, requiring most vessels to discharge and load with their own gear. The other four wharves can accommodate only two vessels each. The National Railways of Mexico have tracks to all wharves. The current of the Panuco River is moderate enough to allow vessels to anchor mid-stream while waiting for berthing space. The depth of the water at all of the wharves is 28 feet or better. Tank steamers load, both above and below the city, at the tank farms of the various oil companies, and from shallow-draft oil barges.[70]

Assessment of Enemy Forces (Tampico)

One thing glaringly missing in all three of the Green War Plans is any assessment of the military capabilities of the Mexican government overall. This is understandable on several accounts. First and foremost, the situations of the War Plans almost all introduce changes in the Mexican Federal Government—which could potentially have substantive changes on the size and nature of the military.

There is one exception to this—a 1916 assessment of the military forces at Tampico. While this might change if there was a civil war in Mexico, or a new hostile government, it is still the best possible assessment of the military forces that the landing US Marines might find themselves facing:

Tampico is unfortified. Before the recent revolution, the garrison at Tampico rarely exceeded 150 men. Peace and order were kept in the district by 30 trusted Indians, paid and equipped by the Mexican Petroleum Company but under orders of a Government official and subject to the call of both State and Government authorities.

About 800 Huerta Government troops occupied the city in the latter part of 1913 and dug a line of trenches from the Tamesi River to the Laguna Carpintero, along the high ground northwest of the city.

At this date, January 1916, the Carranza Government is reported to have 250 men stationed at Tampico Alto, about 10 miles south of Tampico.

It has been estimated that about 3,600 Mexicans with six 8-inch guns could be available for the defense of Tampico in 24 hours, and that in 10 days this force could be increased to 10,000 men by reinforcement from the force usually kept in the State of Vera Cruz.

The Mexican soldier is small in stature, poorly trained and his morale has never been considered high. Mexican arms are a mixture of rifles including Mausers, Springfields, and a few Remingtons.[71]

While estimates are varied in the War Plans, it was assumed there would be a minimum of 350 defenders in Tampico and the region with a significantly larger number of troops that could be brought in for defense. The worse-case-scenario estimated that 3,600 Mexican Federal Troops could be engaged with the US Marines in the area within three days' time. These forces would be reinforced with six artillery pieces. Beyond 72 hours, it was impossible to estimate how much force the Mexican Army might toss into the battle.[72]

How Tampico would be Taken

The 1916 War Plan Green (Basic) offers thinking in to how the battle might unfold at Tampico. This assessment was not superseded in future editions of the war plans. As such this summary gives a good indication of how the battle might unfold:

The Naval plans for the actual occupation of the City of Tampico and its vicinity, before the arrival of the Army, provided for the distribution of gunboats in the Panuco River from near La Barra to a point above the city in such a manner that the city, the military barracks, to high ground northwest of the city and the foreign property and oil properties on both banks of the Panuco River will be covered by the guns of these ships.

Under their cover, the different landing battalions are to go ashore at the Custom House wharf, in the city, and at the wharf at Arbol Grande, below the city; these forces will overcome all opposition and occupy the high ground northwest of the city, where the artillery battalion sent ashore is to place its guns in position. Guards are to prevent rioting and disorder and protect foreigners and their property. If a large military force is in the vicinity, it is not planned to use the shore forces beyond the range of the guns on the ships. The Navy plans to mount one-pounders and machine guns on certain tugs and river craft and to use these as patrol boats for the movement of troops in the rivers and nearby canals. Such will probably be the force protecting the city water supply station at Camalote. After the seizure of the city, a movement of our forces towards Ebano to secure rolling stock, oil tanks, etc., will depend upon circumstances. All rolling stock in Tampico will be secured and outposts stationed on the railway line towards San Luis Potosi to hold the line as far as possible.[73]

The Navy being in possession of Tampico...transports upon arrival will be able to go alongside the Custom House wharves to disembark the troops that they carry. These wharves can accommodate 7 vessels at one time. In case more space should be desired, the wharves at El Colfo, Arbol Grande and Dona Cecilia, each large enough to accommodate 2 vessels can be used.

One of the key objectives was the city water supply pumping station at Camalote, on the Tamesi River, nine to ten miles northwest of the city. One battalion of Infantry and four machineguns would be sent to the plant for protection, along with one patrol boat with two machineguns mounted on it. This objective was to be secured three-and-a-half hours after the landing.

At Ebano, the plan was to send one Infantry regiment, one troop of cavalry, and one radio (signal) troop along with eight machineguns to cover Ebano, Chijel and Chila and the railroad bridges at these locations. These forces were to dig trenches and prepare for a Mexican counterattack.

A battalion of Infantry, one machinegun company, one troop of cavalry and one radio troop would go to secure the oil fields themselves. At Casiano; two companies of Infantry, one machinegun company would protect the pipeline and pumping stations from San Geronimo to Garrapatas. Blockhouses and machinegun emplacements were to be constructed near the pump-house facilities.

At Panuco, one battalion of Infantry, four machineguns, and one radio section were sent to protect the East Oil Company wells and tanks. Two troops of cavalry were to be dispatched to Altamira, northeast of Tampico on the railroad line.[74] Once secured, a Military Governor would be named and provost marshal troops deployed to keep civilian order.

The Pacification of Mexico

All three of the Green War Plans call for assuming some degree of control over Mexico. Plans were defined for establishment of Military Governors, Provost Marshals, and the establishment of military courts in order to preserve order—but it would require much more than this to keep the local population in line.

One set of analyses outlined the scale for pacification of Mexico under the plans:

This discussion is based on having available for the purpose a total of eleven infantry divisions, two cavalry divisions and certain field army troops.

Regulars: I, II, III, and IV Divisions and the I and II Cavalry Divisions
Volunteers: V, VI, VII, VIII, IX, X, and XI Volunteer Divisions.

It is assumed that the occupation has been undertaken for the purpose of restoring order and establishing a stable government in the States of Northern Mexico, viz, Tamaulipas, Nuevo Leon, Coahuila, Chihuahua, and Sonora; that to carry out this purpose a force of approximately 250,000 mobile troops will be necessary; that to obtain that number the Regular Army has been increased so as to permit the organization within the continental limits of the United States of four divisions and two cavalry divisions, and that volunteers to the number of 150,000 have been called for, from which are to be organized seven infantry divisions.[75]

Detailed plans were devised for each of these geographies outlining the seizing of strategic assets (coal and oil being predominant) and the garrisoning of forces for keeping orders. Given the size and scope of just the northern portion of Mexico, a long term occupation would be a stretch both from a manpower and financial perspective.

Summary Evaluation of the War Plan

The three Green War Plans provide a wealth of information and detail as to how the United States would cope with a Mexican threat. But all three variations had flaws which would hinder their overall executions. Some of the most obvious gaps include:

- The plans do not address a guerilla or insurgency type of warfare. Given the raiding styles of Pancho Villa, this should have been a consideration—but is overlooked. Mexico's vast geography meant that garrisons would be essentially outposts and the territory that would be open between them would be subject to potential enemy attacks and strikes. The number of rebellions and rebel leaders clearly point to the Mexican government lacking political and military control of regions of their country—a problem that the Americans would be destined to inherit. There is an underlying assumption, though never spelled out, that the Mexican people would either welcome the US Army/Navy or would be, at worst, ambivalent to their occupation of their nation.
- All of the plans assume a rush of enlistment volunteers. The small size of the Regular Army in 1929 necessitated this kind of influx of personnel. The Spanish American War did have such a rush of volunteers, and with it came a number of logistical issues. The Regular Army alone could not deal with the threats in Mexico, and having a large number (over a hundred thousand) volunteers early in a crisis was going to be critical for the success of any of the Green War Plans.
- War Plan Green #2 provided for the landing of Marines and the US Army in the taking of Veracruz but had few provisions on objectives, communication, and coordination. Depending on the resistance faced and the complexity of operations—

this lack of command and control between the two diverse military branches might lead to dangerous issues that would favor the defenders.

- There is a presumption in War Plan Green #2 that taking Mexico City equated to taking out the Federal Government. Leaders would know the American forces would be approaching the city and would most likely flee it. Mexico City, while an administrative hub for the Mexican Federal Government, did not guarantee that Mexico would be taken out of the fight. In fact it might serve as a rally-point for anti-American activities.

- While the planned attack on the Tampico–Tuxpan area provided for local governing and administration, the overall Green War Plans lack any details of how the United States would govern or handle the civilians under their control. Military troops, while useful for attacking the enemy, in that time period, lacked the training and skills necessary to police a potentially hostile civilian population.

- War Plan Green #2 did not offer any plans as to how a friendly new government would be brought into power. After toppling the hostile government—how would the United States go about establishing (electing) a new government? With no plans, it can only be assumed that this process would be a long and arduous ordeal, during which time the US forces would be required to essentially run Mexico.

The 1932 Plan for Intervention in Cuba
War Plan Tan

Introduction

Cuba presented the Joint Board military planners with a unique situation. Unlike many different invasion scenarios, Cuba was one where the United States had an armed base already established—in this case, Guantanamo Bay. The United States had successfully invaded Cuba during the Spanish-American War and the Cuban Pacification of 1906. And while the Spanish-American War had been successful in the hearts and minds of the public, military planners understood the complexities of fighting a war in Cuba— where malaria and inhospitable terrain would impact any operational planning.

War Plan Tan (and War Plan Brown—the Philippines) took a different perspective of military planning. Rather than outright invasions, these were more of interventions. The Joint Board view of Cuba was that the United States was the powerful parent nation that, from time to time, had to discipline her children and step in to correct the problems they may be suffering.

Cuba, and the US base at Guantanamo Bay took on more importance with the completion of the Panama Canal. Cuba was instrumental in maintaining a naval defense of the canal, integral to American military planning.

The First American Conquest of Cuba

To understand the War Plan Tan, the invasion of Cuba, one must first understand the US involvement with Cuba. This was best manifested as Spanish-American War invasion of the island by the United States. Cuba had been a colony of Spain prior to the conflict. There had been a revolution against Spain in 1895 which had broken down to a guerilla war against the Spanish, who resorted to brutality to attempt to suppress the rebellion. American President William McKinley pressed the Spanish to allow Cuban independence, which fell on deaf ears.

Matters between the Spanish and the Cuban (and America) reached a boiling point when the US battleship, USS *Maine*, exploded in Havana Cuba. The Spanish claimed that it was an internal explosion that had sunk the ship, taking with it 266 sailors. The American inquiry into the matter pointed to an external explosion, allegedly from a

Spanish naval mine in the harbor. The American press clamored for war with Spain as a response and retribution. Spain broke off diplomatic relations while the Americans pressed for Spain to allow Cuban independence.

Both powers were poorly placed for a global war where the winner was the nation that was the least ill-prepared. The United States had a small but well-trained Navy but the Regular Army consisted of twenty-eight thousand troops.[1] The US Army's weapons and gear were out of date, in some cases almost antiquated compared to their Spanish counterparts. Spain, for its part, had colony holdings in the Philippines and Cuba which were already garrisoned, but her navy was even less prepared than the United States.

The war initially resulted in two successes. A blockade of Havana and much of the northern coast of Cuba was initiated swiftly. Meanwhile the Asiatic fleet led by Commodore George Dewey aboard the USS *Olympia*, attacked and destroyed Admiral Patricio Montoyo's naval force of wooden vessels in Manila Bay. The Spanish countered by sending a squadron into the Caribbean, avoiding the American blockade and making port at Santiago de Cuba on the south side of the island. The Americans moved into the vicinity to keep the Spanish in check by blockading them in port.

The checkmate in the Caribbean still left the Spanish-led forces on the island of Cuba that had to be dealt with. Major General William Shafter led a sloppy transfer of the Fifth Army Corps from its assembly points in Tampa, Florida, to near Santiago de Cuba at Daiquiri and Siboney. The US Navy pressed for Shafter to lead his troops along the coast via a longer route where they could be covered by naval gunfire. Shafter favored an interior route inland, fearing the long-term effects of disease on his men.

The Spanish garrison did not oppose General Shafter's landings. Instead they deployed to three defensive lines. The first line, centered on the San Juan Heights, was lightly defended but was a strong defensive position. Shafter's plan of attack called for two operations. One assault would be aimed at El Caney to protect the American flank on the main assault—against the San Juan Heights.

The military maxim that no plan survives contact with the enemy came into play. The assault on El Caney was held off for long hours. The rest of the Fifth Corps was ponderously slow in get into position. The operations, which were supposed to be coordinated, were anything but that.

When the Americans did move against the line of defense, it was the First US Volunteer Cavalry under command of future President Theodore Roosevelt that managed to attack and secure nearby Kettle Hill. His actions, combined with fire from US Gatling Guns, forced the Spanish to fall back to their second line of defense. The exhausted US Fifth Corps moved into the Spanish positions on the San Juan Heights and began to dig in to lay siege to the Spanish. The battle had become iconic in American history as the charge of the Rough-Riders up San Juan Hill—historical accuracy be damned.

The partial American success forced the hand of the Spanish. Fearing their squadron would fall into American hands, a call was made to sortie. The US Navy's blockade of the fleet was less-than-stellar and was not aided by the fact that the Navy Commander,

Admiral Sampson, had left the American ships in command of a junior officer while he went to meet with General Shafter. Four of the five Spanish ships were sunk in the channel while one managed to break out, only to be overtaken later and scuttled to avoid destruction.

With no hope of relief and with the loss of any glimmer of naval support, the Spanish garrison commander capitulated. With victory, US President McKinley and his Spanish counterpart signed a protocol which called for Cuban independence, the end of Spanish claims to Puerto Rico, and Guam. The later Treaty of Paris signed in December of 1898 ceded the Philippines to the United States for $25 million to compensate the Spanish for their property and holdings on the islands. On Cuba proper, the United States leased the port at Guantanamo Bay which it had turned into a naval base.

The Cuban Pacification—1906–1909

What emerged post the Spanish-American War was an independent Cuba (in 1902) but one whose government was anything but stable. With the collapse of Cuban President Palma's regime due to a liberal revolt—he called upon the United States to intervene to restore order. Under treaty, the United States reserved the right to intervene directly in Cuba if a government was established that was not deemed in-line with the best interests of democracy and freedom/independence of the Cuban people.[2]

President Theodore Roosevelt attempted to dodge direct intervention, sending Secretary of War William H. Taft and Assistant Secretary of State Robert Bacon to Cube in late 1906 to attempt to mediate the situation. Neither side was amiable to talks to resolve the matter peacefully. In October of 1906 President Roosevelt signed an executive order that called for the establishment of a Provisional Government. He further ordered the US Navy to land a brigade of Marines to protect American citizens and interests.

The intervention became known as The Second Occupation of Cuba and the Cuban Pacification. The deployment authorized upwards of 18,000 troops being sent to Cuba though the numbers were below 700 enlisted men and officers that actually set foot on Cuban soil. The American military presence remained until 1909. During that period it was credited with creating a new network of roads and surveying the island for future potential military operations. The occupation force struggled with typhoid, malaria, and gonorrhea which inflicted more harm than any Cuban force—resulting in ten percent of the occupation force being afflicted by illness. The Americans put a US provisional governor in power who oversaw free elections. The Cubans elected José Miguel Gómez to the Presidency in November 1908 and the US withdrew its occupation forces in early 1909 after he was sworn into office.

There were precedents in American history. After the Spanish American War the US had not only taken over the Philippines from the Spanish, but had also inherited the Philippine Revolution—a bid by the native population for full independence. Full fighting erupted in 1899 with the Second Battle of Manila. The United States response to the insurrection of this new protectorate was to apply military force. The war, one of America's more overlooked conflicts, generated over 22,000 military casualties and upwards of 200,000 civilian casualties among the Philippine people. American soldiers were accused of war atrocities. The Philippines struck like guerilla terrorists. It was a horrific conflict that ended in 1902. Ultimately this intervention on the part of the US was to be a template for War Plan Tan.

America had demonstrated a willingness to intervene in Cuban affairs in recent history. So much so that in 1919 the first true draft of War Plan Tan was produced. This plan outlined military intervention and invasion of Cuba given the right circumstances. The plans were in a continuous state of updating with a major overhaul taking place in 1928–1929. The version presented here is the 1932 draft of War Plan Tan, which represents one of the most complete editions of the invasion plans.

Trigger Points for US Invasion

War Plan Tan outlines several instances which the United States felt might call for American intervention in Cuba. All of these were tied to the 2 July 1904 Treaty between America and Cuba. These points were as follows:

Article I. The Government of Cuba shall never enter into any treaty or other compact with any foreign power or powers which will impair or tend to impair the independence of Cuba, nor in any manner authorize or permit any foreign power or powers to obtain by colonization for military or naval purposes, lodgment in or control over any portion of said island.

Article II. The Government of Cuba shall not assume or contract any public debt to pay the interest upon which, and make reasonable sinking fund provision for the ultimate discharge of which, the ordinary revenues of the Island of Cuba, after defraying the current expensive of the Government, shall be inadequate.

Article III. The Government of Cuba consents that the United States may exercise the right to intervene for the preservation of Cuban independence, with the maintenance of a government adequate for the protection of life, property, and individual liberty, and for discharging the obligations with respect to Cuba imposed by the Treaty of Paris on the United States, now to be assumed and undertaken by the Government of Cuba.

Article IV. All acts of the United States in Cuba during its military occupancy thereof are ratified and validated, and are lawful rights acquired thereunder shall be maintained and protected.

Article V. The government of Cuba will execute, and, as far as necessary, extend the plans already devised, or other plans to be mutually agreed upon, for the sanitation of the cities of the island, to the end that a recurrence of epidemic and infectious diseases may be prevented, thereby assuring protection to the people and commerce of Cuba, as well as to the commerce of the Southern ports of the United States and the people residing therein.[3] *Note: It was this provision in the treaty that led to the Cuban Pacification.*

In drafting War Plan Tan, the Joint Board outlined that the United States had intervened before in Cuba, thus establishing the necessary political precedent should any of the conditions of the treaty be violated. The underlying implications of the Monroe Doctrine are highlighted in the plan as well, though there is an arrogance in the interpretation of that policy—where America knows what is best for Cuba and her people.

Planners also established several assumptions in their work. One was that the Cuban government would not have any issues or instances where organized resistance to an American intervention would take place. "On the other hand, opposition may be offered by discontented political factions, guerillas or bandits."[4]

Likewise planners did not consider the organized Cuban navy to be any sort of true threat:

> On account of the almost insignificant naval strength of Cuba and the strong probability that any operation of a military nature required will involve the use of Army forces only, it is considered that the Army have paramount interest.[5]

The Two Scenarios for Intervention in Cuba

War Plan Tan consisted of two potential scenarios where the United States might attempt to enforce the conditions of the treaty with Cuba. These were identified as Variation A and B.

Variation A called for US intervention without military support. Variation B called for the establishment of a Provisional Government with full military support to enforce the US treaty and Cuban stability. Under Variation B, the Joint Board believed that "serious organized resistance to intervention is not anticipated. Nothing in the international situation indicates that the intervention will be opposed by any foreign power."[6] The planners did not anticipate that a formal declaration of war was necessary to execute War Plan Tan, most likely because a Presidential Executive Order had sufficed during the Cuban Pacification earlier in the twentieth century.

While Variation A did not require a great deal of military assistance, Variation B called for a large scale intervention and incursion into Cuba by the Army. In the event of any Army force landing in Cuba, it was to be designated as the AIF—the American Intervention Force.

In Variation B the "National Mission" in Cuba was broad:

> While protecting UNITED STATES and other foreign interests in the REPUBLIC OF CUBA, to intervene in that country for the purpose of preserving CUBAN independence

and maintaining a government adequate for the protection of life, property and individual liberty, either without military support or with military support, as my be directed by the President.[7]

The Army Mission was defined as one of nation building:

To establish a stable and efficient Government in the REPUBLIC OF CUBA, either without military support (Variation A), or with military support (Variation B), as may be directed by the President; and to protect UNITED STATES and other foreign interests in the REPUBLIC OF CUBA.[8]

The Navy's mission was somewhat different given the nature of that Department:

To extend to UNITED STATES and other foreign interests in CUBAN seaports such protection as may be required prior to the arrival of Army forces; to support and assist the landing of Army forces in Cuba; and, thereafter, to cooperate with the Army in the execution of the Army Mission and to render such assistance to the Army as may be requested by the Commanding General, American Intervention Force.[9]

The theaters of operation for the War Plan Tan was defined as all Cuban territory including the US Naval Station at Guantanamo Bay and the entire Cuban coastline (in the case of the US Navy.)

War Plan Tan Variation A

At first glance it might appear that under Variation A, the military did not have any role in the matters that might unfold in Cuba. In reality, the Joint Board saw the role of the military as advisors and consultants to the Cuban Government already in place there:

In accordance with the National Mission, under Variation A, U.S. Army and Navy Officers will serve as advisors to, or, if necessary, as replacement for CUBAN officials; the officers required for these duties being furnished by the war Department, and the Navy Department upon request of the War Department.[10]

The Army's tasks under Variation A were to ensure that a proper number of qualified officers were available to act as military advisors.[11] The Navy was required to provide officers as well in the same capacity.[12] The Army had the additional burden of "rehabilitating" the Cuban government—implying a training or re-staffing of a new Cuban government.[13]

In fulfilling any staffing needs, the US Navy would be providing men under the following conditions:

To furnish Naval Officers as requested by the War Department, to serve as advisors to, or if necessary, as replacements for, CUBAN Officials. Note: One Captain or Commander, U.S. Navy, one Enlisted man (Yeoman branch).[14]

The Navy's Bureau of Navigation was charged with selection of the men in support of the needs.

How these needs were to be determined, what skills were necessary, to perform what specific duties were never fully defined. There is an almost casual approach to Variation A, where the US would have ample time to make such decisions after careful consideration.

War Plan Tan Variation B

One of the first steps of implementing War Plan Tan's Variation B plan was the establishment of a Provisional Governor. This role was to be appointed by the President of the United States. The Plan strongly suggests that the Provisional Governor was to also be the Commanding General of the American Intervention Force—but that was not seen as a requirement for the plan.

The role of the Provisional Governor was twofold:

(1) To establish a Provisional Government in CUBA for the maintenance of good order and the restoration of the financial standing of the Cuban Government.

(2) To use the American forces for the preservation of law and order only when the civil and military agencies of the CUBAN Government are unable to cope with the situation.[15]

The Army's tasks under Variation B of Tan were written to be deliberately vague, allowing for a wide interpretation and flexibility by the AIF (American Intervention Force) Commanding General. The Army was to ensure that qualified officers were available to fill positions that were to be defined by the Provisional Governor—presumably replacing Cuban officials.

The Army was also to provide troops or Cuban occupation:

To send to CUBA for the support of the Provisional Government an American Intervention Force (A.I.F.) of such strength as may be required to initially support that government; and to prepare to augment this initial force upon request of the Provisional Governor.[16]

Additionally the Army was responsible for furnishing its own transportation for the AIF once it arrived in Cuba. The assumption, as outlined in War Plan Tan, was that the AIF was to be employed for operations in support of the newly created Provisional Government.

The last task for the Army outlined the hope that the operations would maintain the support of the Cuban people. "To make every effort to establish friendly relations with the CUBAN population and prevent clashes between American forces and the natives of CUBA."[17]

The Navy's role in War Plan Tan was more prescribed and detailed than the Army's, mostly because the scope of their operations was not left to the changes driven by combat on the island. The Navy was expected to send the appropriate naval forces to Cuba in order to ensure success of operations. Their mission was not just to protect American interests, but those of other nations as well:

> To extend to UNITED STATES and other foreign interest in CUBAN seaports such protection as may be required prior to the arrival of Army forces in CUBAN territory.[18]

In short, until the Army could arrive, the US Navy and Marine Corps was to shoulder the burden of protection until the US Army could arrive.

The Navy was expected to provide the landing support for the Army coming ashore:

> After the arrival of the Army forces in CUBAN territory, to extend to UNITED STATES and other foreign interests in CUBAN seaports such protection by the Naval forces afloat as may be required; and such protection by Naval forces (including Marine Corps) ashore as my be requested by the Commanding General, American Intervention Force.[19]

The Navy was anticipated to cooperate fully with the Army in rendering assistance as needed.

On top of these assignments, the US Navy was to provide close observation of the Cuban waters and those adjacent to Cuba—presumably to assure that foreign intervention did not take place. The Navy was also tasked to: "… prevent the importation of munitions of war by factions hostile to the Provision Government of CUBA."[20]

The final assignment the Navy had was the protection of the US Naval Station at Guantanamo Bay. Guantanamo Bay was seen as the primary naval base for the defense of the Panama Canal, a vital American strategic asset—so the defense of this post was seen as critical in War Plan Tan. The Navy noted that officers selected for any assignments under the Commanding General AIF were to be graduates of the Naval War College.[21]

The Forces to be Used

War Plan Tan Variation B defined the Army troop requirements much more clearly than the US Navy's. For the Army:

> Under Variation B, the American Intervention Force initially will consist of approximately one infantry division at peace strength plus certain auxiliary troops. The War Department will be prepared to augment this initial force, upon request of the Provisional Governor, by another infantry division at peace strength plus certain auxiliary body of troops.[22]

Oddly enough, later in the plan the full force was further defined as a much larger force:

> To send to CUBA for the support of the Provisional Government an American Intervention Force (A.I.F.) of approximately one general headquarters; three infantry divisions; one general headquarters air force; one reinforced cavalry brigade; plus certain auxiliary troops.[23]

The discrepancy in the number of troops may have been deliberate to the Joint Board Planners. While the discrepancy is not directly explained in War Plan Tan, it can be assumed that the larger force was the one most anticipated for the operation. One thing is clear, the only designated Infantry Division that was named which would be utilized in the operation was the First Infantry Division.

The Army force is broken into two initial landing forces—Havana and Santiago. The priority of movements from the United States would be (1) elements of the 1st Division and attached units; (2) ground elements of the air force; (3) the reserve division.[24]

The Havana force was to be moved to Cuba by boat from New York and Key West Florida. The designated reserve division was to be transported to Key West by rail and from there would be ferried to Havana. The General Headquarters of the Air Force would assemble first in Miami Florida and would then fly to Havana, presumably after the Army ground forces landed.

The Santiago Force would first assemble in Galveston Texas and then would be transported by boat to Santiago Cuba. The only exception to this was one motor repair company which would move by boat from New York.[25] Army supplies would be drawn primarily from the Brooklyn Supply Depot.

By comparison the US Navy was given much more discretion in the force they could send to Cuba: "Under Variation B, the Navy Department will make available such Naval Forces as may be required to accomplish the Navy Mission." While the Navy seemed to have the greatest amount of flexibility, they were hindered by requirements around the globe—as evidenced by additional memorandums on War Plan Tan:

> ... Bureau of Navigation informed of developments as they could occur. Navy Basic Plan, TAN, contains specific directives for normal conditions but presence of U.S. Fleet in the Pacific makes special provisions to increase personnel on ships operating with reduced compliments.[26]

Further notations indicate that a higher degree of planning was required and performed to allocate the potential US Marine forces that might be put into action prior to the arrival of the Army forces.

The Navy put together three possible mobilization scenarios based on the needs of the Provisional Government. These are broken down as follows:

Table: Large Marine Mobilization—War Plan Tan

Port of Embarkation	Officers	Warrant Officers	Enlisted Men
Philadelphia	26	1	569
Quantico	118	15	1,436
Galveston (units mobilized at San Diego)	51	4	979
Port au Prince	34	2	483
To this force is added the 1st Bn, 7th Marines now on the USS *Wyoming*	23	1	475
Total	252	23	2,942

This organization includes:
    Six (6) infantry battalions
    One (1) battery 3″ mountain artillery (West Coast)
    One (1) battery pack howitzers (75mm.) (Quantico)
    Ten (10) planes from Haiti
    Twenty-three (23) planes from Quantico

Table: Medium Marine Mobilization 1—War Plan Tan

Port of Embarkation	Officers	Warrant Officers	Enlisted Men
Philadelphia	25	1	569
Quantico	67	5	569
Total (including 1st BN, 7th Marines from USS *Wyoming*)	116	7	1,737

This force would be organized as an infantry regiment of four battalions without artillery or aviation.

Table: Medium Mobilization 2—War Plan Tan

Port of Embarkation	Officers	Warrant Officers	Enlisted Men
Quantico	47	4	593
To this force is added the 1st Bn, 7th Marines now on the USS *Wyoming*	70	5	1,158
Total	117	9	1,751

This force would be organized as a regiment (7th Marines) less one battalion.[27]

The Naval force estimate provided under War Plan Tan was loosely defined as:
Operating Forces, all under command of the Commander in Chief, UNITED STATES
Fleet, consisting of:

(1) The Fleet Flagship,
(2) The Scouting Force,
(3) Train Squadron One, Basic Force
(4) A detachment of the Marine Corps, EAST COAST Expeditionary Force, if required.
(5) Certain united of the Naval Transportation Service, if required for logistical support,
(6) Certain Surveying Vessels now on Special Duty, and
(7) The District Forces, Naval Station GUANTANAMO BAY[28]

The naval commander also anticipated additional forces from the Naval
Communication Service, the Naval Intelligence Service and the shore facilities at
Guantanamo Bay.[29] The Naval Intelligence Service was to assume the task of all island
intelligence and counter-intelligence activities.

If the AIF were to be dealing at all with guerilla operations on the island, the
Commandant of the US Naval Base at Guantanamo Bay was to assume command of
activities directed against rebels/guerillas.

Oddly enough, while the US had a substantial military base at Guantanamo Bay, the
base was to play very little role in Variation B of War Plan Tan other than as a naval
base of operations. While the base had extensive facilities that would have been of use,
its geographic location on the south coast of Cuba, to the far east of the island, put
it out of reach of many of the ports where operations were likely to be centered. It is
entirely possible that planners still were burdened with the memories of the Spanish-
American War and did not want to exercise a massive landing on south coast with
the Army slogging its way through the heart of Cuba—lacking good roads and facing
jungle conditions complete with malaria and other diseases. Rather than risk repeating
the previous landings, the plans were more comprehensive in nature.

In order to demonstrate the American military presence, the US Navy was to deploy
warships to the key ports in Cuba at the start of operations. The following plan was
devised to outline the number of types of ships required:

Table: Cuban North Coast Ship Assignments

Port:	Name of Ship or Type to Be Ordered:	Additional Ships When Available:	Logistics Facilities:
Havana	CA or CL plus 2 DD's	DD's as relief when available	
Bahia Honda	DD		
Matanzas	DD		
Antilla	DD		
Nuevitas	DD		
Cardenas	DD		
Sagua la Grande	DD		
Caibairen	DD		

Table: Cuban South Coast Ship Assignments[30]

Port:	Name of Ship or Type to Be Ordered:	Additional Ships When Available:	Logistics Facilities:
Cienfuegos	DD		
Santiago	CL or 2 DD's		
Manzanillo	DD		
Batabano	DD		
Guantanamo		USS *Wyoming* DD's as reliefs when available	USS *Henderson* USS *Nitro* USS *Woodcock* USS *Hannibal* Available AM's as necessary from Norfolk or Coco Solo

The Army was to assume all plans for the mobilization, supplying, organization, and transportation of the troops that were to be sent to Cuba.[31]

Command and Control

Under the Commanding General, American Intervention Force, War Plan Tan provides for the following command structures:

a. The senior line officer present with the Havana Force will command the units therein. Headquarters of the Havana Force will be established at the port of embarkation, New York, on M-Day (the designated day of mobilization of American armed forces), or as soon thereafter as practicable, and at Havana upon the debarkation of headquarters thereat. b. The senior line officer present with the Santiago Force will command the units therein. Headquarters of this force will be established at the port of embarkation, Galveston, on M-Day, or as soon thereafter as practicable, and at Santiago upon debarkation of the headquarters thereat.

c. The senior line officer present with the reserve division will command the units therein. Headquarters of this force will be established at Havana upon the debarkation of the headquarters thereat.[32]

The US Navy and US Marine Corps, which might already be in place would maintain command locally in Cuba until the Army was fully debarked, beginning with the Commanding General of the AIF:

Command of joint forces of the Army, Navy, or Marine Corps, operating within the Navy Theater of Operations will be vested in the Army under the Principle of Paramount Interest.[33]

In short, once the US Army arrived on the island, the entire Cuban operation would fall under its command authority.

Plan for Operations

The AIF mission in Cuba clearly was built with the thinking of more a restoration of order to the island than a full-fledged military invasion. The plans called for several missions for the Army:

(1) To establish a Provisional Government in CUBA for the maintenance of good order and restoration of the financial standing of the CUBAN Government, the following procedure to govern:
(a) The framework of the present Government is to be preserved as far as practicable.
(b) CUBAN officials to be replaced by American only when this step is desirable in the interests of the policies to be pursued.
(c) Vacancies arising in Government positions to be field, as far as practical, with competent CUBANS.
(2) To announce the establishing of a Provisional Government through a proclamation....
(3) To use American forces for the preservation of law and order only when the civil and military agencies of the CUBAN Government are unable to cope with the situation.
(4) To make every effort to establish friendly relations with the CUBAN population and to prevent clashes between American forces and the natives of CUBA.[34]

There were two classes of ports that were targeted for the AIF once the Havana and Santiago forces landed. The first target port cities were those where the United States maintained consular representatives. These included: Havana, Matanzas, La Isabella (Sagua La Grande), Caibarien, Nuevitas, (Pastelillo and Puerta Tarafa), Antilla (Nipe Bay), Santiago de Cuba, Manzanillo, and Cienfuegos.[35]

Once these ports were secured and American interests were preserved, operations would be expanded to the other First Class Cuban Ports. These included: Behia Honda, Mariel, Puerto Padre, Gibara, Macabi (Bahia de Banes), Sagua de Tamano, Baracao, Guantanemo (Caimanera and Boqueron), Manzanillo, Santa Cruz Del Sur, Jucaro, Trinidad, and Los Indios (Island of Pines).[36]

Three days after US mobilization, the US Navy would begin operations by sending warships into the key Cuban ports to demonstrate. The arrival of the AIF would commence the following day, with large scale debarkations at Havana and Santiago. In Havana, the Headquarters for the AIF would be established and the staff activated.

Variation B of War Plan Tan did not call for the immediate landing of the US Marine Corps, only if American and foreign interests were placed at risk. If there was general unrest or organized resistance before the two Army Task forces could be fully deployed, the Commanding General would order in the Navy to debark the US Marines. The extent of their military operations would be limited under War Plan Tan to securing facilities and protecting the US or foreign interests in the ports where they were landed. The AIF would have the option of moving the Army forces to the ports by land or to have the US Navy transport them.

Summary Evaluation of the War Plan

When compared to other War Plans developed by the Joint Board, War Plan Tan demonstrates a level of sophistication in planning. Whereas most of the War Plans envisioned all-out invasions or wars, or variations thereof, War Plan Tan is much softer. Even the landing force was termed as an Intervention Force rather than Expeditionary. As such the plan details a more friendly form of US imposition of its political will. Rather than approach Cuba with overwhelming force under the auspices of a full invasion, the Joint Board embraced a more complicated approach of a gentle intervention on the island.

The basic premise of War Plan Tan is that the United States would not face any serious armed opposition to intervention. On the surface, this seems highly optimistic. Rebellion on the island of Cuba was not unheard of, nor was the government a stranger to instability and insurrection. This premise, while at the core of the plan, was a dangerous assumption.

War Plan Tan did account for this in the form of the Commanding General, AIF being able to designate missions for his force as needed. While that capability existed, it also meant that planning for such operations would be done on-the-fly.

War Plan Tan was concentrated on the ports of Cuba rather than the interior of the island. The ports represent the only connection points between the Cuban Government and the outside world. It was only through the ports that commerce, communication and trade could take place. It was here were the interests of foreign nationals were also concentrated.

If the United States were forced into striking out after an armed enemy in the interior of the island, it might be facing some logistical strains that War Plan Tan did not account for. At no point are jungle or hot-weather gear called upon for the Army forces—meaning that depending on the time of year when the operation was initiated, they may be ill-equipped for the jungle conditions of the Cuban interior. On top of this, disease remained an issue in planning military operations in Cuban up through the Cold War, meaning that a 1932-ish intervention would have to cope with this as well. While resources could be called upon to help mitigate the effect of the weather or disease, it would take time and would hinder swift reaction on the part of the AIF.

The 1940–1943 Plan for the Invasion of the Azores War Plan Gray

Introduction

Early Joint Board drafts of War Plan Gray envisioned it as a general set of various war plans to invade a number of islands in the Caribbean, with the exception of Cuba which was addressed in War Plan Tan. At the time these plans were not even listed under a color coding—they were simply noted by the islands they were intended for. The planning for these invasions was documented starting in the late 1920s by the Joint Board, but for the most part these plans were little more than memorandums and correspondence in terms of the depth. Most of the islands were not strategic in nature and lacked standing militaries beyond a hundred or so men.

The concept in early War Plan Gray planning called for invasions only if foreign nationals violated the Monroe Doctrine and started using the islands' forward bases for threatening the United States. Most had harbor facilities and coaling stations but were not large enough to pose a serious threat even if a foreign government assumed control. Strategically the Caribbean and outlying islands had the *potential* to be useful in military operations, but not on their own.

What changed from the early 1920s in the 1930s was the advent of military airpower. Suddenly islands could have airstrips which could support military aircraft which could pose a threat to merchant and military shipping. Even the smallest island could have the capability to project military power. And while most of the island countries could not afford an air force of any size to warrant notice, there were other powers around the globe that could—namely Germany, Italy, Japan, France and Britain. If one of these powers were to seize one of the islands in the Atlantic or Caribbean, they could move a sizable air force onto that island, greatly extending their strike capability into the vial Atlantic shipping lanes. The Joint Board took notice of this starting in 1939 and began to reevaluate the islands covered under War Plan Gray.

The 1940 Threat

The Azores were (and remain) an integral part of Portugal. While Portugal was neutral in the war that was unfolding around the globe, it did have strong pro-fascist leanings which were misinterpreted by the United States. While António de Oliveira Salazar was a dictator, the Azores and Portugal were pro-British in their leanings. Britain maintained a long-standing alliance with Portugal and the population was very friendly with Britain given the amount of trade between the islands. Washington DC, however, tended to lump all dictator's in the same proverbial bucket, a decided flaw in their perception of the Azores. Planners clearly were concerned that Germany would be able to take the Azores with little or no resistance on the part of Portugal, if not by their consent.

President Roosevelt, in the spring of 1940, expressed a concern that Germany might invade the Azores. Their position in the Atlantic would provide the Germans with a forward naval base and air facilities to extend their reach against the convoys being sent to supply the British. At the time German U-Boat operations were nearing their peak in terms of success. The thought that the Germans might gain a foothold out in the Atlantic might cause serious problems.[1] While militarily the Azores were not equipped for a war footing, the thinking was that it would take very little to convert the island into a potent armed base.

An initial plan was drawn up for an American invasion and seizure of the Azores in 1940 as a result of the President's concerns. As the plan reveals, "The President has stated that it is in the interest of the United States to prevent non-American belligerent forces from gaining control of the Azores, and that it is in the interest of the United States to hold these islands for sue as an air and naval base for the defense of the Western Hemisphere."[2] The problems with this plan were many. First, the United States did not have excess troops at the time to commit to such an operation. America was still not at war. Seizing the islands of the Azores in a preemptive attack would be seen by the American public as a deliberate move by the US to interfere in the then-European war. Some diplomatic talks were begun in 1940 with the British and Lisbon governments with the thought of positioning American troops on the island without an invasion, but these soon fizzled out.

In late May of 1941 there were signs that Germany might be preparing to invade the Azores and adjacent islands. There was even a hint that Germany might be preparing to place forces in Brazil as well. In response to this, War Plan Gray was formally drafted by the Joint Board on 29 May 1941.

Military Analysis of the Azores

Per a Joint Board 1941 review of the Azores, the islands were reviewed with renewed interest. Their analysis of the islands drove the military planning regarding War Plan Gray's operational parameters.

The Azores consists of nine islands, with a total land area of 922 miles. The group is located in the Eastern Atlantic about 800 miles from Portugal, 1,300 miles from our base in Newfoundland, 2,070 miles from New York, and 1,800 miles from Bermuda.

These islands are administered as an integral part of Portugal. The three key islands are San Miguel, Terceira, and Fayal. Occupation and defense of these three islands, with observation of the other six, would be essential to the control of the Azores. The principal ports are Ponta Delgada, Island of San Miguel; Horta, Island of Fayal; and Praia and Angra Bays, Island of Terceira. Only the first of these ports have docks and other facilities required for a base site.[3]

In 1933, the population was reported as about 234,000. Most of the inhabitants are of Portuguese origin. There are a few English, Scotch, and Irish. The settlement of the people are reportedly as pro-Ally, and friendly towards the United States. Economic conditions are generally bad. Agriculture and fishing are the principle occupations.[4]

Of key interest to the military analysis were the airstrips on the islands. Only two airfields exist for land planes, both on the Island of Terceira. One is located four miles northeast of Angra, has grass runway, and an area of 1,640 by 650 feet. The other is located on the beach of Parala Bay and has a sand runway 3,000 feet long. Neither of these fields is suitable for the operation of modern military aircraft until further developed. There are comparatively few sites suitable for the development of additional landing fields. Pan American Airways has a seaplane base at Horta, Island of Fayal. Considerable stocks of gasoline are maintained there. Seaplanes can also land at Ponta Delgada, Island of San Miguel, and at Praia and Agra Bays, Island of Terceira.[5]

The military defenses of the Azores almost seemed laughable. But when you factor in the thinking in the United States, there had to be a fear that Germany would realize that the weak defenses would make the Azores a tempting target for the German Reich. From an armed forces perspective, the Azores possessed the following:

> The garrison of the islands consists of an infantry battalion of 285 men at Angra (Terceira), and infantry battalion of 285 men, and a coastal artillery battery (caliber unknown) of 115 men at Portal Delgada (San Miguel) and a detachment of about 40 men at Horta (Fayal). These Portuguese troops are poorly armed, trained and equipped. They would offer little resistance.[6]

The garrison, however, appeared to be increasing according to intelligence reports in May of 1941:

> In the possession of the War and Navy Departments are very considerable amounts of information concerning the military features of the Azores. The most recent summary is that the best Portuguese troops are being transferred there from Portugal. It is estimated that approximately 10,000 regular and reserve troops are in the islands or will be there; it seems likely about one-half are on the island of San Miguel, and the other half divided amongst the other islands. Most of the troops are infantry, although there seems to be a small proportion of field artillery, some anti-aircraft artillery, and several medium-sized coast defense batteries. Combat quality of these troops probably is not high. Information indicated that no airfields are in use, but that Portugal is preparing one or more airfields for use by a small number of airplanes.[7]

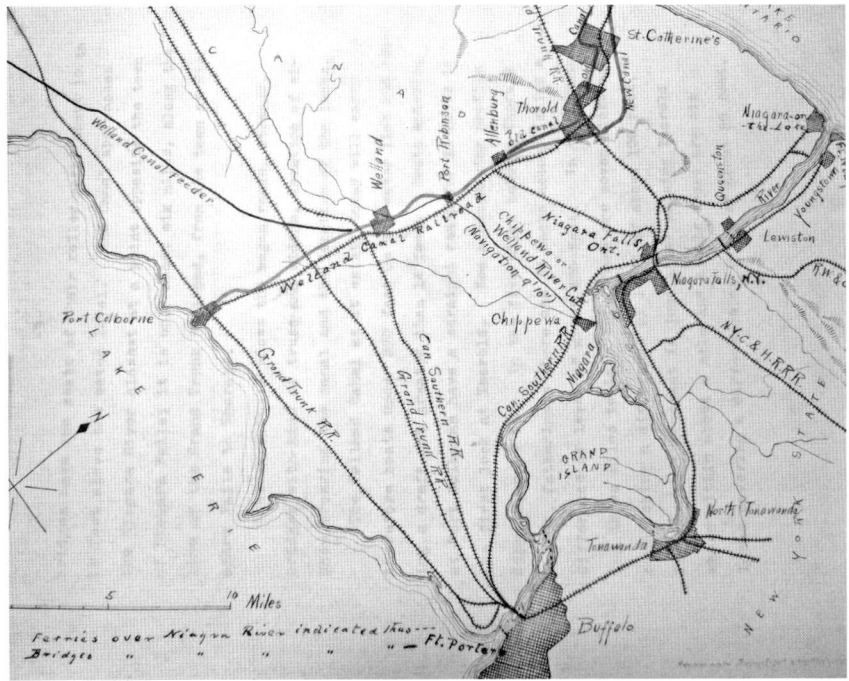

1 War Plan Crimson—This hand-drawn map details the primary invasion of Canada in the 1905 War Plan. (*US National Archives*)

2 War Plan Crimson. The Canadian Fusiliers—1904—These troops would have had to defend against invading US troops in War Plan Crimson. (*Library of Congress, Prints & Photographs Division*)

3 War Plan Crimson—Army intelligence provided this image as part of the planned invasion of Canada—showing the International Bridge, one of the early targets. (*US National Archives*)

4 War Plan Crimson—A more detailed view of the mid-span of the International Bridge (*US National Archives*)

5 War Plan Green—This map was used to provide the planning for the US planned invasion of Mexico (*US National Archives*)

6 War Plan Green. Pancho Villa and his command staff—one of the reasons that War Plan Green was drafted. (*Library of Congress, Prints & Photographs Division*)

7 War Plan Green—The Tampico docks—one of the early targets in the invasion of Mexico. (*Author's private collection*)

8 War Plan Green—Mexican forces in defense of Vera Cruz in 1929. These would be defenders if the US had invaded Mexico. (*Author's private collection*)

9 War Plan Green—The detailed map of Tampico and the defenses of the Mexican port as documented in War Plan Green (*US National Archives*)

10 War Plan Green. US troops search Mexican locals in Vera Cruz. This scene would have been commonplace if the US had invaded Mexico. (*Library of Congress, Prints & Photographs Division*)

11 Brooklyn Army Supply Depot—1919. This facility would have played a key role in several of the war plans. (*Library of Congress, Prints & Photographs Division*)

12 War Plan Tan. The Roughriders Troop H with their eagle mascot. The Spanish-American war forced the formulation of War Plan Tan. (*Library of Congress, Prints & Photographs Division*)

13 War Plan Gray— Ponta Delgada, the capital of largest island, San Miguel, in the Azores, taken in 1940 at the time of their planned invasion by the US to possibly thwart Germany's move against Gibraltar. (*US National Archives*)

14 War Plan Gray. The artificial harbor at Ponta Delgada, the capital of largest island, San Miguel, in the nine-island archipelago that makes up the Azores, with US submarines in the harbor, *c.* 1918. (*Pedro Cordeiro*)

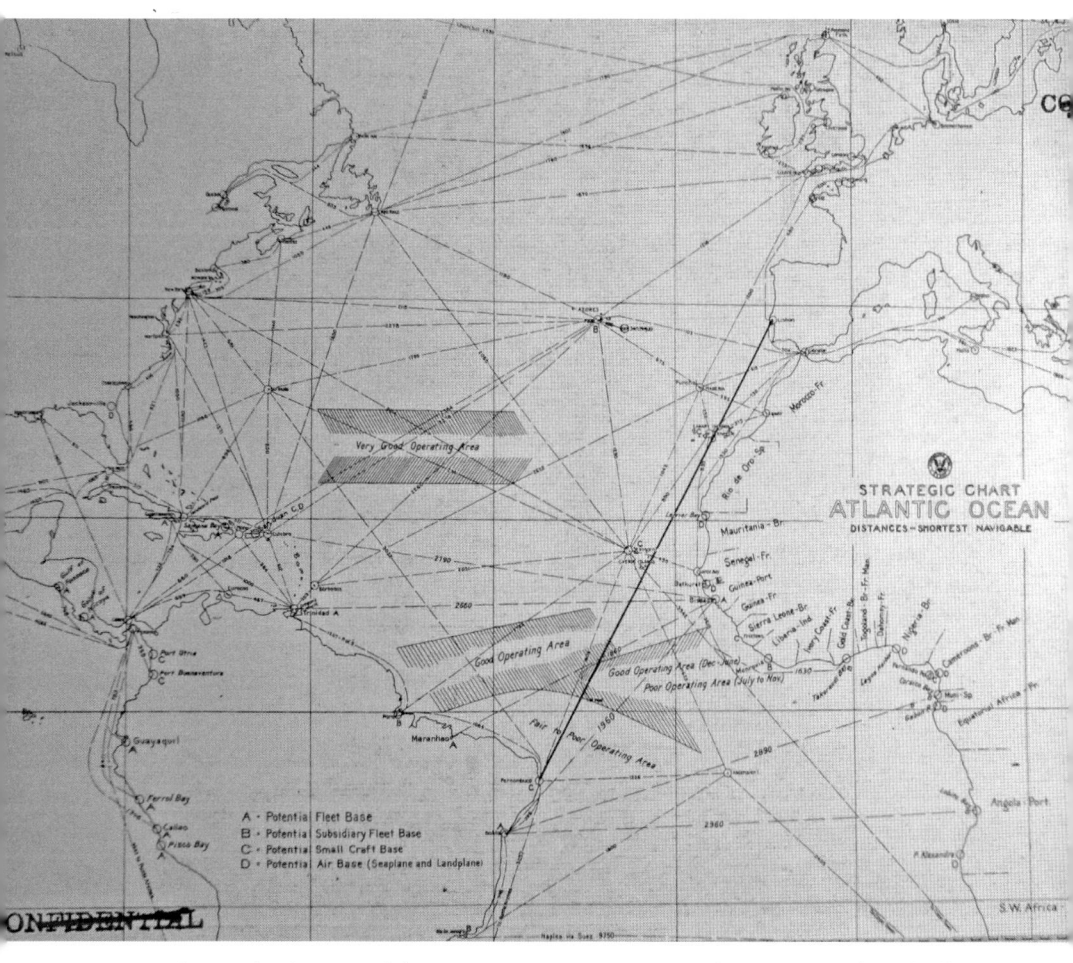

27 War Plan Red—As part of the war against Great Britain, the US Navy plotted where best to raid British merchant ships during the war. (*US National Archives*)

25 War Plan Black—This US siege gun (*c.* 1914) would have been employed inside of the District of Columbia as part of the defense of Washington DC. (*Author's private collection*)

U. S. Battleship "New Hampshire."

26 War Plan Red—The USS *New Hampshire* would have been part of the task force to engage the Royal Navy in the north Atlantic. (*Author's private collection*)

Above: 23 War Plan Black—These New York stationed troops would have been a thin line of defense against the planned German invasion of the US mainland. (Author's private collection)

Below: 24 War Plan Black. German field headquarters units like this one shown in 1914 would have been common during the siege of Washington DC. (*Library of Congress, Prints & Photographs Division*)

21 War Plan Black. The USS *Nevada*—1916—which would have squared off with the Germans if War Plan Black had been enacted. (*Library of Congress, Prints & Photographs Division*)

22 War Plan Black. This 1914 image of a German siege gun would have been commonplace as Germany invaded the US as assumed by War Plan Black. (*Library of Congress, Prints & Photographs Division*)

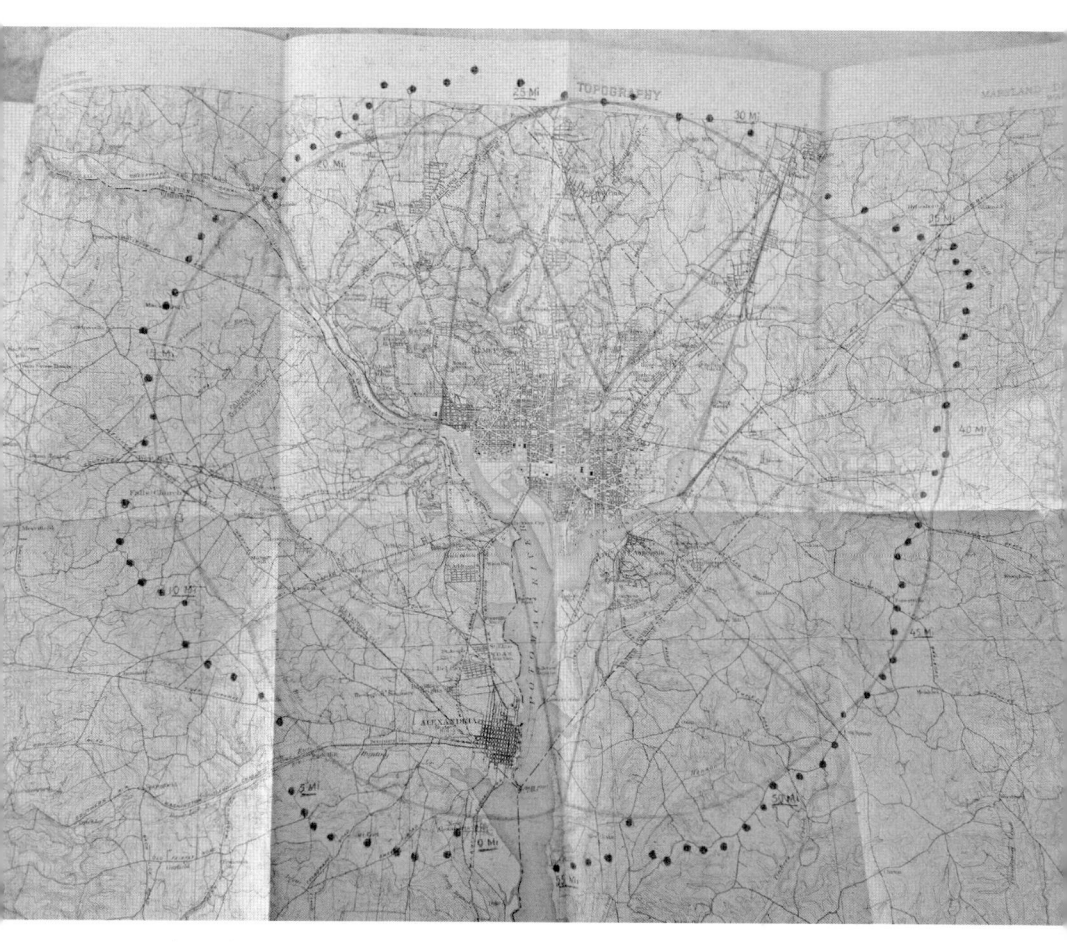

20 War Plan Black—The map of the defense perimeter planned around Washington DC. (*US National Archives*)

18 War Plan Black—These German Officers from 1914 would have been an unwelcome image for those in Philadelphia or Washington DC as they executed their operations on the US mainland. (*Author's private collection*)

19 War Plan Black—In 1914/1915 these men would have been pressed into the defense of the siege of the US capital. (*Author's private collection*)

16 War Plan Black—The USS Wyoming at Cuba's Guantanamo Bay in 1914—one of the early assumed target in Germany's invasion of the US. (*Author's private collection*)

17 War Plan Black—The US Fleet anchored in Guantanamo Bay 1914. The US assumed that Germany would seize the base quickly to coal her fleet for a US mainland invasion. (*Author's private collection*)

15 War Plan Yellow. Canton China as it would have appeared to invading US troops if War Plan Yellow had been enacted. (*Library of Congress, Prints & Photographs Division*)

The military analysis as to the value of the Azores was outlined in the analysis as well:

> The Axis powers could conduct raids against the Azores by aircraft from bases in France (a distance of 1,200 miles), by fast vessels that evade the British Fleet, and by submarines. A major attack against the Azores is unlikely, unless Gibraltar falls.[8]

The Germans did have a plan to seize British-held Gibraltar, dubbed Operation Felix. While really not much more than a staff-study, the Americans had no idea as to the depth of the German thinking. An attack on Gibraltar was not only possible—but probable.

Gibraltar was seen a lynchpin in the thinking of invading the Azores:

> Prevention of Axis occupation and successful use of bases in the Azores is vital to Great Britain and important to the United States. If Gibraltar should fall, a base in the Azores would be essential to the British in order to restrain the activities of the Axis fleet and protect her own vital sea lands. Great Britain may not have forces available for the seizure and occupation of Azores and she may, therefore, look to the United States to accomplish this task.[9]

Other documents related to War Plan Gray indicate that the Azores were strategically important:

> Naval forces based in the Azores would have important strategic possibilities. They could operate across the sea lanes between Europe and South America and between Europe and the United States. They also could operate towards Gibraltar and towards the Caribbean. Because of these possibilities, seizure of a base in these islands offers attractive inducements to the Axis. If Gibraltar should fall, the Italian fleet would have access to the Atlantic, and an Axis attack against the Azores could be expected, particularly if the islands were then defenseless or lightly held. The Axis could also seize the islands now by surprise action with small forces of air infantry dispatched from bases in France (1,200 miles away). Once established ashore and supported by aircraft and submarines, such forces would be difficult to dislodge.[10]

There were implications tied with an American seizure of Azores. These were identified as follows:

(1) Since the Azores are a province of Portugal, a neutral state, and lies outside of the Western Hemisphere, their seizure by the United States might be considered a *casus belli* by Germany and Italy, and possibly Japan.

(2) Our successful seizure and occupation of these islands would have a favorable moral effect upon the British and probably upon the States of South America. On the other hand, if we should undertake this operation and fail to attain complete success, this

failure would entail a tremendous loss of prestige and might prove a catastrophe to the cause of the democracies.

(3) Our occupation of the Azores is not essential to the defense of the Western Hemisphere. These islands are probably too distant and too exposed to warrant their occupation or retention if Great Britain should fall and her fleet be lost. We should not undertake the seizure and occupation of the Azores until we are ready to enter the war in concert with Great Britain, and have the forces necessary to insure the complete success in this undertaking and to meet the requirements for the defense of the Western Hemisphere.[11]

Weighing the Option

The planners of War Plan Gray carefully contemplated taking action in the Azores. This analysis of the political implications was a distinct step up from the planning that took place by the Board between 1904 and 1940. Clearly the expertise of the Joint Board had broadened as the world had slid into the abyss of global war:

> The only strategic justification for the occupation of the Azores by the U.S. forces is the necessity for assisting Great Britain to maintain its war effort by preventing German use of the islands as air and naval bases and by making the islands available to British or U.S. naval and air forces in case Gibraltar is lost. German occupation of the Azores does not in itself constitute a serious direct menace to the security of the Western Hemisphere because of the distance of those islands from any vital American objective. With a powerful American air defense, the threat of such bombing attacks as might be made from the Azores can be minimized.
>
> German occupation and successful use of the Azores will have a serious and possibly disastrous effect on the ability of Great Britain to maintain its ocean supply routes and thereby constitute an ultimate indirect threat to our security. German long range bombers, submarines and surface vessels will be able to maintain effective operations over the 800 and 1,300 miles separating the islands from Portugal and Newfoundland respectively. Furthermore the operations of these forces will interdict to a large extent any efforts by the United States or British surface naval vessels to operate in mid-Atlantic.
>
> The Germans can, at will, occupy Portugal. With air bases in Portugal the Germans can easily seize one or more of the islands with parachute troops. It is unlikely that the Portuguese resistance will be serious. Once in control of the islands the Germans can prepare one, possibly two, airfields suitable for the use of bombers. Protected by aviation and submarines the Germans can move surface cargo and passenger vessels to the Azores with relative freedom. They will be able to convert the Azores into a strong air and naval base. The only way in which the Germans can certainly be prevented from seizing the Azores is the prior seizure and occupation by British or United States forces. In view of the importance of the islands in determining the outcome of the war with England, is highly probable that the Germans will seize them as soon as practicable unless they believe that they can give England a knock-out blow during the early summer.[12]

The United States was not at war in early 1941 when the analysis by the Joint Board was conducted. As such the planners fully acknowledged that any seizure of the Azores by the United States would precipitate active war with Germany and possibly her ally, Japan. While the invasion would boost morale in the United States and in South America (if successful) planners had to come to grips with what the capabilities of the US were in 1941.

> The Army will not be prepared to provide suitable air forces for the defense of the islands until after October, using pursuit and bomber units which are now set up to operate in the British Isles. Prior to that date the Navy will have to provide air defense.

There were other considerations that factored into their thinking at the time:

> At the present time, a critical defense requirement of the Western Hemisphere itself is the occupation of the Natal area. Only the Air and anti-aircraft forces to be used in the Azores are not available for this task. The probable intent of Germany to utilize Dakar as a base, and the impracticability of the seizure of that place by either Great Britain or the United States within any reasonable time greatly increase the dangers of our position in South America. With the support of German aviation flown from Dakar, and of munitions which may be sent by ship, the Nazi adherents in Brazil may seize power, establish a strong base in Natal and make future operations of American forces in that area exceedingly difficult. The security of the Panama Canal and the Western Hemisphere may be seriously jeopardized by the neglect of the Natal area at this time. An ultimate victory by combined U.S. and British forces over Germany will purge the situation in a Nazified Brazil.[13]

War Plan Gray Plan of Attack

The Joint Board did not allocate a great deal of time or effort in detailing the assaults that would be necessary to secure the Azores given the limited number of defenders on the islands and their relatively small size. Instead they concentrated on the organizational aspects of the attack.

The plan was devised to be a secret attack on the islands. The American Expeditionary Force was to department rapidly with no diplomatic or political forewarning of the pending assaults. The plan did not contemplate the use of the US Marine Corps for the initial landings, only US Army troops. The Army was to be divided into three distinct task forces for the assaults: Fayal, Terceira, and San Miguel. Under the air cover the US carrier aircraft, the transports carrying these troops were designated to land at the available ports on their target islands. From there the troops were to negate and capture the Portuguese forces garrisoning the island and secure it for use by the United States.

Task Force Fayal was to secure the harbor of Horta and the Pan American Airways seaplane base there. The Army was then to move in and secure the cable center for telegraph and phone traffic which was on the island as well.

Task Force San Miguel was going to be landing on the largest island in the Azores. The landings would take place at the harbor of Ponta Delgada.

Task Force Terceira would have one of the more complicated missions. Terceira was the headquarters of the garrison force in the Azores and would be most likely where resistance would be the heaviest—if at all. It also had the government center—and administrative center for the island, which was to be captured intact. Finally this task force was to seize the two airfields (four miles northeast of Angra and on the beach of Praia Bay) on the island so that the engineering units landing could begin work to outfit these fields to accommodate modern military aircraft.

Work was to immediately begin to extend and harden the airfields on the islands for use by the British and Americans. Establishment of anti-aircraft units would be of paramount importance as well. Planners assumed that once the United States made its play to take the Azores, that the Germans would strike back to prevent this. They would do this initially with long range bombers—and possibly submarine (U-Boat) forces. These counterattacks, especially from the air, were expected the second day of the occupation if not sooner.[14]

A prerequisite for the operation was that the Royal Navy was to maintain control of the Eastern Atlantic. This did not need to be a long-term situation, only long enough for War Plan Gray to be initiated. A sortie on the part of the German Reichsmarine could place the operation in jeopardy.

One of War Plan Gray's assumptions was that the garrison on the islands would most likely lay down their arms at the sight of thousands of American troops debarking. Because of the overwhelming force being applied in the operation, even if there was resistance, it would not be for long—nor would it be of a nature to endanger the operation.

American Forces to be Used

An estimate of forces, drawn up by the Joint Board in May of 1940 envisioned a division-sized invasion force, augmented with additional troops. This estimate became the basis for the final planning. The original estimate of American forces required was as follows:

Table: Original Estimated Forces Allocated for War Plan Gray[15]

	Officers:	Warrant Officers:	Nurses:	Enlisted Men:
Division HQ	26	2		37
HQ and MP Co.	7			148
1st Signal Co.	8			230
1st Quartermaster Bn.	18			273
1st Med Bn.	29			339
1st Engineering Bn.	21			570
Two Infantry Regiments Three Artillery Bns.	246	2		6,068
One Medium (105)	32			698
7th FA Bn. Two Light Bns.	54			1,038
Division Artillery HQ	12			135
Total First Infantry Division Personnel	453	<u>4</u>		9,536
Two Machinegun Batteries (AA)	10			352
One Truck Company	5			159
29th Ord. Co.	6			140
Plat Co. B 99th QM Bn. Bkry)	1			35
Plat Co. A 67th QM Bn. (LM)	1			68
7th Sta Hospital	20		30	150
Total Attached Units	43		30	<u>904</u>
Grand Total	496	4	30	<u>10,440</u>

As the Joint Board reviewed the plans for the Azores, and with changes to unit availability, these troops allocations and compositions were changed.

Overall Task Force Compositions

The planners arrived at the final overall composition for War Plan Gray:
   1st Infantry Division (less 5th Field Artillery Bn.), reinforced by:
   1 Bn. 244th Coastal Artillery (155mm guns)
   61st and 68th Coastal Artillery (AA)
   3 Batteries, 99th Field Artillery (75mm Pk)
   2 Dets. Signal Corps
   2 Dets Medical Sta. Hospital
   1 Bn. 21st Engineers
   1 Plat Co. C 66th Quartermaster Bn. (LM)
   1 Plat Co. A 84th Quartermaster Bn. (LM)
   1 Plat Co. B 84th Quartermaster Bn. (LM)
   2 Plats Co. A 95th Quartermaster Bn. (Bakery)
   7th Pursuit Wing Headquarters and Headquarters Squadron
   8th and 31st Pursuit Groups
   7th Bombing Group
   3rd Observation Squadron
   2nd Air Base Group (Reinforcements)[16]

This overall force was broken down in the task forces as follows:

Fayal Task Force

   1 Infantry Regiment (less 1 Bn.)
   1 Bn. 75mm guns
   1 Battery 244th Coastal Artillery (155mm gun)
   1 Regiment Coastal Artillery (AA) (less 2–37mm gun Batteries and
   1 Machinegun Plat)
   1 Detachment Medical Sta. Hospital
   1 Coll. Co. Med. Bn. (reinforced by 1 Plat clearing Co and Det. HQ and
   Service Co. (Total strength 11 officers and 170 enlisted personnel)
   1 Engineering Plat.
   Detached 1st Ordnance Co. (1 officer and 20 enlisted personnel)
   Detached 1st Quartermaster Bn. (1 officer and 20 enlisted personnel)
   Detached Signal Co.
   1 Plat. Co. C 66th Quartermaster Bn. (LM)
   1 Plat. Co. A 95th Quartermaster Bn. (Bakery)

Note: Each detachment will consist of 20 officers, 30 nurses, and 150 enlisted personnel. Details would be provided prior to the invasion by the Surgeon General.[17]

Terceira Task Force

1 Infantry regiment (less 1 Bn.)
1 Battery 99th Field Artillery Bn.
1 Bn. 75mm gun (less 1 Battery)
2 Batteries Coastal Artillery (AA) (37mm guns)
1 Plat. Coastal Artillery (AA) (Machineguns)
1 Engineering Co.
1 Coll. Co. Medical Bn. (reinforced by 1 Plat. clear Co. and dets HQ and Service Co.)
1 Detached 1st Ordnance Co. (1 officer and 20 enlisted personnel)
1 Detached Quartermaster Bn. (1 officer and 20 enlisted personnel)
1 Detached Signal Co.
1 Plat. Co. A 84th Quartermaster Bn. (LM)

Note: The detached Signal Company will consist of 1 officer and 20 enlisted personnel with the specifics being worked out prior to departure by the Chief Signal Officer.[18]

San Miguel Task Force

1st Division (less 5th Field Artillery Bn. And elements included in other two task forces)
2 Batteries 99th Field Artillery Bn.
1 Bn. 244th Coastal Artillery (155mm gun)—Less one Battery
1 Regiment Coastal Artillery (AA)
1 Plat. Co. B 84th Quartermaster Bn. (LM)
1 Plat. Co A 95th Quartermaster Bn. (Bakery)
Detached Signal Co.
Detached Medial Sta. Hospital
1 Bn. 21st Engineers

Note: Each battery of the 99th Field artillery were to be equipped with six light wheeled tractors and six trailers (¾ ton). No animal transportation. The detached medical unit would consist of 20 officers, 30 nurses, and 150 enlisted personnel— details to be worked out by the Chief Medical Officer prior to departure. The detached Signal Company will consist of 1 officer and 20 enlisted personnel with the specifics being worked out prior to departure by the Chief Signal Officer.

The Joint Board planners did not anticipate a great deal in the way of resistance:

It is contemplated that one infantry battalion in the FAYAL Force, one reinforced battalion combat team in the TERCEIRA Force and two reinforced battalion combat teams in the SAN MIGUEL Force will be combat unit loaded. Not more than one reinforced battalion combat team will be loaded on a single ship.[19]

While the Army was landing forces on three islands, it was an expressed part of their mission to provide surveillance, security, and observation on the other islands of Azores. How this was to be accomplished was never specified in War Plan Gray. It is assumed that the Commanding General of the First Infantry Division would have to provide for this observation at his own discretion.[20]

The Air Corps units designated for the Azores were not going to be needed in the initial landing operations. These would not accompany the invasion force because there were no facilities to support them on the island, until the landing fields were expanded. That, and the mobilization of the air units might tip off Axis intelligence agents as to possible targets. The Air Corps would arrive only when the landing fields were ready ... which was anticipated to be a week or two after the landings.[21]

In order to provide security, the First Infantry Division was to be at its port of debarkation ten days after the initial notice for mobilization for the operation was given. Command of the operation was to reside with the senior naval commander present in the task force until such time that the Commanding General of the First Infantry Division went ashore, at which time command authority for the Azores would pass to the Army.[22] Secrecy was crucial for the invasion.

> ... it is of the greatest importance that secrecy as to the preparation and dispatch of the expedition be preserved, and that such information as might leak out indicate that the expedition is to go to another destination, as for example Trinidad, Martinique, or Brazil.[23]

In terms of logistics, the Army was to equip with summery clothing, plus heavy tentage, mosquito bars, headnets and helmets. In terms of munitions, the plan was to for an extended stay on the Azores.

> There will accompany the Army forces 60 days of supply of all classes except ammunition, 15 times the initial allowance of ammunition (mobilization) for anti-aircraft weapons and 7 times the initial allowance of ammunition (mobilization) for other weapons. There will accompany air corps units sufficient ammunition for 45 days of operation at approved mission rates.[24]

Naval Support and Missions

War Plan Gray anticipated a significant naval task force for late 1941. Units designated were as follows:

> Two Aircraft Carriers—assigned for direct landing support and air coverage for the operation.
>> Fifteen troop transports
>> One Cargo vessel or tanker for gasoline and oil
>> Four Light cruisers for naval gunfire in support of the landings

Twenty-seven destroyers
One Seaplane tender for eighteen VP planes[25]
One hospital ship
Three Navy tugs
A heavy ammunition ship
A converted refrigerator ship[26]

The actual ships that would have been involved in the operation were identified in May of 1941 as the following:

The Army would turn over to the Navy the following transports: the *Hunter Liggett*, the *Leonard Wood*, the *Dickman*, the *Orizara* [sic], the *Hahhattah*, and the *Washington*.

The identified Navy transports were the *Barnett*, the *Harry Lee*, the *G. P. Elliott*, the *Heywood*, the *Fuller*, the *W. P. Biddle*, the *Neville* and the *McCowley*. The converted passenger ship *America* was also to be used for the transportation of the Army contingent to the islands.

The naval mission included the following:

1. To procure, man, equip, and operate the vessels necessary to transport Army personnel, equipment and supplies.
2. To assemble the necessary transports at the New York Port of Embarkation, at the times specified by the commander of the port of embarkation.
3. To provide for security of transports at sea.
4. To provide for the messing of Army forces en route.
5. To provide adequate reconnaissance.
6. To provide the defense against enemy naval forces during the landing operations.
7. To provide, man, equip, and operate the small craft required for landing operations.
8. To cover the landing by mine sweeping, gunfire, aircraft and screening operations.
9. To provide signal communications between ships and shore.
10. To organize, operate and maintain the sea lines of supply for the Army forces after establishment ashore.
11. To establish a base for seaplane and light forces at Ponta Delgada
12. To maintain a carrier in the vicinity of the Azores until army air forces are established ashore.
13. If practical, provide for the movement of the Army aircraft to the Azores by carrier. [27]

The execution signals for the invasion to proceed were:

The Army: "Execute Gray"
The Navy: "Execute W.P.L. Forty-Seven." [28]

Summary Evaluation of the War Plan

War Plan Gray represents one of the last colored war plans that were created and refined before the Joint Board evolved into the more structured Joint Chiefs of Staff. Few of the War Plans were ever executed, and in this case, Gray was one that was very nearly executed.

It is a what-if scenario that is tantalizing. What if Germany had attempted to seize the Azores? Would it have prolonged the Battle of the North Atlantic? What if America had taken the islands—or better yet, was forced to try and remove Germany from them? Would Terceira have joined the pantheon of famous battles of World War II? How would Portugal have reacted under either situation? Could the Azores have altered World War II, or have remained as a mere footnote to the events?

America was contemplating doing something that clearly violated the neutrality of Portugal in planning an invasion and occupation the Azores. Much has been written about President Roosevelt's disposition to get America into the war earlier than December of 1941—and this invasion plan certainly supports this thinking. The alteration of War Plan Gray from invasions of some Caribbean Islands to a direct assault on the Azores to secure them from German use, certainly supports Roosevelt's strategy.

One thing is clear, the organization of the War Plan was substantial—much more than some of the other War Plans there were drafted during the tenure of the Joint Board. It was the only one that factored in the impact of the United States potentially *losing* the battle—and ensured that overwhelming force was going to be deployed.

War Plan Gray is also interesting because it was drawn up just before the United States was attacked and forced into the war. Given America's neutrality, the thought that they were planning to attack another neutral nation under the thin veil of protecting America and the Western Hemisphere demonstrates just how far toward the precipice of war President Roosevelt was leaning—even in the early summer of 1941.

Would the invasion of the Azores have been successful? Even if the intelligence sources were accurate it is clear that with air and naval superiority, the United States would have been hard pressed to fail in taking the islands. Modifications were made to War Plan Gray up through early 1943. This indicates that even after the potential threat to Gibraltar had faded, the US was still considering attacking and using the islands as bases for the Battle of the Atlantic.

As it was, the plan was not needed. The British and Americans leased basing rights in the Azores in 1943—achieving peacefully the solution War Plan Gray sought to take by force.

The 1929 Plan for the American Incursion/Invasion of China
War Plan Yellow Variations A and B

Introduction

After the Great War, China is best described as "The Wild West," from an American perspective. China was not the monolithic centrally managed government we know today. Instead it was almost a city-state form of government—where local warlords raised their own armies and military forces to protect their holdings. Even the state structure was more of a loose alignment of these warlords, who often turned on each other with no one seeming to achieve the upper hand.

Complicating matters greatly was the fact that China had become a vast market for the surplus weapons of war from the Great War. While all of the governments formally frowned on the sales of arms to China for fear that it would only increase their instability—the reality was that every country with leftover arms was selling weapons of war to the warlords. Suddenly a self-proclaimed general could own fighter and bomber aircraft, rapid-fire artillery, and machineguns. This allowed bands of highway and street thugs to evolve into well-armed (albeit sloppily led) militia units. While many of these weapons were out of date, almost antiquated by the rapid technological advancement that the Great War had introduced, they made mainland China a deadly place.

This instability had many governments negotiate to place their troops in China, under the auspices of protecting key infrastructure and their own national interests. The United States had participated in the Boxer Rebellion and had simply left a garrison force in-country after the end of that conflict. While they were in position, no external government was large enough to be considered significant enough to enforce any true stability to China. The result was that garrisons from countries such as the United States, Britain, and France were simply part of the overall mish-mash of military forces in China.

War Plan Yellow exists today mostly in fragmented parts. What has been assembled in this chapter has been culled from a number of different archival sources.

China—Historical Context

The assembly of War Plan Yellow required context to the plan ... an estimation of the Chinese situation. This was pulled together in May of 1924—outlining the historical, political, and military assessments of China which would serve as the basis of the War Plan.

The members of the Joint Board still remembered America's most recent intervention into Chinese affairs, the so-called Boxer Rebellion (1899–1901). This was a general uprising across China by the Yihetuan Movement to drive out the western powers, Christianity, and attempting to reform China with a new wave of nationalism. The British, French, Austrian, German, Italian, Japanese, Russian and American governments first moved to protect their nationals in China, reinforcing them with small numbers of troops. The British sent several expeditions into China to quell the rebellion—and the Russians used the uprising as a pretext for an invasion of Mongolia. The Americans also sent in military force.

The Chinese were unable to defend their nation, even against these relatively small military incursions and eventually the rebellion was squashed. Memory of it stung China, it was a humiliation that was to be long remembered. For the Joint Board Planners, the Boxer Rebellion provided a stage on which their own more contemporary analysis of China was played out:

Prior to the overthrow of the Manchu Dynasty in 1911, the rather decentralized government was ruled over by an Emperor who was regarded with religious veneration as the "Son of Heaven." Following the Sino-Japanese war (1894) and the competition of the European powers for concessions from the 1896–1898 inclusive ("The Battle for Concessions"), there was a great popular demand for reform. Though some changes were later made in the Central Government, complete steps were not taken to provide for a constitution and a popular assembly.

In 1911 a revolution broke out which finally resulted in the overthrow of the Manchu Dynasty and the establishment of a Republic in 1912 with Yuan Shih Kai as President. The Republic first functioned under a Provisional Constitution which had been drafted in 1911. The majority of the Parliament belonged to the Kuo Wing Tang [sic] party which was in opposition to President Yuan. By December 1913 President Yuan Shih Kai felt strong enough to dissolve this Parliament and from January 1914 to 1916 he ruled as a dictator. A Provisional Constitution was adopted in May 1914 by a commission of 60 members elected from the various provinces and dependencies. This Constitution gave the President complete autocratic powers.

On October 8, 1915, a bill was promulgated calling for a referendum on whether or not a monarchy should be proclaimed with Yuan as Emperor. Voting took place in November, and by fair means and foul the country was made to declare unanimously for a monarchy, Yuan accepted the Throne on December 12, 1915, but, due to widespread opposition especially in South China, he was forced in March 1916 to cancel his acceptance prior to the date of the ceremony. Yuan then attempted to organize his government on approved modern lines but died suddenly in June 1916.

When the Vice-President, Li Yuan Hung, became President in 1916, he reconvened the National Parliament which had been dissolved by Yuan but, under pressure of the militarists, he again dissolved it in 1917. The Kuo Wing Tang [sic] members of Parliament withdrew to Canton insisting that the 1911 Provisional Constitution was the legal instrument that prescribed the duties of the President and Parliament. A Republic called [the] South China Constitutional Government was set up in Canton of which Sun Yat Sen became President in November, 1920. The South China Government was overthrown by troops of General Chen Chiung Ming on June 16, 1922, and Dr. Sung Yat Sen was soon forced to take refuge in Shanghai. Chen Chiung Ming troops acknowledging nominal allegiance to Sun Yat Sen. Sun Yat Sen returned once more to Canton in February, 1923, since which time he has maintained a precarious hold on that city. In July 1917 an attempt was made in Peking to restore the Manchus but this movement was quickly overcome just as similar movements are sure to fail in the future.

In April 1922 Wu Pei Fu, military prop of the Chihli Party, decisively defeated Chang Tso Lin, the Manchurian Dictator, in a campaign for control of Peking. The latter, returning north of the Great Wall, then declared the practical independence of the Manchurian Province. The Chihli militarists, forcing the resignation of the vacillating President, Hua Shih Chang, now recalled former President Li Yuan Hung to the presidency (June 1922). One of President Li's first mandates reconvened the twice dissolved old Parliament. Li, in turn, was forced to flee from Peking in June of 1922 because of the threatening attitude of the Chihli militarists and, from June 13, 1923 until October 10, 1923, the Peking Government functioned without a quorum in Parliament and with only a portion of a cabinet in office. The Chihli Military Party finally succeeded in buying the election of its head, Tsao Kun, from Parliament so Tsao assumed office on October 10, 1923. A new constitution was promulgated the same day.[1]

Politically, China was seen as little more than bands of thugs rigging a string of elections that seemed to do nothing to advance the nation as a whole:

Following the death of the dictator Yuan Shih Kai in 1916, the various presidents who followed were merely puppets of one or the other of the strong military cliques. Parliament, often dissolved by presidential mandate, has proved, when it is in session, to be only a troublesome group of dishonest obstructionists, seldom able to assemble a quorum or effect legislation. On October 5, 1923, Tsao Kun, Tuchum [sic] (Military Governor) of Chihli, Shantung and Honan provinces and head of the Chihli Military Party, was elected President of China. This election was secured by open bribery, the members of Parliament receiving a check for $5,000.00 as their ballots were cast. With Tsao Kun as President, the Chihli military clique became in effect the Peking Government with control, actual or nominal, of a number of provinces.[2]

Military Assessment of China in 1928

With so much political instability and corruption, it is easy to see why China of the 1920s had done little but devolve into a state of petty warlords ruling their city-states. The Joint Board assessment of China during this period pinned this point down to specifics:

> Following the election it was freely predicted that all factions hostile to the Chihli militarists would unite to secure the downfall of President Tsao Kun and his party. On the contrary, there have been no major operation in recent months. With headquarters at Mukden, Marshal Chang Tso Lin, the Manchurian Dictator, has been busily engaged in training an army numbering over a hundred thousand men. Smarting under his defeat in 1922 by Wu Pei Fu, military prop of the Chihli militarists, Chang is erecting new arsenals, importing aeroplanes and employing foreign instructors to train his troops. Some experts believe he awaits the disintegration of the Chihli Party though internal dissensions, other believe that his desire for revenge will cause him to assume the offensive before many months. One can only see in the future a continuation of civil wars coupled with even more complete chaos.[3]

It is this very climate of chaos that forced the members of the Joint Board to draft War Plan Yellow for the protection of Americans in greater China:

> In many provinces, as for example, in the three Manchurian provinces, in Chekiang, in Kwangsi, and in Yunnan, the Central Government has not a vestige of control. In others such as Szechwan, Kwngtung and Fukien the Chihli militarists are fighting for possession.
>
> There are some hundreds of thousands of armed bandits in the country, the distinction between whom and the selfsupporting [sic] soldiery is hard to draw and is not apparent in their long suffering victims, the agricultural population and small merchants. The bandits may be groups into two categories. First: bandits proper, that is, those group of armed men operating usually in remote and inaccessible parts of the country who have for generations practiced the gentle art of robbery on the highways of commerce both on land and sea. Second: those groups of armed men who having started on the military career as legitimate soldiers, find themselves in the death or political eclipse of their original leaders, in the situation of military orphans and so forced either to go back to work as coolies or to fend for themselves as military units. Very few take the former alternative as it involved not great change for their ordinary pursuits for such soldiers to rob and squeeze for themselves and for minor self-appointed leaders, instead of for military leaders and Tuchuns appointed by the Peking Government or by the provinces, as the case may be.[4]

While large armed bands of outlawed mercenary soldiers existed, China did maintain an army—at least on paper:

> Any army is generally understood to be an armed and disciplined force of men, subject to the orders of the Government, and available for the defense of the nation against external

aggressive and the maintenance of internal order. In this sense China possessions no army. There are, exclusive of some tens of thousands of bandits in various parts of the country, probably upwards of 1,000,000 men under arms in various units, a larger number of armed men than is maintained by any other country in the world. Of the million and more men who carry rifles and wear uniforms of some description or another, there are not thirty thousand who would be capable of offering effective resistance to half their number of properly equipped and well disciplined Japanese, American or European troops. The Chinese armies are not under the orders or control of the Central Government or of Parliament, but are employed by, and recognize no authority other than that of the Tuchuns. Each Tuchun raises his own army, maintains his own arsenal and, by seizing some source of public revenue, finds a way to provide clothing, food and a little pay for his troops. No serious attempt is made, today, to standardize arms, uniforms, equipment or ammunition. At least seven types of rifles are known to be in use, and there is an even greater variety of artillery and machine guns. There is no central command, the War Ministry and General Staff exercising no control whatsoever over the Tuchuns' forces. There is no practical plan of mobilization or concentration. Unless two provinces happen to be under the control of the same Super-Tuchun, no force located in one province would be available for operations in another. President Tsao Kun has nominal control over the troops of a number of provinces but this control is due to the fact that he is the head of the Chihli Party rather than any authority growing out of the office of President of China.[5]

As a defense against foreign invasion, therefore, China's armed forces are of little value. But for the difficulties of communication, due to the absence of roads suitable for wheeled transport, one well-equipped foreign division, supported by a small naval force, and equipped with aeroplanes and modern artillery, could affect a landing in any part of China assessable to vessels of modern draught, and its radius of action would be limited only by the problem of transport. There is hardly a General in the Chinese forces who has even an elementary conception of modern strategy or tactics.

As a factor in the maintenance of internal order, the Chinese armies are equally useless. For the most part they are the fomenters of disorder rather than the guardians of the public.[6]

Ultimately the instability was what drove the Joint Board into creating War Plan Yellow:

Never since the Boxer uprising when the foreign legations in Peking were subjected to siege has the prestige of the white man in China been so low. The past year has seen an ever growing list of outrages against foreigners by bands and soldiery. A number of foreigners have been killed and many foreign subjects including women and children have been seized by organized bands numbering thousands and carried captives around the countryside. Numerous cases of piracy involving foreigners have occurred in South China while the instances of indiscriminating firing on foreign vessels on the Yangtze and West Rivers have been too numerous to record.

With the prospect of a continuation of the civil war between rival military cliques in which foreign lives, property and treaty rights are certain to be endangered, and with a growing disregard for foreign treaty rights among all factions, one is convinced that some day [sic] a spark may light the magazine and force the Great Powers into either a forcible assertion of treaty rights or a relinquishment of them.[7]

Potential Triggers for War Plan Yellow

The planners of the Joint Board outlined a series of potential events that might lead to an American intervention or invasion in China. The criteria that they adopted in War Plan Yellow were as follows:

a. To enforce the provision of the protocol of 1901, viz., to maintain open communication form Peking to the sea.

b. To protect Americans who are endangered as a result of factional warfare between Chinese armies.

c. To protect American citizens from attack by radical, anti-foreign groups, some of which might be armed in opposition to the existing government or which that Government might be unable or unwilling to control.

d. To protect American citizens from attacks by organized armed forces of the existing Chinese Government or by independent groups.[8]

The United States believed it would have ample warning of when the political/military situation had devolved to a point where intervention was necessary:

There is usually some warning of the probability of large scale disorders or of situations threatening the safety of Americans residing in China; and it has been the policy of the American Government to advise its citizens residing in threatened or dangerous area to leave such localities and proceed onto ports where adequate protection can be afforded or from which they may be evacuated.[9]

The underlying assumption was that the US would maintain this policy should China destabilize. This thinking would be crucial to the architects of War Plan Yellow.

Yellow was devised to approach unrest in China is two aspects. Variation A, for which little information exists, called for a limited application of military force to evacuate Americans from an unstable or outwardly hostile China. Variation B saw a larger military incursion in China centered around Shanghai and Peking with the intent of restoring stability.

War Plan Yellow—Variation A

War Plan Yellow's Variation A does not have a great deal of supporting documentation still existing to outline the plan in minute detail. From what can be cobbled together, from a variety of archival sources, it appeared to be primarily a US Navy and Marine Corps operation to secure key port facilities with the purpose to effect the removal of American citizens (and other friendly foreign nationals) from China.

A high-level analysis of Variation A outlines its boundaries:

> After careful study undertaking in collaboration with the G-2 Division, this Division concludes that the use of armed forces of the United States in China would be limited to seaport areas. The majority of the American citizens and the major portion of their interests are in the immediate vicinity of treaty ports. Furthermore, it is the policy of the United States to advise evacuation of American citizens in times of danger to seaports where they would be provided a greater measure of safety. In view of the foregoing any operation into the interior of China with its attendant difficulties is precluded.[10]

Under Variation A, the Army would only provide minimal troops which were to be drawn from the Philippines or Hawaii garrisons—though the exact numbers or specific unit designations were never fully defined. These would augment the US Marine Corps which would ensure a stronger American military presence. This was clearly intended to be a short-term intervention, essentially long enough to mount an American evacuation from China.

Variation A called for a relatively short time span for a military operation. The US was not to secure the ports for long-term use, but simply evacuate Americans and withdraw—leaving Navy patrols for the key waterways. In short, Variation A was a, "get in and get out," solution for instability in China.

War Plan Yellow—Variation B

Under the terms of Variation B, the United States would be essentially invading several key cities in China with the expressed intent of assisting in restoring order and protection of US citizens and friendly foreign nationals:

> …Variation B, provides for a total of five infantry divisions. Since interposition will be limited to the vicinity of seaports and probably undertaken at not to exceed three such areas, it is been concluded that a maximum force of this size is excessive and the revised plan (1929) employed only two modified divisions.[11]

While the plan outlines two infantry divisions as well as US Marine support, there was a feeling that no matter what—China was going to involve more divisions of troops.

The US Army already had some boots on the ground in China during the planning of War Plan Yellow:

> Tientsin is now garrisoned by an international force, including the 15th United States Infantry (less one battalion) The American Legation guard at Peking numbers

approximately 500 United States Marines. The total foreign forces in the Peiking–Tientsin–Shanhaikwan [sic] areas as of September 1, 1929 was 5,551 officers and men of which 1,320 were in Peking.[12]

While these forces were considered adequate to assist (albeit augmented by additional US Marines) in Variation A of War Plan Yellow—they were woefully undermanned to meet the demands of Variation B.

The intended incursion zones/cities were tentatively designated as Peking, Chinwangtao, Shanghai, and Taku. These were targeted for a variety of reasons. First and foremost they were strategic targets—centers of commerce, railway traffic, and China's most formidable military garrisons. Secondly; these cities had the most advanced transportation systems, namely rail lines, control of which would limit the ability of any large-scale movement by the Chinese military. Third, these cities (or installations in the case of Taku) would severely limit the ability of China to trade with the outside world, cutting off funds that might be used to pay for weapons to resist the US action.

Taku was actually a set of forts located at the mouth of the Hai River near Tianjin. This set of forts could control all commerce coming down river, essentially cutting off this vital province. The forts themselves had been dismantled after the Boxer rebellion but their placement alongside the river would allow the Americans to rearm them and secure transport on the rivers.

Creating a stranglehold on Chinese commerce was critical:

> The guarding of the important railway sea terminals of Chinwangtao and Taku will also present difficultness which will make heavy drains on our combat forces.[13]

War Plan Yellow Variation B called for the Army to not just secure the cities to establish control and protect citizens—but to secure the key railroads. This mission was one that was not without risk for the invaders:

> It is the further opinion of this division that the guarding of the Peiping–Tientsin–Taku–Chiwangtao railway alone will require at least one Army Corps of three divisions and that the guarding of the seaports and Peiping will require one additional division.[14]

So while the initial plan called for the landing of two divisions in China, further examination of the plans called for four to five divisions of strength.

In China—this was not merely a matter of landing troops—but transportation animals as well. While the 1929 US Army was in the middle of a period of modernization to trucks for transportation, such vehicles would actually present a burden to the invading forces. While the major cities maintained paved roads (for the most part), such was not the case outside of the urban areas. For all of its size, China only maintained 25,000 miles of roads that were suitable for motor vehicles. Many of these could not support two-way traffic however, even in the dry seasons. These were unpaved, for the most part—consisting mostly of graded earth. When the rains came, and they did, the roads were a quagmire.[15]

Road development in the area of operations for the American "relief" forces under War Plan Yellow was detailed as follows:

(1) Peiping is connected with Tientsin and Taku by a good dirt road wide enough for cars to pass at any point and practical for travel by all types of automobiles except after heavy rains.

(2) Peiping is connected with Shanghai, by a well graded road 50 feet wide. Important bridges are well built but culverts are constructed of tree limbs covered with corn stalks and mud which must be crossed carefully.

(3) Chefee [sic] is jointed to Weihsien [sic] in the interior of Shantung by a good dirt motor road.

(4) Tsingtao, Shanghai, Nanking, Amoy, and Canton only have short motor roads leading into the country.

The ordinary country roads in the Peiping–Tientsin area and vicinity of the ports traverse densely populated territory dotted with towns and covered with a network of canals, irrigation ditches, lakes, streams and rivers. The road net, developed through centuries, conforms to the terrain and is well adapted, naturally, to the ordinary Chinese forms of transportation, that is, the narrow two wheeled cart, the wheelbarrow, pack animals and coolies. The very narrow roads wide enough at the infrequent points for the passage of carts follow the tops of dykes in the lower country and wind through cuts, often as deep as 200 feet, in the higher sections. Under such conditions cross country ravel is impracticable, and the use of most of the roads by our wide tread motor vehicles, escort wagons and artillery is impossible.[16]

The impact of this terrain would force the US Army to adopt a more early twentieth-century solution to movement outside of the ports/cities. Motor vehicles heavier than the usual commercial 1½–2 ton truck should not be employed in the field. Light motor vehicles would be of limited use where there are no motor roads. Heavier trucks have a limited sphere of usefulness (even at) the ports. The Army escort wagon in unsuitable to field service in China. Pack trains could be used successfully but it is believed that the native transportation would do the same work satisfactorily. Artillery (75mm) should be tractor-drawn using the smallest tractors possible. Native carts, pack animals, wheelbarrows and pack coolies can be utilized satisfactorily and will always be available in sufficient numbers. Animals of the size to which we are accustomed and for which our harness and vehicles are designed are not procurable in China. Only a very limited number of comparatively small horses could be procured in Japan. Since all horses in Japan suitable for military use are subject to draft by the army the permission and cooperation of the Japanese government would be necessary to make possible the purchase of such animals in Japan.[17]

Another consideration leaning away from the use of vehicles was the lack of gasoline in China to drive them. The US Navy would find itself in a position of having to bring in a constant supply of petrol to keep the Army even marginally mobile. Operations in the countryside of China would make the stalemate of trench warfare in the Great War appear to be highly mobile. The US Army would be severely limited in where it could effectively go and how fast it got there.

The Army would not even be served to bring their own pack teams of mule and horses to China. The Chinese, however, were well suited to the modes of transportation native to their country. The Divisions of the US Army that landed as part of Variation B would find themselves reduced to walking as the only organized means of movement.

The US Navy's role was not just to assist in the seizing of the key port installations. While roads and railways were instrumental means of transport in China, the Navy also recognized that China relied heavily on its network of rivers for transport. The Navy would not just support the transportation of the Army and the Marines for the initial landings; they also would secure the key rivers in China. Detailed plans were drafted for securing at least parts of the following rivers:

Canton River Delta
Nimrod Sound
Yangtze River
Kiao Chau Bay

These plans called for patrolling the rivers with smaller craft, riverine armed monitors, to ensure that the Chinese could not employ these routes for the movement of munitions, arms or Chinese troops.[18] The Navy would have to transport these vessels or convert local ships into armed river monitors. Since no provision was provided for either contingency in War Plan Yellow, it was not a solution that would have been affected quickly.

Studies were drawn up against a wide range of coastal or strategic targets that the US Navy would have to potentially deal with. An analysis of the Kiang Yin Forts, their antiquated coastal artillery and the placement of their powder magazines was detailed for potential naval bombardment. Similar analysis was done for the Tachiang, Chu-Sou Pagoda, and Shinnimu Creek, Chinkiang, and Silver Island, Kukau, Kiukiang Split Hill (Pwampien) and Yen-Tse Ke fortifications. The gun emplacements of the Nanking Forts were drawn up too, though many of these relied on information from foreign nationals providing covert data to the US Navy. Many forts like the Matung and East and West Pillar Forts (and the Split Hill fortifications) were either not manned (Matung) or were equipped with muzzle loading cannon which would be no match for the US Navy.[19]

Just attempting to execute Variation A or at minimal Variation B in War Plan Yellow was going to stretch US Navy resources:

Protection at or evacuation from Chinese ports, with the possible exception of Tientsin, Shanghai, and Canton can ordinarily be effected by the United States naval forces maintained in Chinese waters. The complement of the United States naval craft ordinarily in Chinese waters is approximately 6,000, of which one-third to one-half could, in an emergency, be used for landing operations ashore. This is exclusive of the United State Marines now at Peking and Shanghai, number approximately 1,500. Most of these naval forces could be used within 48 hours, after notification, at any port or ports between Tangku and Canton inclusive, provided the fleet had been warned of serious disorders (a logical assumption)

Evacuation form ports of Tientsin, Shanghai and perhaps Canton might be possible or greatly delayed on account of the considerable numbers and interests involved. It is therefore to these ports or to any one of them that the United States Army troops might be dispatched for the protection of American citizens residing or taking refigure therein.[20]

Chinese Resistance

Would the Chinese resist this kind of direct invasion?

It may be stated as axiomatic that the Chinese Republic will no longer submit passively to any occupation on its territory by any foreign power or powers, and that we can expect serious opposition on the part of the Chinese forces to our occupation of Peiping (Peking) and the guarding of some one hundred odd miles of railway.

It was estimated that in the region of operations where the United States would be landing would number roughly 300,000 troops, equipped with modern weapons, including some medium artillery and some combat aircraft.[21]

Despite analysis to the contrary, there was a belief that the arrival of the US forces in China might serve as a rallying point for the Chinese people … providing them with a common enemy to face. This was the primary driving force for the Army requesting upwards of four-to-five Infantry Divisions for War Plan Yellow.

Summary Evaluation of the War Plan

Significant portions of War Plan Yellow were missing, misfiled, destroyed, or have been lost over the years. Thus identification of the gaps in the plan is difficult, since a complete copy of the plan was not available for review. Aside from being the most politically incorrect name for a War Plan, it is one which had one of the higher levels of vagueness about its goals and intended objectives.

Some level of analysis can be performed based on the notes and memorandum of the Joint Board in regards to the plan. These were focused on two specific topics. First, there was no specificity as to where the two-to-five divisions of troops were going to come from. In some of the correspondence there are references to pulling troops from the Philippines and from the west coast of the United States, but the numbers and designations were not specified. The Navy raised the issue as to logistically how many troops could be moved at one time across the vast distances of the Pacific. While the plan called for the troops, the United States simply did not have the excess capacity to handle such a plan. War Plan Yellow did not provide for a mobilization effort in terms of US volunteers for service, so where these troops might have come from remains something of a mystery.

The second area of concern was that there was no defined exit strategy from China. While the US could, almost freely, engage in an invasion of the nation; there was no defined point on how the United States could *leave* China. Taking over her key port facilities and managing them did not ensure they could or would be turned over easily to the civilians authorities. China had the potential of being a war that the United State could not fully win, but would be difficult to extract herself from.

The final point of analysis regarding War Plan Yellow is that any action there might not just involve the United States alone. The War Plan did not account on the British or French participation in any invasion of China. Given past histories, both of these governments would most likely want to be a part of any incursion into China, if only to keep the United States in check (as well to protect their own citizens and interests there.)

The 1914 Plan for War with Germany
War Plan Black

Introduction

War Plan Black detailed a massive war between the United States and Imperial Germany in 1914, at the dawn of the Great War. While the war plan itself exists mostly in fragments, the Naval War College and the Army War College both undertook detailed analysis of the plan and that information allows for the reconstruction of the War Plan. Their analysis, while not done in conjunction, provides a scenario of war that is both intriguing and frightening.

The 1914 copy of War Plan Black was the earliest that has been located. Future editions, especially the 1916–1917 edition are more widely known but even these only exist in bits and pieces in various archives. While the later editions may be more realistic about a war with Germany in the midst of the Great War (seen as primarily a naval conflict) this edition is perhaps the least known and most interesting given its scope of dealing with a superior German force overwhelming the United States on her home soil.

Background

War Plan Black, is also referred to as "Blue (US) vs. Black (Germany)" in archival references and was drafted late in the summer of 1914 as the flames of war were igniting in Europe. The plan assumed that war would be declared by the United States on Germany on 1 November 1914. Prior to that declaration of war, the presumption of hostilities between at least France and Germany was assumed as well.

Under War Plan Black's premises, France collapsed relatively quickly to Germany. The fate of England, Russia, and Austro-Hungary was not addressed. The assumption laid out assumed that England had either capitulated or had engaged in a decisive naval battle and lost, forcing armistice with a triumphant Germany.[1] Even at this time the thinking of US planners mirrored that of Europeans, that the Great War was going to be fast, decisive, and over quickly.

The 28 June 1914 assassination of Archduke Franz Ferdinand set into motion a series of events that led into the Great War. Much has been written about the start of the Great War. The simplified version is that a series of alliances, and political misperceptions sent the nations of Europe on a collision course which embroiled the continent and much of the world in a state of war. Essentially Emperor Franz Joseph of Austria-Hungary declared war on Serbia which forced Russia (an ally of Serbia) to mobilize. Germany declared war on Russia in response, followed three days later with a declaration of war with France (Russia's ally). Germany, following most of the tenets of the Schlieffen Plan attacked neutral Belgium in an attempt to make an end-run on France. Britain, not even a claimant in the unfolding, declared war against Germany under the auspices of supporting her allies (Belgium, France and Russia) but more out of fear that a German victory would leave the continent under German rule. British guarantees' for protecting the security of Belgium compelled them further into the conflict. Fear of a new balance of power ruled the day in terms of decisions.

While most people think of the Great War as one of trenches and stalemate, the first few months of the war were highly mobile. Russia, for all of her size and might, was defeated soundly in the Battle of Tannenberg. Only a few weeks into the fighting, France was reeling, finally grinding the German advance on Paris to a stall in the First Battle of the Marne.

Even though the Germans had been checked, there was no way to know if that was a temporary state or not. Russia, staggering back from Tannenberg like a boxer reeling from having been given a nearly knock-out blow; would either rally or crumble completely. If they collapsed, Germany would be able to divert hundreds of thousands of troops from the eastern front the western front and potentially finish off France with a decisive blow.

To military planners around the globe and the US, evidence seemed to support the concept that the war would be won fast. French experts believed, at best, the war was a six to nine month affair. When one reviews the premises in War Plan Black, the American thinking was even faster. They estimated that France would surrender much faster and that the United Kingdom would either capitulate, sue for peace, or likewise be defeated on the high seas.

On the naval front by fall of 1914 Great Britain and Germany both were armed with the strategic weapons of the era—dreadnoughts. The dreadnought was possessed of speed via a steam turbine engine system, and massive caliber guns for unprecedented firepower. With dreadnought-type ships, a government had the ability to extend its influence around the globe. Britain had an edge in terms of numbers of this type of vessel, but Germany did not lag far behind. While formidable, these ships on both sides had never been used in war. France had a sizable fleet as well, but was forced to defend not just the Atlantic and English Channel but the Mediterranean as well.

Both Britain and Germany harbored the illusion that the war at sea would be settled in one massive battle. Both concentrated their fleets accordingly. Germany augmented her fleet with a new weapon of war—the U-boat. The U-boats had some initial dramatic successes against the British, changing the face of naval warfare. Both fleets danced around the North Sea with each other, laying mines and striking in a limited fashion, waiting for the opportunity to deliver a knock-out blow to the enemy in the form of an epic naval battle.

Naval planners had no idea how the change of weapons on the high seas would impact naval strategy and tactics. The idea of a Battle of Trafalgar-type engagement still dominated thinking—an all or nothing contest with one decisive and clear winner. As such, there was a distinct chance that Germany might well sink the Royal Navy— just as much of a chance as the Royal Navy sinking the German High Seas Fleet.

Joint Board war planners had to struggle with the premise of fighting a militarily superior and potentially victorious Germany. First, and foremost, the United States Army in the summer of 1914 was less than 70,000 men.[2] A fully mobilized Germany was going to be fielding an army in the millions. The German Navy was seen as numerically superior to the US Navy. Even worse, with France collapsing, there was the distinct possibility that her navy would be absorbed by the Germans as well, actually adding to their numbers. This premise of a surrendered fleet was not out of line and was mirrored with the eventual real-world surrender of the German High Seas Fleet in 1918. In other words, the US would be facing a vastly superior foe oozing with combat experience ... something the Joint Board acknowledged that the US lacked.

Even as early as 1914, Germany had experience managing an Air Service. While aircraft were primarily used for reconnaissance, they had played a key role already in the German victory at Tannenberg, detecting the strategic moves of the Russian army. America had used an airplane in pursuit of Pancho Villa in 1916 but that was the extent of their experience. General John J. Pershing said of the fifty-five training aircraft, "Fifty-one were obsolete and four were obsolescent."[3] America did not have a single pilot with air combat experience, even in a reconnaissance role. Again, the edge seemed to favor the Germans from the onset.

Adding to the complexities facing American planners was that in August of 1914, the world's largest construction project, the Panama Canal, was opened. While this gave the United States a fantastic strategic advantage in terms of moving a fleet from one ocean to another—it also presented new problems ... mainly that the canal was going to have to be defended. This defense was no small feat. On the Pacific Ocean front, the canal would have to be garrisoned against possible threats from that sea, namely Japan. The Atlantic would have to be protected as well. This meant that the defense forces for the canal would have to be divided to the two seas. Adding to the woes of the Joint Board was the fact that the forces to defend the Panama Canal had to be drawn from the Army's continental forces. This would leave less troops in the United States proper. While the canal was a powerful strategic sword in the arsenal of the United States, it was also a burden that required significant assets to defend both from the Army and the Navy.

The original premise of War Plan Black was for the United States to go toe-to-toe with Germany alone after France was out of the picture. As with all of the War Plans there were two elements to the plan, Navy and Army. These approached the issues with the war in a very different manner.

What Would Lead to War Between Germany and the United States?

The Joint Board planners demonstrated a good understanding of just how vulnerable the United States really was:

> Many intelligent and otherwise well informed people, among whom are included some of our statesmen and lawmakers, have rashly assumed that we are safe from attack by any European power. A close study, however, of the growth of population and commerce in the first-class European powers, and of the already existing causes of irritation in our international intercourse with them will, it is believed, convince any impartial investigator that war with at least one, and possibly two, European powers is not only possible, but probable unless we take steps to remedy our present state of unpreparedness on land and sea.[4]
>
> In studying the question of a land and naval attack on our Atlantic coast, it may be assumed at the outset that our antagonist will be a European power or an alliance between a European nation and some other power. This will be evident when we consider that the sea power of no other American nation is great enough to demand serious consideration in comparison to that of the United States.
>
> Prior to the present European War, Great Britain, France and German were the only European powers that had sufficient naval strength to make it likely that they would, single handled, undertake a war with the United States, and our relation with all three powers were outwardly friendly. Great Britain, notwithstanding occasional irritation over such matters as the Panama Canal tolls law, the Venezuelan boundary, the European situation, etc., has always been particularly cordial, largely for reasons for sentiment, kinship, etc., but even more so for reasons of self-interest. It has been the policy for some years of both Great Britain and the United States to look to each other for support in putting forward any doctrine of international relationship. When it is remembered that more than one-fourth of the exports from the United States go to Great Britain, and that these consist mainly of the necessities of life, cotton and the manufactured products of iron, steel and copper, it will be seen why chances of a war with her are remote.
>
> France for many years has been unusually friendly, and it would seem that this attitude is sincere.
>
> Germany, with an area of only 206,830 square miles, already has a population of 69,000,000 and her population prior to the war was increasing at a rate of a million per year. Since 1890 the annual increase in her population has been 1.34% per year, and it was only a question of a few years before she would have outgrown her borders. Expansion was, therefore, a necessity that became more pressing with each year that passed. Germany has long been fully alive to the necessity of securing outlets for her rapidly increasing population, and her comprehensive naval building program was inaugurated with the idea of leading to her commercial supremacy. Thus far she has been unfortunate with her colonies, and as the temperate regions of the world that are feebly held are already preempted, she turned her attention to South America where there were rich localities in temperate regions that might be seized from the holding nations were they the only

obstacles. But the Monroe Doctrine stood in the way of such an enterprise, which, in view of their need for expansion, not unreasonably appeared unfair to the German mind. It also stood in the way of their getting a foothold in the Caribbean, which would be desirable for trade reasons if no other. There are large communities of Germans in southern Brazil. Of these, prior to the war, between 400,000 and 500,000 Germans lived in a body, speaking their own language, and preserving the customs of the Fatherland in their provinces of Brazil, principally in the State of Rio Grande de Sul. Though these colonists had lost their close touch with their native land, yet the trade with the Fatherland was maintained with them, and within this fertile territory Germany, in accordance with a well digested plan, was pushing her interests with an aggressive spirit and a thought for detail which promised well for the future. Under peaceful conditions Germany controlled nearly one-half of the trade of the western coast of South America, while by for the larger part of what remained was in the hands of Great Britain. The opening of the Panama Canal must virtually affect this trade. New York is only 1,981 miles from Colon, while Southampton, her nearest European rival, is 4,540 miles from Colon. New York is, therefore, nearer to the west coast of South America by 2,500 miles than her nearest competitor, while New Orleans enjoys a handicap of 3,100 miles. The opening of the Panama Canal should, therefore, give us complete control of the trade of the western states of South America, which would mean the ultimate destruction of the British and German trade in that region. When in addition to the above, it is recalled that the United States was largely instrumental in preventing the partition of China, it is plain that there were latent causes that rendered a break with Germany more probable than with either Great Britain or France, and more probable, moreover, than with any other European power.[5]

All of these controlling diplomatic factors are now in abeyance during the present tremendous struggle in Europe, which has involved already six first-class powers, and four minor ones. This great war has, however, largely increased our chance of friction leading to hostilities with one or more of the World powers. A complete success by either of the warring alliances will almost certainly develop in its members, a confidence and an arrogance that will lead shortly to a very offensive dictation in the world affairs, strategic, diplomatic, and commercial. Blue (the United States) possesses or controls of many attractive fields for foreign exploitation or domination, the Panama Canal, the Philippine Island, and the large unoccupied areas of the American continent, which our Monroe Doctrine has so far been able to protect only as a result of inter-jealousy existing between the great powers.

Collision Course

Given the analysis of the European powers, the Joint Board opted to focus their planning efforts on the one nation that seemed to present any sort of true threat to the US—Germany:

It is a fact well known to the authorities, that for years Germany has been quietly but secretly conducting a diplomatic campaign directed with the sole object of discrediting the

Monroe Doctrine with European powers. Had she succeeded, the crisis would not have been long delayed, even had not the European War intervened.

If the present war places either of the great alliances in a preponderant military position, it is more than probable, following the precedents of history, that Blue will either have to submit to the most distasteful dictation in her affairs, or fight to defend her views.

Assuming the possibility if not probability of the war with an European power, we shall pass on to the probable nature of its opening stages.

It may be assumed that no war waged by a European power against the United States could be successfully terminated with seizure of territory in the United States, or in its possessions, or in some other part of the Western Continent in violation of the Monroe Doctrine. We will then have as possible objectives for the principle operations of the campaign any one or combination of the following:

(a)   The coast of the United States
(b)   Porto Rico [sic]
(c)   Panama Canal Zone
(d)   The West Indian Islands and the Caribbean coasts of the mainland
(e)   South America[6]

The German Objectives in a War with the United States

Germany clearly would be asserting itself in terms of establishing a true global empire to rival or surpass that of Great Britain. The defeat of France and perhaps Britain would put Germany on a collision course with the United States when it came to the former French colonies in the Caribbean.

The Joint Board felt that Germany's military objectives in a war with the United States was not to acquire territory. That would happen automatically when France was defeated. Instead, its goal was to force the United States to acknowledge Germany's right to acquire a foothold in the Caribbean and to establish colonies in the West Indies, Central and South America. In essence, it was to compel America to abandon the Monroe Doctrine:

> … it will be understood that she (Germany) does not desire to become involved in a long and expensive campaign in Blue territory, which would surely be the result if she does not strike a paralyzing blow before Blue can bring her immense resources into play. To accomplish her purpose Black must capitalize her own readiness and Blue's un-readiness for war.[7]

Speed and a devastating blow to America were the criteria that the Joint Board War Planners envisioned with the strike against the United States. If that could be accomplished, America would be forced to the negotiating table and would have to give up much of her dominance in the region.

The Naval War at the Start—A Clash in the Caribbean

The US Navy planners on the Joint Board and at the Naval War College presumed that a triumphant Germany in Europe would attempt to consolidate its new holdings. With the anticipated collapse of France in War Plan Black, a number of French colonies in the Caribbean and South America (such as French Guiana, Guadeloupe, Îles des Saintes, Marie-Galante, Martinique, la Désirade, Suriname, and others) would have been ceded to Germany. At some point, quickly, Germany would have to establish German control and possession of those colonies. It was to Germany's advantage to do that while her military was mobilized and to build upon the momentum of the victories that War Plan Black anticipated she would be savoring.

The Joint Board felt that this was going to be the impetus of war between Germany and the United States. When Germany would assume possession of these colonies, it would be interpreted as an infringement of the Monroe Doctrine. Through diplomatic channels, the United States would attempt to persuade Germany from taking ownership but the Board felt that these efforts would fail. With control of much of the Atlantic shipping lanes (with Britain out of the war one way or another) and the addition of the French fleet to the High Seas Fleet, Germany would feel that they possessed the military might to send a fleet to the Caribbean and take control of what they had rightly won in war.

In the Naval War College planning for this eventuality, this set the stage for a confrontation that could end the conflict. The US Navy would deploy to the Caribbean and lay a trap for the German High Seas Fleet. When the Germans arrived, they would spring their ambush, defeat the Germans, and destroy the threat of German naval power and the war would reach an impasse and force both side to seek a diplomatic solution.

But even the Navy admitted there were issues. If war was indeed declared with Germany, there was a chance that Germany might not strike to seize the former French colonies. Instead they might opt to shell the American coastal cities of Boston, New York, and others. Guantanamo Bay and the US Navy's base there, critical for the defense of the Caribbean, were also painfully exposed. Also there was America's newest strategic asset, the Panama Canal—a potentially ripe target for a German squadron.

The US Navy acknowledged fully that while they were laying a trap for the Germans, the Germans would also fully anticipate such a trap and be prepared. What would unfold was not an ambush of the German navy, but instead a well-planned and anticipated fight.

This would have forced the United States to move away from a strategy of concentrating a fleet in the Caribbean to ensure that it had adequate protection of her homeland and other assets. This flaw was corrected in the 1916 edition of War Plan Black—which called for a concentration of the US Fleet off of the New England coast which would sortie only when the true intentions of the German High Seas Fleet were known.

Both the 1914 and 1916 versions of War Plan Black were flawed in that the technology had eclipsed naval tactics. Massive naval battles happened, but they were not decisive in nature. Jutland showed that in 1916 when the British and German fleets tangled in the North Sea with neither side being able to claim a true overwhelming victory. The 1914 War Plan Black still assumed a single massive naval battle with one side or another securing utter victory.

The key difference with the 1914 version of War Plan Black was the chilling assumption that the United States Navy might actually *lose* the fight in the Caribbean against the Germans.

Anticipated American Forces

War Plan Black assumes that the United States has not initiated a draft or begun a full-fledged mobilization of her potential military assets. Some National Guard units would be activated early on in the planning and be available for use, but those would be limited in size.

The American order of battle for War Plan Black was as follows:

I Division: 1st Brigade, 33rd, 34th and 35th Infantry
2nd Brigade, 9th, 17th and 32nd Infantry
3rd Brigade, 36th, 37th and 28th Infantry
2nd Cavalry
1st Brigade, Field Artillery, 3rd and 7th Field Artillery

II Division: 4th Brigade, 23rd, 26th and 27th Infantry
5th Brigade, 4th, 7th, and 19th Infantry
6th Brigade, 11th, 18th and 22nd Infantry
6th Cavalry
2nd Brigade Field Artillery, 4th Field Artillery
(reorganized and complete) and 8th Field Artillery

III Division: 7th Brigade, 20th, 21st, and 39th Infantry
8th Brigade, 40th, 41st, and 42nd Infantry
9th Brigade, 43rd, 44th, and 45th Infantry
1st Cavalry
3rd Brigade Field Artillery, 5th and 9th (Regular) Field Artillery

1st Panaman [*sic*] Brigade, 5th, 10th, and 28th Infantry
2nd Panaman [*sic*] Brigade, 3rd, 29th, and 31st Infantry
3rd Panaman [*sic*] Brigade, P.R. Infantry—1st and 2nd Panaman [sic] Militia

Cavalry Division: 1st Brigade, 3rd, 14th and 15th Cavalry
(15th is fully organized)
2nd Brigade, 9th, 10th, and 16th Cavalry
6th Field Artillery (less Batteries A & B)
3rd Cavalry Brigade, 12th, 13th and 17th Cavalry (Battery A, 6th Field Artillery Attached.

4th Cavalry Brigade, 5th, 11th and 18th Cavalry
(Battery B, 6th Field Artillery Attached.

XVI Division: 46th Brigade, 2nd, 5th and 7th California Infantry
47th Brigade, 2nd Montana, 2nd Idaho, and 3rd Wyoming Infantry
48th Brigade, 2nd Washington, 3rd Oregon, and
2nd Colorado Infantry
16th Mil. Cavalry
16th Brigade Field Artillery, 31st and 32nd Field Artillery

IX Division: 25th Brigade, 1st, 2nd, and 3rd North Carolina Infantry
26th Brigade, 1st, 2nd South Carolina and 1st Florida Infantry
27th Brigade, 1st, 2nd and 5th George Infantry
9th Mil. Cavalry
9th Brigade Field Artillery, 17th and 18th Field Artillery

X Division: 28th Brigade, 1st, 2nd and 3rd Kentucky Infantry
29th Brigade, 1st, 2nd and 4th Alabama Infantry
30th Brigade, 1st and 3rd Tennessee and 1st Mississippi Infantry
10th Mil. Cavalry[8]

Once fighting started the United States would be increased as National Guard units were mobilized. It was assumed that Assuming that Germany struck quickly, the United States would be able to field fifteen divisions of regular and militia units with between 500 and 600 guns. This would amount to 324,000 to 485,000 men. These forces would not necessarily all be concentrated into one fighting force.

Anticipated German Forces

There are two primary ground forces as defined for War Plan Black. The first was to be targeted at the first landing in the Caribbean against the German objective. These forces were defined as follows:

A Black (German) Army Corps on a war footing consists of the following:

1. Commanding General and Staff   13
2. Two Infantry Divisions   35,485—144 guns
3. One Company Pontoniers [sic]   154
    One division heavy bridge equipage
    One telegraph detachment
4. Four Infantry Ammunition Columns
    Eight Artillery Columns
5. Six Supply Columns

Seven Wagon Park Columns

Two Mobile Remount Depots

6. Twelve Field Hospitals

7. Two Field Bakery Columns

8. One Battalion Heavy Artillery   509—16 guns

9. One Aeroplane Detachment.

10. One Battalion of Pioneers   820

Furnishes one Company to each Division and one Company to the Army Corps

Initial Combatant aggregate forces for an Army Corps: 36,981—160 guns. *Note: Each infantry division was to have one regiment of cavalry, 600 men, as a divisional cavalry, included in the total above.*

A Cavalry Division consists of:

Staff:	3
Three brigades of two regiments each	3,606
Two batteries of horse artillery	264—8 guns
A detachment of machineguns	100
A detachment of engineers	34
A signal detachment	
Combat aggregate:	4,007—8 guns[9]

The German Forces for the Invasion of the United States Mainland

The numbers above were listed as what was necessary for the Germans' Caribbean target. For the actual landings on the continental United States, the following were determined to be the requirements for a successful operation—and upwards of 225,000 troops. These forces would not be necessary as part of the initial landings—which would utilize the force designed for the Caribbean (having already achieved that objective).

Naval Defenses of the Coastal United States

The United States East Coast had not endured an invasion since the raid by Britain during the War of 1812. The coast supported a large number of forts, but many of these were antiquated relics from the American Civil War—kept relatively up to date, but outclassed by the weapons fielded by the navies of the world. Still, these forts protected strategic cities and ports of commerce—and would have to be overcome by Germany if it planned on launching an invasion of America.

Table: American Forts, Coastal Defenses, and Armaments—1914[10]

Fort:	Place:	State:	12"	10"	8"	6"	5"	4.7"	4"	3"	Mortars 12"	Mined?	Submarines or Torpedo Boats?
Baldwin	Portland	Maine				4				2			
Lyon	Portland	Maine				3				3			
McKinley	Portland	Maine	2		8	4				4	6	Yes	Yes
Levett	Portland	Maine	3	2		2				3			
Preble	Portland	Maine				2				3			
Williams	Portland	Maine	2	5		3				2		Yes	
Foster	Portsmouth	New Hampshire		3						2			
Stark	Portsmouth	New Hampshire	2			2				4			
Constitution	Portsmouth	New Hampshire			2					2			
Heath	Boston	Mass.	3										
Banks	Boston	Mass.									16		
Strong	Boston	Mass.		5				2		8		Yes	
Standish	Boston	Mass.		4		5				9			
Warren	Boston	Mass.	2	5					2	3		Yes	Yes
Andrews	Boston	Mass.				2	2			2	16		
Revere	Boston	Mass.	2			6	2						
Rodman	New Bedford	Mass.			2		2			4		Yes	Yes
Adams	Narragansett Bay	Rhode Island		2		3		2		2	16	Yes	
Wetherill	Narragansett Bay	Rhode Island	4	3		5				4		Yes	
Getty	Narragansett Bay	Rhode Island	3			2				2		Yes	

Fort:	Place:	State:	12"	10"	8"	6"	5"	4.7"	4"	3"	Mortars 12"	Mined?	Submarines or Torpedo Boats?
Greble	Narragansett Bay	Rhode Island		3		3				2	8	Yes	
Philip Kearny	Narragansett Bay	Rhode Island				6				2			
Mansfield	Long Island Sound	New York			2		4						Yes
Wright	Fisher's Island	New York	2	2		7				4	8	Yes	
Michie	Great Gull Island	New York	2	2		4				2			
Terry	Plum Island	New York	2	2		6	2			10	8	Yes	
Tyler	Gardiner's Point	New York				2	2						
Slocum	New York Harbor	New York				2	2				16		Yes
Schuyler	New York Harbor	New York	2	2	2	2	2			2			
Totten	Willett's Point	New York	2	2	2	2	2			7	8	Yes	
Wadsworth	New York	New York	8	4	2	4				14	8	Yes	
Hamilton	New York	New York	6	7		12		2		4	8		
Hancock	Sandy Hook	New Jersey	4	5	3	4	1			10	16	Yes	Yes
Delaware	Delaware River	Delaware	3					2		6			
Mott	Delaware River	Delaware	3	3			4			2			
Du Pont	Delaware City	Delaware	2		2	2	2			2	16	Yes	Yes
Howard	Baltimore	Maryland	2			2	2			4	8	Yes	Yes
Smallwood	Rock Point	Maryland				2				2			
Carroll	Baltimore	Maryland	2				2			2			
Armistead	Hawkins Point	Maryland	1		3			2		2		Yes	

Fort:	Place:	State:	12"	10"	8"	6"	5"	4.7"	4"	3"	Mortars 12"	Mined?	Submarines or Torpedo Boats?
Washington	Fort Washington	Maryland		6		2			2	4	8	Yes	Yes
Hunt	Sheridan Point	Virginia			3		2			3			Yes
Monroe	Hampton Roads	Virginia	5	7	3	2				4	16		Yes
Wool	Hampton Roads	Virginia				6				6		Yes	
Caswell	Southport	North Carolina	2	4	4	2	2			4	8	Yes	Yes
Sumpter	Charleston	South Carolina	2										
Moultrie	Charleston	South Carolina		6		5		2		5	16	Yes	Yes
Fremont	Port Royal	South Carolina		3				2					Yes
Scriven	Savannah	Georgia	2		4			3		2	8		Yes
Taylor	Key West	Florida	2	4	2	2		2		8	8		
Dade	Key West	Florida			2	4				5			
De Soto	Key West	Florida								2	8		
Pickens	Pensacola	Florida	2	4		2		2		4		Yes	Yes
McRee	Pensacola	Florida			2					4			
Morgan	Mobile	Alabama	2		4			2		2	8		
Gaines	Mobile	Alabama				3				3			
St. Philip	New Orleans	Louisiana		2	2	4		2		4			Yes
Jackson	New Orleans	Louisiana			2					2		Yes	
S. Jacinto	Galveston	Texas		2				2		2	8		Yes
Travis	Galveston	Texas			2					3			
Crockett	Galveston	Texas		2						2	8		

While this table presents a considerable amount of data, what it also does is expose just how much of the American east coast was *not* protected in any way. While key port cities were sheltered and under cover of American forts and guns, much of the coast was not. Also, those forts that were in place were often equipped with weapons that were old and obsolete against modern warships.

Germany's first Attack

The planners assumed that Germany was going to need a forward base of operations:

> To render the movement of an expedition consisting of a large army reasonably safe, and it insure the security of their communication, it is necessary to gain command of the sea. To do this our enemy must disperse, blockade, or neutralize our navy.[11]

The US Navy was faced with a daunting task in terms of the defense:

> Captain F. K. Hill of the Navy in a recent (1914) lecture at the War College delineated the strategic front along which the Navy proposes to cover our Atlantic and Gulf Coasts, and from which it will operate against a hostile invading fleet. The front is a line including the region of Narragansett Bay, the entrance to the Chesapeake Bay, Guantanamo and the Panama Canal Zone.[12] This was a front of nearly 2700 nautical miles.
>
> As a step to this command of the sea, the enemy must have, and must securely hold, a base in the vicinity of the operations.
>
> There are unfortified places along our Atlantic coast where deep draft ships can enter and be secure from the elements, and some of these admit of improvised defense to a greater or less extent. That such a place could be seized seems certain, but that it could not be made secure with our undefeated fleet threatening it on the sea and our military resources opposing it on the land, seems equally certain. Hence, the enemy would be obliged to look elsewhere for a base, which restricts his choice to the Caribbean or South American coast.[13]
>
> For these reasons, the first operations of an enemy would necessarily be directed to the Caribbean, quite apart from the consideration of the great interest of the United States which center there, or of the blow to our prestige resulting from such a defiance of the Monroe Doctrine.
>
> Great Britain and France already possess harbors in the West Indies more or less suitable for naval bases. Of these, Kingston only is fortified. The only other European possessions in the West Indies of consequence are the Dutch Island of Curacca [sic] and the Danish Islands of St. Thomas and Santa Cruz. Germany possesses no port in the West Indies, but should she contemplate war with the United States, it is safe to conclude in the light of recent events in Belgium that she would not hesitate to violate the neutrality of Cuba, Haiti, Santa Domingo, Venezuela, or Columbia, by the seizure of ports on their shores if such seizure were considered necessary for the success of her naval operations.[14]

Determining where Germany might strike in the Caribbean was not a new topic for the Joint Board. In 1903 and 1905 the Naval War College had tackled this problem before. Their findings were:

It is believed that any of the following places are liable to seizure by Black (Germany): In the West Indies, Margarita Island, Cartagena, Porto Rico [sic], Samana, Port Liberty Bay, Guantanamo, and one or more ports on the Cuban Coast.[15]

Political doctrine drove much of the military planning by the Navy to protect the Caribbean. The political considerations included:

1. The protection of Porto Rico [sic] , as an outcome of the sovereignty of the United States over the island.
2. The protection of Guantanamo Bay, as a result of the lease of the port from the Republic of Cuba.
3. The guarantee of independence and good government in Cuba, in accordance with the United States Laws and the Cuban Constitution.
4. The guarantee of independence of Panama, the government and protection of the Canal Zone as the result of treaty obligations, and the preservation of the neutrality of the Panama Canal.
5. The preservation of the republican form of government of the Western Continent not now in the possession of European powers and the preservation of the further acquisition of territory by the European nations on the Western Continent or the West Indies, as a result of our adherence of the Monroe Doctrine.[16]

Panama and the newly opened Canal drove much of the thinking of planners in terms of defense:

Our national interests in the Isthmus of Panama are enormous and our responsibilities commensurate. The control and defense of the Canal lie solely with us and we have no co-guarantors. By the terms of the Hay-Pauncefote Treaty we stand before the world as taking full responsibility for the integrity of the Canal, and of transit through it. It will have cost us, when occupied, something like $500,000,000.00 and is, moreover, a work of such interest and value to mankind that even a temporary interruption of traffic through it would greatly damage our prestige. On account of its international value it is, at least, open to question where neutral nations would permit our enemies to make it the scene of hostilities, but to count too much upon such support would be to shirk our responsibilities deliberately incurred. The present war involving all of the great powers, is likely to leave at its close, no neutral nation capable of assisting us in the protection of the canal.[17]

Assuming that the enemy's first efforts will be directed to the Caribbean, Guantanamo is our only base in that region having any pretense of security; and, until the Army has completed the installation of the permanent defenses, that security must depend upon the fleet. As an advance base from which the armored cruisers and scouts can cooperate during the approach of the enemies combined fleet, Culebra is favorably situated. Of this port the 1905 Conference of the Naval War College said: 'Culebra is a strategic, advanced scouting centre for Blue's armored cruisers and scouts during the approach of Black's combined fleet; but as this anchorage is limited, exposed to the weather, and open to torpedo attack, the battleships and destroyers should anchor at Fajardo—only 20 miles to the westward— which anchorage, by reason of its chain of reefs and islands, affords excellent protection against night attack.'[18]

The result of this thinking was that America's defense of the Caribbean would be centered on Guantanamo Bay and Culebra:

With Guantanamo as a fleet base and with Culebra as a scouting center, the naval war plans contemplate striking the enemy's fleet at the first favorable opportunity, preferably just before he reaches the shores of the Western Atlantic, when he will labor under the disadvantage of a long sea voyage, and will be burdened with the care of a considerable convoy of supply ships closely following his. At the same time the United States fleet should be coaled and is in every way free to act, with its personnel unwearied by any unusual duties.[19]

While the US Navy would be spread along the entire east coast of the United States and fanned out to protect the Caribbean, the German Navy would not be hampered with covering multiple targets. Instead they would be able to concentrate their resources on a single target. But where would they attack? The Joint Board arrived at a single conclusion: Guantanamo Bay Cuba … right where the US had planned to stage its defense of the region.

The first battle between Germany and the United States was anticipated to come on the high seas. Unlike almost every other War Plan devised by the Joint Board, in this engagement, the United States would be defeated by the Germans. Somewhere north and east of Cuba, the American Navy would clash with the High Seas Fleet and be utterly destroyed. Unimpeded, the Germans would sail on to Guantanamo Bay and land forces to seize the US installation there. From what the Joint Board saw of the 1914 defenses for the bay, there was little more than a few antiquated cannon that could mount much of a defense. Guantanamo Bay had not been envisioned as a defensive position as much from a sea attack as it was from establishing a defense from the native Cubans themselves.

The War College simulated (gamed) the scenario with the student body and could not devise a situation where the Germans could be prevented from victory at sea and in seizing the US base on Cuba. But where would the Germans strike next? The first phase of the anticipated German moves was the defeat of the US Navy and the seizure of a naval base of operations in the western hemisphere. The second step was seen as more ominous—the seizure of American territory directly. In other words, an invasion of the United States itself.

To the casual observer, the loss of the US base at Guantanamo Bay did not seem devastating. Yes, it would hurt American pride and morale, but it was simply a lone base.

But the members of the Joint Board realized that with Guantanamo in German control, the German Navy would be able to refit, refuel and could launch operations anywhere along the east coast or Gulf of Mexico. Moreover, it also demonstrated another weakness. From Guantanamo Bay, the Germans could essentially bottle up the Panama Canal. The canal had always represented a complicated defense matter for the Joint Board. The Germans could tie up American troops there and could blockade the access to and from the canal using Guantanamo as a base. This would render the canal inert for military use, not risking German resources, and while still forcing the United States to tie up large number of troops to defend it against possible German ground attacks.

Analysis of German Invasion Targets in the United States

The Joint Board proposed twenty different scenarios for Germany to attack the United States to force the goals for the war. Some of the solutions poised included a broad overall invasion of the US, landings on the Gulf Coast, incursions around key cities on the East Coast, landings in Panama to seize the canal, one at Puerto Rico, and one operation where the German force would strike on the Pacific coast. Of these the operations where Germany established a strategic foothold on US territory that could force America to the negotiating table were the most plausible.

The proposed landings in Panama and Puerto Rico were ruled out because of both the terrain considerations and the fact that they might not be significant enough in scope to achieve Germany's war goals. The Pacific and Gulf Coast assaults, while likely successful on the short term, lacked the strategic impact enough to force the US to the negotiating table.

Narrowing the list of options—an invasion aimed directly at the Chesapeake Bay was seen as risky.

Some of the proposed landing sites included:

- A landing at Beverly and Salem for the capture of Boston.
- New York City. Two scenarios for this were outlined including a German landing on the southeast shores of Long Island and another called for landings new Sandy Hook.
- Delaware Bay. This was seen as useful for reducing the forts along the river and providing an invasion avenue to seize Philadelphia.
- One contingency called for seizing both ends of the Chesapeake and Delaware Canal, capturing the forts and entrenching along the peninsula near the canal.
- The Chesapeake Bay. This allowed for thrusts towards Wilmington and Philadelphia, with Philadelphia as a base of operations for the German Army. Baltimore was another potential Chesapeake Bay target. There were options presented to reverse the American Civil War's Peninsula Campaign, seizing Fort Monroe, Norfolk, Newport News and use this as a base of operations to drive north towards Washington DC.

Assuming that the war was initiated in the autumn of 1914, the weather conditions would eliminate some of the targeted cities in New England. Weather would adversely impact road and sea travel in the winter months. This left four potential high priority target objectives that the Germans would consider striking: New York, Philadelphia, Baltimore and Washington DC.

War Plan Black would have unfolded in the US between the coast and the mountains:

The Appalachian Mountain system extended from Maine to Alabama and forms the watersheds which separate New England and the Atlantic states from the valleys of the St. Lawrence and Mississippi. It is completely broken through by an important artery of commerce at but one point, namely at the junction of the Mohawk and Hudson rivers. The Delaware, Susquehanna, and Potomac rivers penetrate this mountain system, but the regions they traverse are too rough and broken to lend much importance to these avenues to the interior. South of the Potomac net a river breaks through the system, and in western North Carolina we find the highest peaks and the most rugged terrain. The system terminates in northern Alabama.[20]

The Hudson River was seen as having strategic value as a potential avenue of advance for the Germans. It is navigable as far as Albany New York and control of this waterway would provide the invading armies with access to much of New England as a result.

The road network of 1914 in America was mostly two lane roads, with many remaining unpaved. Far before the age of the interstate highway system, it was a spider-web of roads. Movement of troops, *en masse*, had to be done by the robust railroad network. For the German invaders, use of the rail network was going to be critical. For the defenders of the American coast, it meant strong lines of communications and transportation.

Detailed analysis by the Joint Board of target US cities were as follows:

Target Boston

Boston, with a population in 1910 of 670,585 and foreign trade of $190,000,000, is the terminus of numerous railroads and the key to a populous and wealthy territory. It is the center of the entire shoe trade of the country. Watertown Arsenal is practically within the city limits and Springfield Arsenal is not far away. The loss of the latter would be a serious blow to Blue. In addition, Boston is a great banking center and presents a tempting objective. The harbor of Boston is well fortified, but it can be attacked either from New Bedford on the south or from Salem or Marblehead on the northeast. From the northeast Boston could, no doubt, be easily captured. But its capture could not have any material effect in bringing the war to a close, as a base from which to operate for the capture of New York, it is too far away and its choice as a base of operations against New York would give Blue what she needs most of all, namely time in which to make her resources tell. However at this season of the year operations would be considered almost impossible on account of the rigorous climate.[21]

Ironically, in the actual German war plans that were drafted prior to the outbreak of the Great War, the Kaiser's advisors had selected Boston as their target city of choice—regardless of the time of year.

Target Narragansett Bay

On this bay lie the cities of Newport, Fall River, and Providence, with a total population of 390,000, with a large foreign commerce and with an enormous coastwise traffic. Numerous rail facilities are available, and within easy reach are some of the richest districts of the world. The harbor is well defended, and the reduction of the Coast Defenses would require considerable time. It is, moreover, distant about 125 miles from New York and is subject to the same conditions as to climate is Boston.[22]

Target New York

Greater New York has, at the present time, a population of about 5,000,000, and is the commercial and financial center of the United States. Its harbor is one of the best in the world and its value from a naval point of view is vastly increased by having two channels of ingress and egress, one to the south and the other through Long Island Sound, while the possession of the city places the great island waterway of the Hudson River in control of her captors.

The great weakness of New York lies in the fact that all the raw materials for her great industries come from the outside. But more important still, she depends on her food supply on the surrounding country, while the failure of a single train of supplies to reach its destination causes a certain amount of distress in the city. Her location on the island makes ingress and egress difficult and the blocking of a few exits paralyses her system. In considering, however, how to deal New York a fatal blow it must be remembered that her commercial wealth depends far more on her domestic than her foreign trade, the proportion being about 670 to 12, while her domestic water borne commerce amounts to more than a million tons annually and is valued at more than seven billion dollars, of which about three-fourths is conducted with New England through Long Island Sound. For the destruction of such a source of wealth, no more blockade the port will suffice.

To arrest New York's traffic the invader must land and sever to the city's connection with the Sound and its communications to the north and west, either by direct assault or by investment.

With the fall of New York, the Hudson River is opened to the invader, and the main railroad and water communications with New England are broken; and the whole section east of the Hudson depends on these lines of trade for its food supplies and the raw materials for its industries, a more serious blow is thus delivered against New England than would result from the capture of Boston and the invasion from that point as a base.

But more serious than all other consequences would be the wrecking of the whole financial system of the country. New York is the financial center of the United States.

It is thus clear that of all the objectives considered by Black, New York is by far the most important from the standpoint of Blue and its capture promises, therefore, corresponding disadvantages to Black.

Let us consider then, the chances of success of a Black attack on New York. All of the approaches to New York by water are so well defended by coast forts that a naval attack is out of the question. There is a landing place east of New London nearer than Narragansett Bay which promises success, and this point is 150 miles from New York in the direct line. A landing on the Jersey coast with the object of capturing Ford Hancock and Wadsworth by land attack and occupying Station Island would not accomplish the object because it would not open the harbor to the Black navy, as the Long Island Batteries would still command the entrance.

The only other avenue of approach to New York City is by landing on the southern shores of Long Island. The direction of the prevailing winds at this season of the year is such that the southern shore of Long Island is more or less sheltered and makes it desirable as a landing place.

… the entire southern shore of Long Island from Rockaway Inlet east is out of range of fire from the coast forts and that it will be possible for the Black fleet to approach close to the shore, embark its forces in lighters and boats, move them through Jones' and Zach's Inlets and through Fire Island Inlet, and land them along the coast from Seaford to Babylon and Bayshore. The salt meadows which exist at many places along the shore of Great South Bay do not prevent landing when not frozen and at this season of the year, when the shallows are frozen, they could be passed over with ease. The troops and supplies having been landed, the transports would at once return to home ports for reinforcements.

A landing on Long Island would soon lead to the capture of Brooklyn and Fort Hamilton, but the entrances would still be closed by the western forts, and the fleet could find no harbor nearer than Delaware Bay. The Black forces could doubtless obtain positions from which New York could be bombarded, and its surrender might be compelled in that way. If, however, vigorous defense is offered and bombardment submitted to, the passage of the East River would be a difficult matter and Black might find himself hopelessly bottled up on Long Island.[23]

New York was a paradox of planning. On one hand, as the financial center of the United States, it was a target that was far too tempting to ignore. While not heavily defended, its sheer size and complexity made taking New York possible, but holding New York under occupation a complex exercise of logistics. In the minds of the American planners, a German invasion force that seized New York would be faced with the painstaking task of keep the armies and civilians fed—which would require cooperation with a determined enemy. This seems to fly in the face with how the German's dealt with provisioning the civilian population of Belgium in the Great War. War Plan Black references that assumption that the Germans would need to feed the population in order to maintain its control. While at the same time, there was a belief that if New York fell, the United States would not be able to resist for any period of time without suing for peace.

Target Delaware Bay
This bay offers a suitable base of operations against the coast defense forts defending Philadelphia and against the city itself. Philadelphia has a population of 1,549,000 and a

foreign trade of over $150,000,000. It is a shipbuilding center and, moreover, contains a large navy yard, of Blue's most important arsenals and her principal clothing depot. The clothing trade of the country largely centers around the city. More important still is the fact that the factories producing the bulk of smokeless powder are located within easy reach of Delaware Bay.

The Harbor of Refuge constructed by the United States at the mouth of Delaware Bay offers sheltered anchorage for a large number of vessels. The entrance to the harbor is rather narrow, at the south and on the north, the shoals and the row of ice breaker piers offer facilities for closing it against submarines. The harbor has no coast defense, though a mortar defense has been recommended.

The approach to the city above the bay is by dredged channel, which, with the buoys and lights removed, would render navigation difficult and dangerous, but not impracticable.

The Harbor of Refuge is 90 miles from Philadelphia.

The advance up the Delaware Peninsula would prove easy, as far as the narrow neck at the forts. A force of 100,000 should have no difficult [*sic*] in reducing Fort du Pont by land operations, and then a transfer to the Jersey side for the reduction of Fort Mott would be practicable. Fort Delaware on an island in the river might present some difficulties, but could probably be overcome by combined boat and naval attack after Forts du Pont and Mott have been eliminated. With the forts captured, advance on Philadelphia would be simple, and unless Blue has collected a large force to oppose Black, its capture would be certain. With the Black navy in the river and suitable land defenses, General Black could expect to hold Philadelphia until reinforced, for an advance on New York on one hand or Washington and Baltimore on the other. In any case, he has a significant base for further Black operations and has fulfilled his mission. The ice in the Delaware River presents little difficulty until after January 1, and the river even later can be traversed by War Vessels without much annoyance. The ice would probably be a vulnerable deterrent to the operations of submarines.

If Blue should attempt to concentrate a force to oppose [the Germans] more rapidly than is expected, the Delaware Peninsula offers the most secure area on the Atlantic Coast in which to defend himself until reinforced.[24]

Target Chesapeake Bay
This bay is undefended at its entrance. For the purpose of this discussion, Hampton Roads must be classed as part of the bay. Norfolk, Newport News and Hampton Roads form a very important base for the Blue Navy and one which is in constant use. Norfolk has a population of 67,452 and Newport News is a town of considerable size. Both have excellent rail connections. Hampton Roads is a fine harbor having shipbuilding yards at Newport News with a large drydock, while Norfolk is the navy yard with a drydock. Hampton Roads is defended by coast forts at Old Point Comfort and on the Ripraps at Fort Wool. Fort Monroe can be attacked by land, from the direction of [the] York River, but its reduction would be a matter of considerable time. Fort Wool is on a small island and its reduction would not be difficult after the capture of Fort Monroe.

The increased value of the submarine, makes Hampton Roads a deadly menace on the flank of a naval expedition if Fort Monroe is not captured. It is doubtful if any modern army would contemplate operations in the Chesapeake Bay, while Fort Monroe remained in possession of Blue.

Washington, with a population of 331,000, and Baltimore, with a population of 558,000, both cities are of great importance. They are both secure from attack by sea by reason of the coast forts, but both are open to attack by land. Both cities have ample railroad facilities. Chesapeake Bay furnishes unlimited anchorage for vessels of the largest size and the shores and generally quite flat enough for landing, although in place they are marshy. Landings cold be made to the advantage anywhere between Chesapeake Beach and Annapolis and the later place could be used as a temporary base. After landing, either Washington or Baltimore may be attacked by land.

The value of Washington as an objective lies solely in the fact that it is the capital, and that it has a naval gun foundry, and its loss would be a serious blow to Blue, both for sentimental reasons and for the practical effect which it would have upon the conduct of the war. It must be remembered, however, that Washington does not possess the same political importance as is possessed by Paris or Mexico City, and its capture should not end the war. The value of Baltimore rises entirely from its commercial importance.[25]

The problem with attempting a drive directly on Washington DC is that the Potomac River which feeds into the Chesapeake Bay cannot be navigated by battleships ... or any other vessel that draws more than 23 feet of water. There are three potential landing points for anyone attempting a direct move on Washington. These are:

- On the Virginia shore of the Potomac below Fort Hunt
- On the Maryland shore of the Potomac below Fort Washington. An additional site was located on Pope's Creek which has easy access to a rail line.
- On the western shore of Chesapeake. The probable landing points would be Herring Bay or near Annapolis.[26]

In compiling War Plan Black the Joint Board analyzed what the German attacker was going to need given the list of probable targets. Germany was going to need a target where they could defend themselves with their fleet nearby at anchorage to provide naval gunfire support and maintain a line of communications back to the Fatherland. As Germany had already demonstrated in the opening attacks in the Great War, its army could move with swift speed. "A sudden dash with a force of the size of his will enable him to land anywhere, unless held off by coast defenses."[27] The German aggressor, in order to sustain himself, was going to have to seize rail and water communications near a suitable base of operations.

The German Landings

War Plan Black assumed that the German would make feints at New York and Washington DC in an effort to draw away defenders from his true landings. These would be pressed by the German Navy, with shore bombardments which would appear to be aimed at reducing the coastal defense forts. The feints would also have the effect of sowing the seeds of fear in the American population knowing that a German land assault was coming.

And it would come ... but not at New York or Washington—but at Lewes Delaware. Defensive entrenchments would be made in the unlikely event of a rapid American counterattack. The Germans were not there to dig in but instead would move across the Peninsula and attack the coastal defenses by both land and by sea.

Once the forts had been seized or forced into surrender, they would turn on their first primary target—Philadelphia, the birthplace of the United States. The High Seas Fleet would move in to provide ample firepower for the infantry capture of the city. Once Philadelphia was taken it would be immediately fortified against land attacks. The good sheltered harbor which lacked any defenses would prove a good base for any German submarines in their attack force as well as sheltering the battle cruisers of the fleet. The key railroads and bridges would be secured as well. Even if an American force were in the vicinity, they would be hard pressed to organize a major assault quickly—giving the German Army time to entrench and fortify their positions. And any land attacks against the German defenses would potentially face long-range naval gunfire as well.

Philadelphia is only 86 miles from New York City, 96 miles from Baltimore, and 135 miles from Washington DC. With good railway and road systems between these major cities, the capture of Philadelphia would offer the Germans the opportunity to engage and defeat the American Army when they attempted to recapture Philadelphia, then strike at any one of these other objectives. The Joint Board planners, in looking at the secondary targets—felt that Washington DC, with its symbolic importance to the American people, would be high on the list for the Germans to move against once the American Army was crushed.[28]

American Reaction to the Invasion

War Plan Black initially called for concentration taking place at various points along the Atlantic Coast:

> One provided for concentration at Plattsburg and Boston only; one for a single point of concentration to cover the coast between Long Island Sound and the Chesapeake Bay, one for five field armies, each in the sections around Boston, New York, Philadelphia, Washington and Atlanta.[29]

Given the winter conditions Boston was taken out of the mix of areas, as were those targets in the South Atlantic. As such troop concentrations would be made in three or more large bodies between New York and the mouth of the Chesapeake Bay.

A call for Americans to rally to the defense of their country would be made:

> Blue, following the practice of former wars, has no doubt called for several hundred thousand volunteers, but as there will be a lack of trained officers and as the organization, training and mobilization of these troops will take considerable time, they need not be considered in the present estimate (of troop strength).[30]

In fact the Joint Board planners recognized that the US was ill-prepared to jump into a major campaign, even on her home soil.

There was also the consideration of expertise:

> The Blue regulars, comprising a force of about 70,000 men, although made up of a large percentage of recruits, are excellent troops. About 40% of the militia have more or less some training, but no war experience. In spite, therefore, of the patriotism, enthusiasm, and high character of the Blue militia, they are inferior to the Black troops. If in addition to Blue follows her historic custom of appointing political generals to high command, the Blue inferiority will still further increased.[31]

In reviewing the port cities and their defenses, the mouths of Delaware Bay and the Chesapeake Bay were for the most part were the only ones not heavily fortified—though many of these coastal defense batteries at the forts were antiques.

> However, the harbors and ports of the Atlantic south of Norfolk, and those of the Gulf Coast, in addition to being far away from the centers of wealth and population, are not first class harbors and cannot be compared, as possible naval bases, with those of the on the Atlantic Coast between Boston and Norfolk.[32]

The plans in War Plan Black, called for initial defense placement of troops as follows:

Boston and vicinity:	Two divisions
New York and vicinity:	Three divisions
Delaware Bay:	One division
Fort Monroe—Norfolk:	One division
Washington DC and Baltimore:	Two divisions infantry —one division cavalry
South Atlantic and Gulf Coasts (to include the Mexican Border):	Three divisions
Pacific Coast (until relieved by volunteer recruits):	One division
Panama and other outlying possessions:	Two divisions [33]

The spreading out of these divisions would work to the disadvantage of the Americans because it would mean that it could take days if not weeks to move divisions to the respond in large numbers to German landings. While the local divisions garrisoned (as above) would be available to respond to the German assaults, they would not be engaging with superior numbers.

The Americans did not contemplate fighting the Germans during the landings themselves:

> … defense should contemplate resistance at the water's edge, it is not believed to be a good policy to provide for this until the hostile fleet is sighted. Rather keep the divisions together where they can be drilled, trained and supplied under the eyes of their commanders until the proper time to send them out.[34]

Under War Plan Black, the American strategy was to leverage time against the Germans until a significant number of volunteers, militia, and National Guard units could be mustered, assembled, and mobilized for crushing the defeat. As such, for the short term, the Americans would need to remain on the defensive until they possessed such numbers where victory was possible.

Ultimately the Joint Board does not say that indeed Philadelphia will fall to into German hands but none of the plans call for a siege of the Germans in the city. Indeed, there is an implied acceptance that Philadelphia would fall. Instead, the US would bide time to build up strength. At the same time the Germans would be ferrying reinforcements in terms of men and manpower. This would be a deadly game of logistics.

The Joint Board planners realized though that the Germans well-understood the concept of maintaining initiative. While they might take Philadelphia, they would not simply sit there, but would launch an offense. Moving north to New York in the winter did not seem likely given the logistics necessary to take and hold the city. If not north to New York, it seemed likely that the German Commanding General would turn his gaze to the south—to Baltimore or Washington DC.

The German commander did not have to take either of these cities in order to be victorious. Laying siege to either of them, especially Washington DC, might be enough to compel the United States to negotiate a truce. Simply taking Philadelphia was not enough to do that. The Germans would have to demonstrate that the war could be brought anywhere along the east coast.

Rather than jump into a fight, War Plan Black calls for the deployment of the III Division reinforced by a Cavalry Brigade. One of their first missions was to secure and rig for demolition the railway bridges over Gunpowder, Bush and the Susquehanna rivers. If these were severed it would cut off communication with the main German body to the north and prevent their ability to rapidly move on Washington.

The American force aimed at stalling the Germans would establish their headquarters at Bowie, Maryland. The III Division would be located in the vicinity of Upper Marlboro, Maryland, astride the Chesapeake Beach Railroad line. The troops would establish their camp along the western branch. The First Cavalry Brigade would be established in the vicinity of Lyon's Creek, across the Patuxent River and the railroad six miles southeast of Upper Marlboro Maryland.

By buying time, this would allow the formation of the VIII Division which was to be composed of militia and National Guard units from New Jersey, Delaware, Maryland, West Virginia and Virginia. The VIII Division would be established just north of Baltimore at Pimlico. If pressed or driven by the Germans it would reform near Linthicum Maryland, at the junction of the Annapolis Short Line and the Pennsylvania Railroads.[35]

What War Plan Black does not address is the impact to American morale over the loss of Philadelphia. While they acknowledge it would cause a surge of nationalistic fever, probably driving up enlistments of volunteers, the long term implications of such a major historical city falling and remaining in the hands of a determined and entrenched enemy were never fully explored.

The Siege of Washington DC

One of the last pieces of War Plan Black was to prepare the capital city for siege by the Germans. Again, keeping with the US strategy, the goal was not just the protection of the city but to tie down German forces in a prolonged fight which would give the US time to bring its manpower and industrial might to bear. Counterbalance to that thinking was that if the Americans took too long to respond to the German threat, public support might falter and compel a negotiated truce and the shattering of the Monroe Doctrine. Joint Board planners believed in this case, a siege would tear away at the one thing the Germans could not afford to lose—time.

There were challenges with protecting the American capital. The intent was to ring the city with a string of forts and entrenchments for in its defense.

> Its location must be such as to keep an enemy at sufficient distance to prevent the destructive bombardment of the capital or the serious injury of the vial features within the city. In this way only can the capital be insured against capture of serious damage.[36]
>
> It is obvious that a line should be selected that will be the shortest consistent with the above purpose in order to economize troops and render the defense simple yet effective. It will not be enough to build and strengthen a part of this line, such as a single front, but the defense protection for the entire circumference around the city must be decided upon first from the map then it must be corrected later by examination of the ground. The works after being planned will probably be built as rapidly as possible, as soon as war seems inevitable.[37]

In other words, as soon as war is declared with Germany, the preparation for the siege of Washington was to commence.

One of the driving factors in erecting any defense of Washington DC is the range of the enemy artillery. The Joint Board felt that the invading Germans would bring only short to medium range artillery—ranging 10,000 to 11,000 yards:

The lines of resistance must therefore fulfill two objects; first, hold off the enemy's artillery beyond bombarding distance; and, second, be impregnable to infantry assault.[38]

Washington DC was a city ripe with targets. War Plan Black recognized the following as points that required defending:

- The Navy Yard
- The Capitol
- The White House
- The Treasury
- Department Buildings
- The War College
- The Library of Congress
- The railway yards at Eckington
- The National Museum (The Smithsonian)
- The Washington Monument
- Fort Myer Virginia
- The "Long: railway bridge"
- The Aqueduct, the Long, Anacostia, Pennsylvania Railway and Bennings bridges

Two points were considered important, but most likely would fall victim to the Germans at the start of fighting. These were the Chain Bridge into Virginia and the Bladensburg Bridge into Maryland. "… they must be allowed to take their chances."[39] Likewise Fort Hunts and Washington, while they protected the approaches to the city by sea, were too far away to include in the defensive rings around Washington DC. These would be reinforced but it was recognized that they would most likely fall.

Mapping out the key institutions and assuming each had a six-mile radius around it in terms of required protective range, made for a massive ring needed to protect the city. Factoring into the defense planning was the number of troops that might be available to defending the earthworks. The length of the longest portion of the defensive line was 77 miles, with the shortest being 50 miles. During the American Civil War, the last time that Washington was so entrenched, the defensive line was 35 miles. The Joint Board planners eventually settled on a defensive ring 55 miles long. "At two thousand infantry per mile, this line would require 110,000 men plus accompanying troops."[40]

Washington's two reservoirs inside the defensive ring were insufficient to supply the city with the water it would need. A small defense force would be sent to Great Falls Virginia to protect the intake tunnel for the water supplies. During the German siege, the citizens would have to rely on the rivers for their water.

Other seemingly strategic targets fell outside of the defensive ring as well. The Firth-Sterling Steel Company's Giesboro Point facility manufactured projectiles for the US Navy. With the assumed loss of the US Atlantic Navy at the onset of War Plan Black, the plant seemed to have lost its value.

The defensive line would begin on the west bank of the Potomac, south of Alexandria, Virginia, the controlling arc lies in the reverse of the slope of the Mt. Erin Plateau. Holding this piece of ground could protect the Long Bridge into the city and was the high ground.

From the Southern Railway to Falls Church the question is whether to go east or west of Holmes Run. The line east of the run is very good and strong, but it is not much shorter than the line west of the run, and although it looks much stronger, there is no second line in the rear of it until Four Mile Run is reached, and the outer line of that line. From Falls Church to the Potomac the choice lies between a line from East End to the Kirby Road, and along that road just east of Longley. The other line runs north from West End through Mackalls Hill, and west of Turkey Run. The flat top of Mackall, and the decision about the line west of Holmes Run taken together make the outer line the better one of the two.

At Glen Echo there is nothing to move the location of the line far away from the controlling arc, and the hill northwest of Bethesda invites the line to go through it. From here around to Avenel there is nothing to govern, except the desire to get through with as short as a line as practicable, and this line seems to follow Rock Creek, and lie between Linden and Forest Glen. It is a bad area and difficult to pick out on a map. A study of the terrain to the east shows the ridge north of Riggs Mill, and the Maryland Agricultural College as the next desirable position, and the northern line is made as short as possible through Linden and Woodside to the ridge just mentioned. The ground south of this line on the north is so broken and rough that a satisfactory line through Bethesda-Silver Spring seems possible.

Between Northwest Branch and the B & O Railway there is a slight ridge just under the controlling arc, but the ridge just in front thereof seems to be better than the one under the arc and is longer.

The line from the B & O Railway is the Pennsylvania Railway at Lanham is like the northern line. There is nothing to recommend it except that the two ends are fixed and the shortest line seems to be as good as any other reasonable line.

The hills at Lanham and Brightseat are the controlling points, and the hills near Bald Hill Branch seem the best route to follow between the two. The section from Brightseat to the Railway follows a ridge in rear of the most open and flat terrain in that vicinity. In fact, the section from mile 20 to mile 40 is taken mainly because it appears to be the first possible position in front of or within 1000 yards of the controlling area.

The line from the Marlboro Pike to the Potomac must like either along the Suitland–Oxen–New Glatz road or the Forestville Camp Springs–Fort Foote Road. The inner line is too far inside the controlling area and so the outer line is chosen. The flat tableland along the outer road also seems to indicate this as the easier line of the two to defend. Whether this line will drop to the south and go through Friendly or follow the line indicated on the map can only be decided on the ground. The drop into Broad Creek Valley is difficult at best, and a map location in such a section is even more tentative than in other parts of the line.[41]

The defensive ring was not a single trench fortification—but a maze of trench lines and communications trenches—clearly influenced by those that were being dug at the same time as the planning during the Great War on the Western Front. Points along the edge would have in-depth trench lines, acting as forts dotting the edge of the ring. These would have 750 yard fire trenches, 2,850 yard fire trenches, 2,850 yards splinter proof bunkers, anti-personnel obstacles—six yards wide, and clearing of 3,600 yards in front of the trenches where possible—meaning that anyone rushing the fortifications would have no cover from defending artillery and those men manning the trenches. Additionally assembly and communications trenches leading back behind the front lines would have to be dug and fortified.[42] The complexity of the US plan to protect the capital was a massive undertaking.

The expenses of creating this citadel around Washington DC was incredible—totaling 79,912 man hours of labor. It would require the work of 4,320 men for three days at six hours per day.[43]

Summary Evaluation of the War Plan:

The opening assessment at the beginning of this chapter in regards to the war in Europe and which powers might be the greatest threat is fascinating. The US clearly felt that Germany had a better-than-average chance to win the Great War and to do so quickly. The French and British were seen as rivals to the US, but not direct threats.

War Plan Black differs from most of the colored War Plans in that it presumes failure on the part of the United States. Failure in the defeat of the US Navy in the Caribbean and the loss of Philadelphia to the invading German Army. While later versions of the War Plan Black, specifically the update of 1916, favored the United States to be victorious—with heavy mining of the North Sea and the eventual forcing of Germany into defeat; this version of the War Plan offers the most tantalizing scenario.

Kaiser Wilhelm II created his own set of plans for invading America starting in 1898. These Operational Plans I–III originally focused on taking of New York and/or Boston—they offer a counterbalance to the assumptions that the Joint Board placed in War Plan Black.

When one considers when War Plan Black was devised, at the start of the Great War, it is easy to see that the US was coming to grips with the possibility that Germany might be victorious in the war. France would fall as would Britain—leaving America alone to face a seasoned and polished German Army.

There would be defeats at Germany's hands—the loss of Guantanamo Bay then Philadelphia. America would have a foreign invader on her home soil, something unheard of since the War of 1812. The Navy would be a shattered sword. The Army would find itself outnumbered and outclassed.

The concept of War Plan Black was based on time—it would take time for the United States to raise an army large and equipped enough to deal with Germany. In the meantime, the Joint Board acknowledged a series of stunning defeats and losses would be incurred. This was a dangerous strategy to execute. The more time that passed, the more Germany maintained the initiative. While the planners clearly felt that a siege of Washington DC was not only possible but probable, there was still a good chance that the Germans would drive north into New York instead. No planning went into defending New Jersey and Pennsylvania to prevent such a thrust. If the Germans did not follow the American plan, the losses could be even more staggering and outright defeat might have been possible.

War Plan Black does not factor in the German Pacific fleet or the American assets there. While the loss of Guantanamo would allow Germany to put a cork in the passage of the Panama Canal, the Americans could send their fleet around the world to eventually arrive and engage. With frequent coaling required (even at neutral ports) the Germans would have advance notice of such movements and could move to counter them. One can only imagine how weary the US sailors would be after such a long journey, only to be then tossed into battle against a more seasoned opponent.

The War Plan does not address some of the logistical issues, namely how would Washington DC receive food for the military and civilian populations during the siege? There is a single line assumption that travel up the Chesapeake Bay would be most likely blocked by the German Navy. This leaves one to wonder how long the city could hope to hold out as its population and defenders slowly starved to death.

One interesting aspect to the War Plan is the notation that there was a tendency in 1914 to allow the placement of political generals, which might hinder operations. When one studies the US Civil War the impact of these ill-trained and poorly disciplined leaders can be seen as one of the aspects that led to the Civil War dragging out as long as it did.

The more widely-known version of War Plan Black (1916–1917) altered the face of the war. It had entire sections for dealing with German merchant raiders—which had already successfully been employed by the time the plan was drafted. It also called for the US to work in conjunction with the Royal Navy to lay fields of mines that would, hopefully, prevent the German High Seas Fleet from setting sail. This well-known later edition nullified that concepts of American losses now that the Joint Board better understood how long the Great War was likely to take and the evolving naval technology and tactics.

Aviation was another area of technological advance that the Joint Board members failed to account for in their plans. By 1915 in the Great War, both sides had begun to master the use of aircraft for reconnaissance and artillery bombardment spotting. Aviation was something that the Germans, in particular, excelled at. They drove many of the dynamic innovations in aviation during the Great War.

If the United States and Germany were to go to war, America would have done so with virtually no air force, no experience in aerial combat or observation, with no pool of ready pilots to fly aircraft. Her air force only existed on paper and in the hearts and minds of the Signal Corps branch where it originally had been shuffled. Many of the early aviation schools were based on the east coast in 1914—meaning they would be next to useless when the Germans eventually landed.

The advantages that Germany would have had against the US during the first year of such a war in terms of aviation might very well have been a game-changer. Even a siege as complex and logistically challenging as one against Washington DC could have proven to be easy for the Germans to control with complete domination of the skies. It would take at least six months for the US to even begin to produce contemporary aircraft and aviators to wage such a war. In that period of time, the entire operation may have come to an end with Germany as the victor.

There is little if no evidence that War Plan Black had any influence on the formation and eventual landing of the American Expeditionary Force under General Pershing once the US did enter the war. The plan was ignored in favor of the US working as part of a greater alliance of nations. War Plan Black drifted into obscurity.

In some respects War Plan Black is a plea to the political leadership of the US, a plea to prepare for a war or face consequences that might be devastating. By remaining neutral, America was not rearming for the new age of warfare that was unfolding in Europe. Her regular army was a joke compared against Germany, even a Germany that suffered losses at the hands of the French, Russians and British in the Black scenario. If Germany had crushed her enemies in Europe, America would have presented a ripe target, almost easy for the taking. War Plan Black demonstrates those vulnerabilities.

An Alternate WWII—the 1935 Plan for the American War with the United Kingdom War Plan Red

Introduction

The Joint Board drew up the first true War Plan Red in 1930 and the plan was in a state of constant amendment and update in 1934, 1935, and 1937. This plan became obsolete in the late 1930s when it became clear that alliances were going to drive the next global conflict and that a one-on-one war with Britain simply was the stuff of fantasy.

So why would the US contemplate going to war with Great Britain? The two nations had been steadfast allies in the Great War against a common foe. British foreign policy was one of developing positive relations with the United States. Outwardly the United States appeared to be friendly as well.

There were the memories of the Venezuela Crisis of 1895 still lingering in US planner's minds. The British had lightly tested the Monroe Doctrine and while in Britain this was not a major news item, for the United States it was a stinging reminder that her friendly relations with the British could turn quickly to conflict.

War Plan Red does hint strongly that economic factors could come into play in sparking a conflict between the two nations. After the end of the Great War and the 1918 Armistice Britain ended up owing the United States £9 billion ... a war debt that was not being paid off because of Britain's own recovering economy. Great Britain renegotiated its repayment schedule with America in 1923 to payments of £34 million for ten years then £40 million pounds for 52 years. The US ended up loaning Germany allowing her repay the massive war debt/reparations to Great Britain, who would in turn pay off its loans to the US Government. The planners seem to disregard how the United States managed to stay out of the conflict for three years, profiting massively by selling arms to Britain and France. US perspectives in regards to Britain were heavily slanted. They viewed the convoluted reparations financing scheme coupled with Britain's irregular payments as fuel which allowed for old animosities towards Britain to resurface.

After the war, Britain (at the behest of the allies including the US) had interred the German High Seas Fleet at Scapa Flow. The Germans scuttled the fleet rather than let it fall into British hands. This attitude led to suspicions in US Navy circles that the British had contemplated seizure of Germans ships to augment the Royal Navy.

The US sponsored the Washington Naval Conference in 1922 to attempt to limit any nation's military growth at sea—keeping naval arms races in check. The resulting Washington Naval Treaty of 1922 marked the end of the Royal Navy's superiority, allowing the United States and Britain to maintain equal quotas of tonnage for their warships.

The US never ratified the terms and conditions of the Treaty of Versailles. Much of this was political wrangling on the part of Republicans who, pressured by constituents with Irish and German backgrounds, felt that the Treaty unfairly favored the British. Despite the fact that the US had initially enthusiastically endorsed the concept of the League of Nations, politics had kept her from officially joining the League. Britain took part in the League directly. The net result coming out of the Great War was that Britain squarely backed the League of Nations and a treaty which the US was unable or unwilling to rally behind. Victory, rather than war, served to divide the two powers.

When the Great Depression hit the global economies, the US responded rather unilaterally by raising tariffs in 1930. This matter did not go over well with the British and Canadians who retaliated with their own raising of tariffs, including those against the United States. Economics, in 1930, were the primary tensions between the two nations. If war were to come, it would be as an expression of economic power between the countries.

A cultural reason for the United States to contemplate war with Britain was the growing admiration of events unfolding in Germany. In 1930 the new political power, the National Socialist Party under Adolf Hitler, was coming into power. With a large population of former Germans, the United States found itself culturally aligning with Germany. Americans admired the underdog and often saw themselves as such.

It is striking that in 1935, when this version of War Plan Red was revised, that the United States did not update War Plan Black with Germany. It was as if military planners were looking at Germany with a blind eye out of some unfounded paranoia/ fear of Britain. In 1935 Germany introduced the Luftwaffe and officially began rearmament in direct violation of the Versailles Treaty. Germany implemented the Nuremburg Laws that year and began building a dozen U-Boats. To many nations, Germany was seen as a threat. American perceptions were colored—in this case Red. They still thought under the premises that if war came about, Britain was the only nation in the hemisphere that stood to risk a loss of territory in the event of war. This perception merely dated and pointed out some of the hypocrisy of the Monroe Doctrine in an ever-evolving world.

It was in this culture of misguided perceptions that the Joint Board began to draw up a new version of War Plan Red—the contingency that the next war might be with her former ally—Great Britain.

Assessment of the British Empire at the Start of Hostilities

War Plan Red attempted to define the British Empire in the 1930s in terms of the scope of the war that was contemplated. This factored in Crimson (Canada), Scarlet (Australia), and the reaction of Orange (Japan).

The Red Empire in extent of territory and population is the greatest in the world. It is distributed in all quarters of the globe. Its land frontiers are nowhere continuous to those of a strong military power, except in the case of Crimson. The United Kingdom is the heart of the Red Empire and the existence of this Empire depends on the maintenance of sea communications between the United Kingdom and the Dominions, Colonies, Protectorates, and Mandates which make up the Empire. To protect such sea communications Red has established a system of naval bases and protected harbors along almost every important trade route throughout the world. This makes it possible for Red to concentrate naval forces to threaten the sea frontiers and the commerce of any probable enemy, while at the same time safeguarding its own. However, the wide distribution of the Red Empire and its seaborne trade tend to demand a considerable dispersion of naval forces to protect them.

The United Kingdom is itself vulnerable to attack by aircraft based on the European Continent, but, without an ally in Western Europe, this fact would be of no advantage to Blue in a war with Red.

In a war between Blue and Red, the Dominions of Scarlet are not subject to attack, and the military and naval forces of these Dominions would be available, in combination with other Empire forces, to attack Blue possessions in the Pacific and Blue commerce therein.[1]

The US considered the far flung parts of the British Empire too remote to pose any real threat ... a dangerous assumption given Australia's position near the Philippines and potentially near Hawaii.

Red maintains large military and naval forces in India and other Red possessions and mandates in the Middle East. Since these portions of the Red Empire are secure against attacks by Blue, these forces, except such as are necessary to guard the frontiers and to provide internal security, would be available to undertake operations against Blue, particularly the Philippine Islands and Guam.

Red further maintains relatively large naval forces and small military forces in the Fast Eastern waters and possessions. These would be available to attack Blue possessions and commerce.

The Red Dominions and possessions in Africa also are so situated as to secure against Blue attack, and their forces would be available to assist other Red forces. On account, however, of their relatively small white populations, such contribution would not be of great importance.

In a war of long duration where the bulk of the Blue naval forces would have to be retained in the Atlantic, the Hawaiian Islands might be subjected to serious attack by Scarlet and Indian forces or by Allied forces in the case Orange should intervene in the war on the side of Red.

In the Caribbean Sea and West Indian waters, Red has potential advanced naval bases at Jamaica (Port Royal), Trinidad, and St. Lucia. In addition Red has an outlying subsidiary naval base at Bermuda. There are suitable harbors elsewhere within Red North American possession (exclusive of Crimson) which are capable of serving as bases for small craft, particularly submarines. Notable among these are the Bahamas and Red Leeward Island.

These harbors are important not only for the protection of Red seaborne trade, but as sally points from which to attack Blue commerce.

Jamaica constitutes a serious menace to the security of the Panama Canal and to all Blue trade routes passing through the Caribbean Sea and is the most important West Indian submarine cable communications center. Bermuda is well located to interfere with Blue seaborne trade to the West Indies and along the Blue South Atlantic coast. In addition it is capable of serving as bases for aircraft carriers designated to conduct air raids against Blue vital areas. The Bahamas are so situated as to afford bases from which to control Blue trade through the Straits of Florida and to Cuba.

Trinidad, St. Lucia, and the Red Leeward Islands lie on the flank of Blue Trade Routes to the East Coast of South America and constitute serious threats to the integrity of Blue commerce engaged therewith.

Of the Red North America possessions, exclusive of Crimson, only Jamaica and Bermuda are at present defended, although the defenses are neither extensive nor modern and the present garrisons are small.

Geographically, Crimson affords Red admirable bases for Naval, Military, and Air Forces close to the vital areas of Blue and so situated as to provide a comparatively short line of sea communications to the Red United Kingdom, which line is not flanked by Blue territory which could be used as a naval base. Due to the eastward projection of Crimson relative to the Blue coast, a concentration of the Red Battle Fleet in Crimson waters, particularly in the Halifax area, would permit Red to transfer forces to Crimson with such freedom as to require only small detachments to safeguard such line of communications. This relative location of Nova Scotia, Cape Breton Island, and Newfoundland would render it difficult for Blue Naval forces to attack successfully the Red line of sea communications. Ports of the Maritime Provinces of Crimson afford strong points from which to initiate invasion of Blue territory, by joint Army, Navy and Air Force operations. Naval raids may be launched from these bases against Blue commerce and blue vital areas. The eastward projection of these Provinces also facilitates the rapid transfer of Red air units to Crimson, even should Blue have control of the St. Lawrence Valley.

Red also has a sea route to Hudson Bay which is easily secured as soon as Red has established naval superiority in the Western Atlantic. Port facilities are being constructed at the terminus of the single track railroad now in operation. During the short season when this route is open to navigation Red forces would be enabled to reach Central Crimson with greater ease and facility, provided transportation through the railroad bottle neck at Winnipeg was uninterrupted. This route would be particularly valuable for the transfer of air units from other portions of the Red Empire to Crimson.

There are harbors with well-developed port facilities on the Pacific Coast of Crimson, notably at Victoria-Vancouver and at Prince Rupert. These harbors have good rail communications eastward, and would afford base facilities for naval operations against Blue Pacific commerce, especially that passing through the Straits of Juan de Fuca and with Alaska. They would be available as ports of debarkation for Scarlet forces or for Orange forces should Orange eventually intervene in the war on the side of Red.

Geographically, while Crimson provides the Red Empire as a whole with advantageous bases at such widely separated points as to invite an initial dispersion of Blue armed forces, Crimson itself occupies an extremely weak position with respect to Blue. While its territory is of great extent, all well-developed parts thereof lie close to the Blue border; hence, they are especially vulnerable to an attack launched from Blue territory. The reinforcement of Crimson forces in the region by strong Red contingents requires free use of the St. Lawrence River and of the rail lines having terminals in the ports of the Maritime Provinces. On account of the severe winter climate of this portion of Crimson, the St. Lawrence River and Gulf are closed to navigation for several months each year. The greatest salient into Eastern Crimson formed by the State of Maine would provide Blue with a base from which to conduct operations to cut communications between the Quebec–Montreal area and the Maritime Provinces, or to initiate land or air offenses against Halifax and St. John, New Brunswick, the ports best fitted for use by the major units of the Red Fleet.

The Ontario Peninsula southwest of the line Midland-Oshawa, inclusive, is the principal manufacturing area of Crimson and contains approximately one-third of Crimson's present munitioning capability. The denial to the Ontario Peninsula of the Niagara power and the coal imported from Blue and the western provinces of Crimson would produce an immediate strangulation of its manufacturing and munitioning industries. Approximately ninety percent of Crimson's present munitioning capacity is confined to Crimson territory bordering and adjacent to Lake Ontario, and the Ottawa and St. Lawrence Rivers. The self-destruction of this munitioning capacity would be effected by the isolation of the Ontario Peninsula from its industrial power sources and an offensive which controls the St. Lawrence River Valley from Ottawa to Quebec. Pending the expected development o the hydro-power in the James Bay area, which development is indicated in the near future by the present rapid growth of the Metallurgical operation from Sudbury towards James Bay and the interconnection of this power with the lines from the Niagara Falls area, the Niagara power is considerably more vital to Crimson then to Blue. The destruction of the Niagara power facilities would have but slight effect on Blue's munitioning capability.

For the industrial life and munitioning capacity of the Blue, the Great Lakes, except Lake Ontario, and the waterways connecting them are of the greatest importance as routes of transportation. In a war of long duration the possession of the Great Lakes transportation routes west of the Welland Canal would be of vital importance to Blue's munitioning capacity. The narrow defiles of the St. Clair River, the Detroit River, the St. Mary's River, including the Sault Ste. Marie Canals, and the Straits of Mackinac along these routes are extremely vulnerable to attack both by air and by mobile artillery. The Welland Canal is of no industrial use to Blue, therefore its disposition would be determined entirely from military considerations.

Winnipeg constitutes a rail bottle neck which connects eastern and western Crimson. Scarlet or other forces landing on the Pacific Coast of Crimson or on the southern shore of Hudson Bay would require the uninterrupted use of this railroad center in order to reinforce eastern Crimson. The vital supply of coal from the western provinces of Crimson passes through this bottle neck in reaching the Ontario and Quebec Provinces munitioning areas; as does the supply of wheat and other grains raised in western Crimson and required in the eastern part of that country. The Winnipeg railroad center is particularly vulnerable to attack from Blue.

The details of terrain and of transportation routes must be carefully studied with respect to each possible local theater of operations in Crimson. IT seems sufficient here to mention the following:

(a) Nova Scotia particularly, and New Brunswick to a less extend, contain so many lake and rivers that successive defensive lines can be organized by Crimson or Red forces to cover important localities such as Halifax and St. John. Rail and road communications in these Provinces are entirely inadequate for the operation of large forces.

(b) The southern shores of Newfoundland, Cape Breton Island and Nova Scotia have a much milder climate than the remainder of Eastern Crimson and the harbors and anchorages are rarely frozen over during the winter. In the Gulf of St. Lawrence fogs are very prevalent, and the Gulf is blocked by ice to navigation for about five months of the year. The Straits of Belle Isle are open even a shorter period o the year. In the Bay of Fundy the tidal range is extreme and the currents are so strong that the landing of troops and supplies for operations in Nova Scotia would involve unusual difficulties and would require special provisions. The coastline of the Maritime Provinces presents a continuous succession of harbors and sheltered anchorages which might be employed by Red Naval forces should Halifax or St. John not be available to them Rail communications to such harbors are however, few in number.

(c) There are three possible routes of invasion of the Montreal-Quebec area from Blue, as follows: from Jackman, Me., to Quebec; the Connecticut River Valley from St. Johnsbury, Vt., to Sherbrooke, and thence by three routes to vital points on the St. Lawrence River; and the Hudson River-Lake Champlain-Richelieu River Valley from Ft. Ethan Allen, Vt., Plattsburg and Malone, N.Y., through Fanham and St. Johns, Quebec. These routes each contain a primary highway and a railroad. The Richelieu River is navigable for small steamers and connects by Lake Champlain and canal to the Hudson River.

(d) The country in the vicinity of Sault Ste. Marie is sparsely populated, and that north of the border is generally poorly developed.

(e) On the Pacific coast, Vancouver, and , to a less extent, Prince Rupert, have adequate water and rail communications with the other ports of Crimson and would be available for use as ports of debarkation for any reinforcements which Crimson might receive by way of the Pacific Ocean.[2]

How the British Empire would deal with war with the United States was something that the Joint Planners wrestled with as well in their creation of War Plan Red:

The government of Red is well suited for war making, the cabinet ruling the state in the name of the Sovereign by virtue of its control of Parliament. The government is subject to change as a whole only through failing to command the support of Parliament or by defeat in a general election of the party to which it belongs. In future wars, as in the World War, it is probable that the Prime Minister will be advised on all war policies by a small group of the cabinet known as the "War Cabinet". It is believed that in war, there will be no greater likelihood of a major change in the government than there is in the case of Blue. The Prime Minister and the cabinet of the United Kingdom to all intents and purposes dictate the policy of the Red Empire as a whole, although, in certain major foreign policies the self-governing Dominions are consulted.

Based upon the fundamental understand by all Red citizens of the vital character of Red trade and the necessity for its protection and of the evident necessity for keeping the war away from Red territory, the cabinet is unlikely to find any difficulty in obtaining appropriations for making, preparation for a foreign war should it be deemed vital to Red commercial interests. Propaganda to such ends would be intensive and thorough. The solidarity of the Red race in cases dealing with national interests is proverbial where a foreign government is concerned.

While there has been no act of Parliament since the World War designed to produce national plans for war, it is believed that the lessons of the War have well been digested and the Chiefs of Staff of the three fighting services may be assumed to have well-considered war plans for the conduct of any probable war ready at any time to present to the Prime Minister.

It may be taken for granted that no Red government will undertake to commit the Empire to a major war unless it is assured of the full support of the labor elements of the United Kingdom. Since the laboring class constitutes four-fifths of the population, its support is essential to the success in war.

In the Irish Free State, while the irreconcilable elements are no longer in position to interfere with the policy of the State, it is believed that Irish support of Red in a war with Blue will be far from unanimous and the internal security of this Dominion will be a matter of concern to Red. On the other hand, on account of the economic situation it is believed that this Dominion will remain loyal to the Empire.

In the Dominions of Scarlet, while feeling against Blue is not likely to be pronounced, it is believed that the principle of Empire solidarity will prevail. However, in case Orange should intervene in the war on the side of Red, these Dominions will probably insist upon guarantees of their paramount interest in the South Seas and their participation in any territorial readjustments that might take place after the conclusion of the war.

In the dominion of South Africa, Imperial feeling is divided; however support of Red in a war with Blue by this Dominion will probably be of small importance.

In India, and, generally, throughout Red possessions, protectorates and mandates in the Near and Middle East, unrest is always prevalent, but it is believed that Red will be able to maintain sufficient forces in these regions to suppress promptly any uprising as well as to repel attacks on the frontiers by warlike tribesman.

In Crimson, Imperial feeling is strongest in British Columbia, and quite strong in the Maritime Provinces, Newfoundland, and Ontario. It is weakest in the Prairie Provinces (exclusive of Manitoba). In Quebec Province, Crimson feeling, rather than Imperial feeling, is strong. However, it is estimated that in the event of war between Red and Blue, local feeling would have little effect and the Crimson Provinces would take united action.

The possibility that Crimson may declare neutrality, which, under the rather loose constitution of the Red Empire (or, rather, Red Commonwealth of Nations), the Dominion is in a position to do so, should receive careful consideration. Such action on the part of Crimson would necessarily involve permanent or temporary secession from the Empire, but there are several reasons why such step appears to be advantageous to Crimson. Not only is this Dominion more closely bound to commercial, financial and cultural times to Blue than to any part of the Red Empire, but it appears inevitable, in case Crimson does not declare neutrality, that large parts of Crimson territory will become theaters of military operations with consequent suffering to the population and widespread destruction of the country as well as almost total suppression of normal trade and industry. Such action, moreover, might be considered advantageous to Red, as it would relieve the Empire of the moral obligation to defend this far-flung Dominion against the full military strength of Blue, and would permit the concentration of Red military and naval strength against Blue commerce and overseas possessions. On the other hand, it would deprive Red of the best suite base from which to conduct war against Blue and would thereby bring about a limited war, chiefly maritime in character, of prolonged duration, and leading to no decisive result.

From the standpoint of Blue it would appear advantageous for Crimson to be allied with Red. In this case Blue would be free to employ her greatly superior man-power in overrunning Crimson and holding that Dominion to offset such losses as Blue might suffer elsewhere. Crimson neutrality would be of little military advantage to Blue since the duration of such neutrality would always be a matter of doubt, and might be employed to protect Crimson during the period when the Dominion was weakest. In any case large Blue military forces would have to be retained in readiness to advance into crimson should that country enter the war on the side of Red. It appears to be almost certain that Crimson will not ally herself with Blue, unless in the highest improbable event that Red fails to respect neutrality declared by Crimson. Unless Crimson goes so far as to declare her independence of Red and to ally herself with Blue, it would appear to be advantageous not to accept such neutrality unless accompanied by guarantees. Among such guarantee Blue should demand and insist upon occupation, until the end of the war, but Blue military forces, of the ports of Halifax, Victoria, and St. John, New Brunswick, and the bridgeheads, in Crimson territory, in the vicinity of Sault Ste. Marie, the St. Clair and Detroit River, and of the Ontario Peninsula along the line of the Welland Canal.[3]

The Joint Board assumed that war would not happen between the two powers without some sort of preamble and build-up. This concentration of forces came with concerns on the part of the United States.

When it becomes apparent that war with Blue is possible, it may be expected that Red will begin secretly to increase her military, naval and air forces in her American possessions in Northwestern Atlantic waters, although such increase will be gradual at first. Among the first of these possessions to receive consideration will probably be Jamaica, Bermuda, and Trinidad. It is likely that the garrisons in these islands will be augmented by the recruitment of local forces.

While, during this period of strained relations, Red would unlikely to precipitate hostilities by the open movement of considerable land, sea, or air forces to North American possessions, Red light naval forces basing in Halifax will be increased. The land elements of the defense of that base will probably be provided by Crimson contingents, and while it is unlikely that Red will send Air Force combat units to Crimson at this time, Crimson may be expected to provide the base troops and facilities required for the reception with a view to beginning operations immediately on landing. Crimson may also be induced to expand her own air force.[4]

War Plan Red Assumptions

The Joint Board planners drew some parameters around War Plan Red in terms of who the war was going to be against and how the war would be waged. Red (Britain) was acknowledged to be a global empire. The planners assumed that no part of the British Empire would declare neutrality in a time of war. This meant that (from the Joint Board perspective) Crimson (Canada) would be drawn into the fight against the United States early on in the war. If Canada were to embrace a strategy of neutrality, War Plan Red would be thrown into utter chaos and may force the United States to violate Canada's neutrality.

The analysis done by the Joint Board of the military strengths did show some differences—but ultimately the two powers were considered evenly matched.

Canada was going to be the key in fighting a war with Britain. It had a massive border with the United States and represented the best location for Britain to springboard a war to damage the US. This had been the case in the War of 1812 as well, and those historic lessons were engrained in the thinking of this plan.

Given the global nature of the British Empire, it was assumed that the United States would not be caught off guard by the declaration of war. In preparing to fight, the bulk of the US fleet would be moved to the Atlantic prior to the initiation of hostilities.[5] The initiation of hostilities was defined as "M-Day" or Mobilization Day—the first day of the war.

Attempting to understand the enemy goals, the Joint Board planners assumed that Britain's war goals would be as follows:

> The war aim of Red in a war with Blue is conceived to be the definite elimination of Blue as an important economic and commercial rival in international trade. This objective is to be accomplished by the destruction of Blue merchant marine and foreign trade, and by acquisition of Blue overseas possessions, including Red control of the Panama Canal.[6]

The American Strategy in War Plan Red

The US approach to waging the war against Britain was critical to the planning. This "Concept of the War" defined how Britain was to be brought to heel in a prolonged conflict was a driving force in how the war would be waged.

> A war of long duration, involving the maximum effort of the armed forces and civil power of the United States, directed initially toward the isolation of Crimson from Red and the defeat of Red armed forces in North America and the Western North Atlantic, including the Caribbean Sea and West Indian waters, and finally toward the economic exhaustion of the Red United Kingdom.[7]

In other words, war would be waged around the world aiming not at blockading Britain but making it impossible for her to receive the food and other material that her island homeland would need—driving her to the negotiating table as the result of economic pressures.

The Overarching Roles of the United States Army and Navy

Both the US Army and Navy had broad roles that were assigned them under War Plan Red. First and foremost, they would have to protect the territories and interests of the United States. From an offensive responsibility, the Army and Navy were also have to fight the British forces in the Western North Atlantic, Caribbean, and West Indian waters. The goal was to deny Britain the use of these bases in the Western Hemisphere for waging war against the United States.

For the Army this would mean that occupation of Canada and other British possessions as necessary.

For the Navy, the role would not only be military, but one of maintaining communications for the Army with occupied possessions. The Navy also was also tasked with preventing any supply or reinforcement of Canada once the United States attacked her. The Navy was expected to "exercise control of the sea in the Western North Atlantic," to further strangle the Britain.[8] On top of this the Navy would have to protect American trade routes around the world from British response.

Theaters of Operations

The Joint Board envisioned a global war with Britain. Despite that grand vision, the US Army's primary theater of operation would be rather limited, centered on the Great Lakes and all other adjoining Canadian territory since this is primarily where the damage to British Empire.

The execution of the global war would fall to the US Navy. The Navy was designated to operate on a much broader scope of operations than their Army counterparts. Their primary theaters were defined as follows:

The Western North Atlantic
This theater was designated as the primary theater of the war, with all other theaters being deemed as secondary. This would include the Caribbean Sea, the West Indian Waters, the Gulf of Mexico and the St. Lawrence River as far west as Cornwell Inland.

The Asiatic Theater
This is defined as an area between the Meridians of one hundred and fifty (15) and one hundred (100), East Longitude, and between the parallels of zero (0) and forty (40, North Latitude.

The Hawaiian Theater
This theater was comprised of area included within the circumferences and the tangents connecting such circumferences of circles drawn with Midway Island, Honolulu, Hilo, and Johnston Island as centers, with radii of three hundred (300) nautical miles.

The Panama Canal Theater
This was centered on the Panama Canal Zone and the Republic of Panama. It was to include the coastal waters of the Caribbean and Pacific coasts for a distance of 200 nautical miles from the Republic.

The Alaskan Theater
This included the territory of Alaska and her outlying islands.

The Pacific Theater
This large theater of operations included the sea areas adjacent to the Pacific Coast of the United States, excluding those areas designated by other theaters.

The Naval Great Lakes Theater
This was going to include the water areas of the Great Lakes and the St. Lawrence River eastward to Cornwall Island (exclusive). This new theater of operations was to be commanded by the Naval Commandant of the Great Lake Coastal Frontier which would be designated on M-Day. The Naval Commandant would set up his headquarters in Detroit Michigan.[9]

The Forces of the British Empire—1935

War Plan Red relied, for the most part, on data that was several years old regarding the strength of the British military forces. Despite this, the planners anticipated, at the onset, facing a formidable enemy on the global battlefield.

The following is the size and scope of the British forces:

Table: The Armed Forces of the British Empire[10]

Forces	At Home	In Colonies	Total
Regular Army (excluding India) *	110,148	24,648	134,796
Colonial and Native Ind. Ops.		2,137	2,137
Territorial Army	138,011		138,011
Militia		2,140	2,140
Regular Army Reserves	90,906		90,906
Supplemental Reserve	14,061		14,061
Regular Army Reserve of Officers	13,983		13,983

| Totals | 367,109 | 28,925 | 396,034 |

* Includes 3,235 China in excess of normal Garrison. The Jamaica Detachment numbers 827; the Bermuda Detachment numbers 275. The British Army in India is included in Indian Establishment.

Australia
Permanent Force	1,811
Civilian Force	26,184
Total	47,995

India
Regular Army
Aden and elsewhere
Indian Army	166,495
Auxiliary Force	33,181
Territorial Force	20,000
Indian State Forces	36,056
Reservists	29,924
Total	347,243

New Zealand
Permanent Force	514
Territorial Force	20,375
Total	20,889

Union of South Africa
Permanent Force	1,072
Non-Permanent Force	8,381
Total	9,453

Canada
Permanent Force	3,533
Non-Permanent Force	52,105
Reserve of Officers	12,213
Reserves (estimated)	30,000
Total	97,851

Irish Free State
Regular Army	6,976
Reserve	10,000
Total	16,976

Aggregate of the British Empire Armies   936,441[11]

The British also maintained a so-called "Expeditionary Force" consisting for four infantry divisions, two cavalry brigades and a proportion of the corps, army and line communications troops of an approximate strength of 100,000 men capable of being mobilized in one week and designed for minor emergencies within the British Empire.[12]

Breakdown of Canadian Forces

__Canada was divided into eleven military districts, each designed to support a division and quota of auxiliary troops during a time of war. These were organized as follows:

Table: US Estimates of Canadian Force Distribution in 1935[13]

District Number	Area	Headquarters	Troops (as of February 1928 estimates)
1	Western Part of Ontario Peninsula between Lakes Huron and Erie.	London, Ontario	4,802
2	Toronto and vicinity; extends west almost to Fort Williams and Port Arthur; also comprises a small section of Ontario opposite of Buffalo NY.	Toronto, Ontario	9,226
3	That part of Ontario east of District No. 2	Kingston, Ontario	5,902
4	Montreal and vicinity	Montreal, Quebec	5,439
5	Quebec and vicinity and that part of the Province of Quebec east of District No. 4	Quebec, P. Q.	3,844
6	Province of Nova Scotia and Prince Edward Island	Halifax, Nova Scotia	3,890
7	Province of New Brunswick	St. John, N.B.	2,273
10	Province of Manitoba; part of Province of Ontario west of and including Port Arthur and Fort William	Winnipeg, Manitoba	4,876
11	Province of British Columbia; Yukon Territory	Vancouver, British Columbia	3,862
12	Province of Saskatchewan	Regina, Saskatchewan	4,220
13	Province of Alberta and Territory of Mackenzie	Calgary Alberta	3,841
	Total Peacetime Strength:		52,175

Table: *Royal Navy Fleet Strength and Assignment—1935*[14]

Class of Ships	Atlantic Fleet	Mediterranean Fleet	China Station	America and West Indies	East Indies	African Station	New Zealand	Australia	Canada	Home Waters and Reserve	Total
Battleships	4	8								4	16
Battle Cruisers	4										4
Cruisers	5	10	6	5	2	2	3	4		14	52
Destroyer Loaders	2	5	1					1		7	16
Destroyers	19	36	8					11	2	64	140
Minelayers	1										1
Minesweepers		9	2						4	18	33
Submarines		7	6					2		35	50
Aircraft Carriers	2	2	1							1	6

Table: US Estimated Royal Navy Personnel Strength—1935[15]

Branch	Officers	Enlisted	Totals:
REGULAR FORCES			
Royal Navy	7,535	81,029	88,564
Royal Marines	430	9,819	10,249
Royal Canadian Navy	76	450	526
Royal Australian Navy	497	4,764	5,261
New Zealand Division of the Royal Navy	66	905	971
South African Naval Service	15	121	136
Royal Air Force assigned to the Royal Navy	300	2,800	3,100
Civilian Crews of the Naval Auxiliaries	255	3,900	4,155
RESERVE			
Special Reserve of Engineer Offices	124		124
Emergency Officers	225		225
Royal Fleet Reserve		21,914	21,914
Royal Naval Reserve	1,679	7,855	9,534
Royal Naval Volunteer Reserve	420	3,616	4,036
Royal Navy Auxiliary Sick Berth Reserve		1,275	1,275
Australian Naval Reserve	815	8,452	9,267
Canadian Naval Reserve	102	931	1,033
New Zealand Naval Reserve	43	488	531
South African Naval Reserve	50	653	703
Totals	12,632	152,420	*161,594*

Table: Estimated Royal Air Force Strength—1935[16]
Number reflect squadrons of 10-13 aircraft each

Posting	Bombing	Fighter	Army Cooperation	Communication	Total
Home	13	12	5	1	31
Middle East	4		1		5
Iraq	4		1		5
India	2		4		6
Aden	1				1
Totals	24	12	11	1	48

Aircraft allocated for naval operations[17]

Home	18
Mediterranean	4
China Station	5
Total	27

British Reserve Air Force Squadrons[18]Special Reserve (Bombers) at Home 3
Auxiliary Air Force (Bombers) at Home 5
Total 8

Royal Canadian Air Power

The Royal Canadian Air Force in 1935, per US estimates, consisted of 68 officers, 307 airmen and a reserve of 67 officers and 1,390 airmen. This allows the Canadians to field four squadrons of aircraft. Due to the numerous lakes and rivers that occupy Canada, the government concentrated on the use of seaplanes. They maintain a school for seaplane pilots at Vancouver and at Camp Borden, sixty-miles north of Toronto. These schools have 30 officers, 250 enlisted men, and 100 student pilots at any given time.

The Canadian aerodromes for land aircraft were based at: St. Huberts and Chicoutimi, P.Q., including an airstrip tower at the former; Camp Borden, Toronto; Trenton, Hamilton, and London, Ontario; Brandon, Man.; High River, Alberta; and Vancouver, British Columbia.

Joint land and sea plane bases existed at: Fredericton, N.B.; Roberval, Quebec, Three Rivers, Grandmere [sic], Montreal and Lake Osisko, P.Q.; Timagami, North Bay, Sudbury, Ottawa, Remi, Birch Lake, Como, Sault Ste. Marie, Orient Bay, St. Frances, Sioux Lookout and Minaki, Ontario; Vidin, Man.; Yorkton, Regina, Moosejaw, and Saskatoon, Saskatchewan; and Letherbridge [sic], Alberta.[19]

Mobilization

After the declaration of war, the British Empire would be able to tap its vast resources around the globe to fight the United States. The Joint Board analysis of this manpower posted some issues in the event of a prolonged conflict with the United Kingdom:

> Of the white population of the Empire, 66,000,000, about 8,600,000 comprise her military manpower. Of the colored races it is estimated that not more than 2,000,000 will be utilized, thus making her total military manpower 10,600,000. Of this total, 400,000 will be needed for the naval forces, thus leaving available 10,200,000 for the Army and Air Force.[20]

The mobilization of these forces, however, would take time and would be a drain on the Regular forces in terms of training and equipping. The mobilization for both Britain and Canada—the primary field of combat at the start of the war, the mobilization effort was defined as follows:

Table: US Estimate of British and Canadian Mobilization Rates—1935[21]

Date. M + days	Empire Strength Except Canada	Divisions	Canadian Strength	Divisions	Total Strength	Total Divisions
15	537,928	27	60,000	11	597,928	38
30	617,699	30	126,796	11	744,495	41
60	686,899	31	161,698	11	848,597	42
90	727,747	31	167,095	11	894,842	42
120	739,776	31	167,095	11	906,871	42
150	757,701	31	171,057	11	928,758	42
180	1,279,733	44	237,119	11	1,516,852	55
210	1,514,527	44	304,365	11	1,918,992	55
240	1,774,384	48	351,869	11	2,126,253	59
270	2,040,284	54	424,585	11	2,464,869	65
300	2,307,891	60	498,408	11	2,806,299	71
330	2,581,004	66	572,739	13	3,153,743	79
360	2,859,208	72	649,676	14	3,508,884	86
390	3,141,620	78	728,625	16	3,870,245	94
420	3,434,207	84	809,705	17	4,243,912	101
450	3,732,035	90	893,383	19	4,625,418	109
480	4,334,439	96	893,383	19	5,227,822	115
510	4,658,815	103	893,383	19	5,552,198	122
540	4,974,867	109	893,383	19	5,863,250	128
570	5,306,365	115	893,383	19	6,199,748	134

Other colored War Plans always positioned the United States as having an advantage

in terms of manpower that it could mobilize during war ... not so with War Plan Red. In short, the true strength of the British Empire can be seen by the sheer number of troops that it could bring to muster over a prolonged conflict.

Available American Forces

The American Army at the outbreak of hostilities would have a Regular Army force of 102,700:

> ...officers, warrant officers, and enlisted men, including three infantry divisions, one cavalry division and the principal components of three additional infantry and two additional cavalry divisions. Air Corps units included are as follows: pursuit aviation, one group of three squadrons, bombardment aviation, one group but with airplanes for only two squadrons; attack aviation, one group of two squadrons; observation aviation,

one group and six squadrons. The National Guard in this area consists of approximately 175,000 officers, warrant officers and enlisted men, including eighteen infantry divisions, and the principal components of nine cavalry brigades. Air Corps units included consists of eighteen observation squadrons, each with three service airplanes.[22]

These estimates of starting forces presumed that there would be a diplomatic build-up to a conflict with Britain, allowing for the mobilization of some forces prior to the start of fighting.

The US also had Organized Reserves of 113,000 officers and 5,000 men. This allowed for assignment of personnel to twenty-seven Organized Reserve Infantry Divisions, six Organized Reserve cavalry divisions and one Regular Army and National Guard Division.

In the case of War Plan Red, the plan required the US Congress to pass a selective service law, affecting a draft, at the outbreak of hostilities. War Plan Red actually includes drafts of the legislation to help Congress speed up the process. Until that happened they anticipated a volunteer enlistment rate of 25,000 men per day. The draft would also provide an equal number per day as well. Within sixty days there would be three mobilized field armies (nine corps, including nine Regular Army and eighteen National Guard Infantry Divisions).

American forces distributed at overseas possessions were as follows:

Table: US Overseas Garrisons[23]

Location	Regular Army	National Guard	Philippine Scouts	Officers of Reserve Corps	Total
Panama Canal Department	8,800			350	9,150
Hawaiian Department	14,200	1,500		500	16,200
Philippine Department	4,800		6,500	400	11,300
US Air Force in China	950				950
Porto Rico [sic]	1,250	1,475			2,725
Alaska	275				275

The force of the US Navy, compared to the Royal Navy show relative equality, in tonnage if not in number by class of vessel. As of July of 1929 the forces compared as follows:

Table: US Naval Strength Compared to the Royal Navy—1935[24]

Class of Ship	Royal Navy	US Navy
BB Battleships	16	18
CC Battle Cruisers	4	0
CL First Line Cruisers	62	18
CV Aircraft Carriers	6	3
CM (Mine layers, First Line)	1	0
DL and DD (Destroyers and Destroyer Loaders)	175	221
SF and SS (Submarines and Fleet Submarines)	68	57
DM (Light Mine Layers)	0	10

The Joint Board also outlined a detailed plan as to what was going to be required from Congress in order to support a war with the United Kingdom—beyond implementing a draft. This included massive expenditures in the US Navy for the creation of numerous ships to both replace losses and to hopefully surpass the numbers that Great Britain would be producing. Per the analysis, the US had an advantage in terms of the raw materials needed for such construction were within the borders of the nation and she had ample production facilities. Britain would have to import the iron and other materials needed to produce enough ships to keep pace with the US.

What was also needed by the United States was potential allies. The analysis provided in War Plan Red identified countries in the Western Hemisphere that the US government should begin considering talks with in regards to access to ports and other assistance.

Inclined toward the United States
• Brazil
• Peru

Inclined towards Britain
• Argentina
• Chile
• Uruguay

Nations that have no preference to either of the combatants
• Venezuela
• Columbia
• Bolivia
• Ecuador
• Paraguay

The Joint Board strongly recommended entering into diplomatic talks with these countries because of the long-term impact on the war effort. For example:

The probable attitude of all of the above countries, especially the "A B C" Nations, is of the utmost concern to Blue. Of these latter it is estimated that Argentina, while initially declaring neutrality, will assume an attitude of hostility toward Blue, and, on account of the predominant financial and economic position of Red in that Republic, will probably be selected by Red as the base for propaganda in South America. Chile, while including toward Red, will probably be less hostile toward Blue, and on account of the great profits to be expected from her nitrate trade, will probably assume an attitude of strict neutrality. Brazil, on account of its economic ties, will probably incline toward Blue, but may be expected initially to declare neutrality. On the whole, by reason of mutual jealousy between these nations, and with their fear of each other, they may be expected to remain neutral, at least in the early stages of the war.[25]

War Plan Red—The Plan of Attack

The Joint Board looked at several different options when it came to fighting the British Empire. These options were divided by the Army and the Navy plans. The Army's options were broken down as follows:

Army Plan I

> To initiate an immediate general offensive against Crimson with a view to penetrating vial Crimson areas, preventing mobilization of Crimson forces, and disruption Crimson life.[26]

This plan had numerous advantages. It gave the initiative in the war to the United States. Canada could conceivably be crushed before Britain could reinforce her. Early air operations by Britain against the continental US required the use of Canadian aerodromes. If they were lost when Canada fell, the US would be less vulnerable to aerial attack. Finally it removed the risk of invasion by British forces from Canada.

There were disadvantages to Plan I as well. It diverted a great deal of American resources on an objective that didn't necessarily compel the British to negotiate peace. It committed the best American forces into battle at the start of the war which might leave them weakened for later operations. Plan I did not allow for strengthening other US interests overseas, leaving them somewhat vulnerable to British reprisals.

Army Plan II

> To initiate promptly operations to separate Crimson from Red through the destruction of enemy forces in Crimson and the seizure of vital Crimson areas.[27]

Plan II called for:

... a joint overseas expedition against Halifax, which will be dispatched in case the situation at the outbreak of the war indicates the practicability of the operation, otherwise Halifax will be neutralized by air operations.[28]

Plan II also called for an Army advance into the Montreal–Quebec area. At the same time measures would be taken to secure sensitive points of the Great Lakes waterways. These provided for limited incursions into Canadian territory where necessary, such as the narrow area of the Detroit River where shipping might find itself under enemy artillery fire. Also the Army would mount an expeditionary force to cut the Canadian railroad communications and traffic at Winnipeg.

Plan II had its share of advantages. It still allowed the US to hold the initiative. The initial advance on the Great Lakes region would protect vital US interests and cities. At the same time it would hit Canada where it was weakest. The attack on Halifax would provide the US with an ice-free port and would cut shipments of food to the home islands, hitting their economy hard. The operations outlined did not require a strong commitment—*per se*, of the Navy, allowing them greater flexibility elsewhere.

The downside to Plan II is that the operations had to be done quickly at the outset of the war if they were to be successful. If not, the British would be reinforced in Halifax forcing a landing on hostile shores with greater losses.

Army Plan III

This was essentially plan II with no operations contemplated against the port of Halifax. It had all of the advantages of Plan II except that by avoiding the risks of Halifax you also lost the benefits of taking Halifax out of the war. If the Royal Navy still controlled the seas, she could reinforce Canada via Halifax and still ship vital foodstuffs and material back to Britain.

Plan IV

This variant of War Plan Red called for a dramatic change of strategy:

To assume the strategic defensive against the enemy along the Crimson frontier, and to concentrate the Army effort initially in cooperating with the Navy in driving Red from the Caribbean Area.[29]

The advantages of Plan IV was that it ensured a quick and complete control of the Caribbean. It was also deemed the best way to ensure the defense of the Panama Canal. Finally if the war broke out in winter, it allowed operations to take place with relative ease compared to facing the harshness of a Canadian winter which would favor the defenders.

The weaknesses of Plan IV was that it allowed Britain to reinforce Canada and potentially launch a large-scale incursion into the United States. This was a highly probable course of action for Canada/Britain in this scenario. Plan IV did not allow a crippling blow against Britain that would force her to negotiate a peace. Finally, Plan

IV did not take advantage of America's immense manpower since operations in the Caribbean did not require large land forces.

Army Plan V. The nature of Plan V was that it was a plan that had to be proposed but had little chance of being adopted:

> To assume the strategic defensive on all fronts. This plan contemplates deploying such troops as may be necessary for covering missions; reinforcing overseas garrisons; and building up in the meantime forces suitable to a major offensive. This is in reality the taking up of a position of readiness pending the building up of strong forces.[30]

Plan V's advantages was that that did provide for the immediate protection of the frontier and the border with Canada. It allowed the orderly organization of training of American forces and allowed for the war production to catch up to the army mobilization. When the time came for the Army to go on the offensive, it would do so with overwhelming strength and deliver a concentrated blow against the enemy.

The disadvantages of Plan V was that it surrendered initiative to the British. Canada would be allowed to strengthen and reinforce for a potential assault onto American soil—forcing the US to respond with defensive and siege resistance. This strategy applied no pressure on Britain or Canada. Plan V also ensured a very long and protracted war. Worse yet, this strategy would not play well with the American people or Congress who would be pressured by British operations for the US to take action.

The Navy's plans for war against Britain consisted of three options. These were broken down as follows:

Navy Plan I
This plan called for the US Navy:

> To adopt the strategic offensive with the Blue Main Fleet and seek out and engage the Red Main Fleet decisively while conducting secondary operations in other theaters for the purpose of weakening Red's economic power.

The Navy's Plan I did allow for the US to seize the initiative in the war and would allow for a quick resolution to the war. If the plan was successful, it would provide the United State with unfretted control of the sea.

The disadvantages to the Navy's Plan I was that it was risky. The US Main Fleet would engage the Royal Navy in a "winner takes all" battle, one where the conditions might not favor the US Navy. If the US lost this epic naval battle, the Royal Navy would have complete control of the seas and they could control international trade globally. While bold and daring, the plan allowed for fate to control the winner of the war.

Navy Plan II
This proposed option under War Plan Red called:

To establish the Blue Main Fleet in the Western North Atlantic in sufficient strength to dominate sea communications between Red and Crimson, while conducting secondary operations in other theaters for the purpose of weakening Red economic ability to support the war and of dispersing her naval power. The above operations to be undertaken with a view of toward attacking in force the Red Fleet or detachments thereof whenever a favorable opportunity arises.[31]

The advantages to Navy Plan II is that it allowed the US fleet to operate close to its home bases on the East Coast. It preserved the ultimate integrity of the US fleet while awaiting for favorable opportunities to strike and potentially cripple British fleets and task forces. This positioning would make Britain adopt a resource intensive convoy system to move troops and vital food supplies between her vast empire and the home islands. In response to this strategy, the Royal Navy would be compelled to concentrate their forces to fight the US Navy—thus weakening their naval forces around the globe. This approach would allow for the gradual attrition of the Royal Navy rather than rely on a massive one-shot battle to determine the winner of the war.

The most significant downside to Navy Plan II is that it prolongs the war and delays the ultimate decision as to who controls the seas.

Navy Plan III
This proposed operation provided the US Navy:

To assume the strategic defensive with the major units of the U.S. Fleet, seizing any favorable opportunity that may arise to defeat Red Naval Force in detail and to exert the main naval effort against Red overseas commerce and seaborne trade.[32]

The plan did allow the US Navy to retain its resources. It would allow the Navy to pressure the British Empire by threatening their vital sea communications and would, over time, disrupt British international trade.

The weaknesses of Navy Plan III was that it gave initiative to the British. It also allowed the British to whittle away at the US Navy, defeating it in detail. Also Plan III provided for no coordination efforts at all with the Army. Over time it would erode diplomatic support of the United States. Even the Joint Board planners concede that this strategy had uniformly failed in the past.

As such, given the options and risks, the Joint Board opted for Plans II for both the Army and the Navy. They expanded on these with specifics. Not only was Halifax to be seized, but the US Navy and US Marine Corps were tasked specifically with seizing, if practicable, Jamaica, the Bahamas and Bermuda at the earliest possible dates. Once the Navy and Marines secured these islands they were to coordinate with the Army to provide garrison forces there. From there the US Navy would further strike out at Trinidad, St. Lucia and other British holdings in the West Indian and Central America.[33]

The Navy was also tasked with securing the US trade routes including the Coastwise Sea Lanes of the Intercoastal Trade Routes via the Panama Canal and of the Seaborne Trade lanes between the Pacific Coast and Hawaii. The Navy would also provide protection for shipping on both coasts of South America.[34] Also the Navy was under orders to wage war against the commercial shipping interests of Britain—aiming to cripple her economically.

The Army would move to secure the Great Lakes. Special operations were to be mounted to secure strategic objective early on in the invasion. These included:

- The St. Mary River Canal
- Sault Ste. Marine Canal
- Securing passage of the St. Clair and Detroit Rivers (both of these operations would call for limited incursions into Canada)
- The Niagara River
- The Welland Canal.[35]

Likewise the Army was tasked to coordinate with the Navy to reinforce the Hawaiian Islands, the Philippines, and Alaska. Where these troops were to be drawn from is not defined in War Plan Red. Given that Britain once exerted nominal control over the Hawaiian (Sandwich) Islands and were intimately familiar with their terrain, it would be a tempting target. Noting that reinforcement was to take place, at a time when the Navy would be concentrating in the North Atlantic would be difficult if not impossible … potentially leaving these islands woefully exposed.

Perhaps the most disturbing element of the plan was a lesson learned on the battlefields of the Great War just over a decade earlier:

> To make all necessary preparations for the use of Chemical Warfare from the outbreak of the war. The use of chemical warfare, including the use of toxic agents, from the inception of hostilities is authorized, subject to such restrictions or prohibitions as may be contained in a duly ratified international convention or conventions which at that time may be binding upon the United States and the enemy state or states.[36]

This meant that the United States was willing, from the onset of the war, to utilize the most heinous weapons in its arsenals to ensure victory.

Probable British Responses to War Plan Red

US Joint Board members assumed that Britain would quickly respond to an American declaration of war. Their estimated response to the US attacking Canada and poising itself for strikes against other British holdings was thought to be one or more of the following options:

(1) While assuming a passive defense on the Canadian border utilizing Canadian troops—Britain would initiate an offensive naval operation directed at the United States. The anticipated target was thought to be the US overseas trade and outlying possessions. This could include operations against the US naval base in

the Philippines or the Hawaiian Islands.

(2) Provide a strong defense in Canada by reinforcing Canada with other forces from within the British Empire—most likely the home islands given their relative proximity and the concentration of troops and equipment there. This would allow Britain to launch offensive operations against the US Navy, Merchant Marine and outlying possessions. Moreover, this option called for a sustained air attack on strategic US centers and cities, both carrier launched and from Canada-proper.

(3) Initiate a strong offensive operation to be launched from a reinforced Canadian Army, driving across the US border. This operation would require complete control of the seas and would be aimed at the crippling of the US industrial and financial centers. It is estimated that this option would require the full force and weight of the British Empire to be successful, thus would require the longest period of time to prepare and stage.[37]

While the third scenario (above) represented the worse-case-option that the United States might face, it was believed that ultimately the British would take a combination of the three options in their war plan.

Under the auspices of War Plan Red, the Royal Navy would move to seize control of all the sea lanes that the US had possession of. They would force passage to Canada so that it could be reinforced. US merchant shipping would fall prey to the Royal Navy in this response.

The Royal Air Force would be poised in Canada to attack government, industrial, transportation (railroad hubs), and financial centers.

The British Army would:

… use the forces in Crimson at and shortly after the outbreak of the war in the defense of the Montreal-Quebec line, Halifax, vital sections of the Great Lakes—St. Lawrence waterway system, critical points of transcontinental railways, and Vancouver.[38]

Then the Army would move to:

… build up strong forces in Crimson as rapidly as practicable and when the situation is favorable to launch a major offensive in the form of an invasion of Blue, directed toward vital objectives.

The first of these was to secure the Great Lakes for the potential use by the Navy and to deny the US the use of industries that relied on these waterways for supplies or industrial power. Securing the power production facilities at Niagara Falls was also high on the list of potential targets.

The Army would then;

… cooperate with the Red Navy and Red Air Force at an early date in the capture of the Philippine Islands, Guam and Samoa, and when forces become available, in the capture of the Hawaiian Islands and the Panama Canal.

They would also then move in to reinforce their garrisons in Jamaica, Trinidad, Bermuda, St. Lucia, Singapore and Hong Kong. This would be done to negate any offensive moves by the US against these holdings.[39] Tapping forces in India and Australia, Britain would have troops close to the Philippines and even Hawaii even before the United States could reinforce these. The British war would most likely consume the American Pacific holdings early in the conflict.

Summary Evaluation of the War Plan

The Joint Board did its own analysis of War Plan Red:

> Blue, initially, will have on the North American continent a preponderance of available military forces. Red had within her Empire a much stronger trained military force which it will probably seek to establish permanently on Crimson territory. At the outbreak of the war, Blue will be unprepared and unable to place in the field at once any but hastily organized forces, with many skeletonized units. Blue also will be lacking in the defensive strength on both coastal and land frontiers. However, at this time Crimson will be far worse off and practically will be unaided by Red. While Blue is perfecting offensive and defensive forces, Red will be coming to the assistance of Crimson. Crimson is the only Red territory so situated as to afford Blue an opportunity to strike a vital blow on land.
>
> The Red Navy is somewhat more powerful than the Blue but not enough so as to prevent Blue engaging in offensive operations, particularly if this superiority be partially neutralized by so staging the operations that Red is at a disadvantage with respect to bases. This is difficult to accomplish due to the number and distribution of Red bases. On the other hand, the extend of Red bases and sea-lanes constitute a Red element of weakness in the resulting defensive requirement.[40]

Matching up the United States against Great Britain is an interesting concept to contemplate because of all of the potential variables. On naval power, Britain possessed a slight edge on the US Navy. In terms of manpower, the sheer size and bulk of the British Empire allowed her to bring massive numbers of men potentially to bear.

At the same time, the great asset of the Empire was a burden. It forced the Royal Navy to dedicate resources around the globe to protect shipping lanes and strategic ports. The vastness of the Empire reduced the ability of the British to concentrate their forces.

At the same time a British opponent would have assets for moving troops against isolated commands such as the Philippines and Hawaii. The fact that War Plan Red glosses over the defense of these islands with vague references to reinforcement, means they would be equivalent to dangling fresh meat in front of a hungry wolf.

The Joint Board, in reviewing the strategy for fighting Britain, realized that the home islands were vulnerable. The British people required food, strategic metals, etc., to be brought to the islands. This meant that the sea lanes had to be kept open or the islands would slowly be starved. The members of the Joint Board realized this. Rather than attempt to encircle and blockade the home islands, they envisioned a fight where British resources would be cut off all around the globe—starting in the North Atlantic. One did not have to blockade the home islands—a nation merely had to ensure that supplies could not reach the islands.

War Plan Red also is one of the handful of plans that came out of the Joint Board that outlined requirements on two key fronts—diplomatic and legislative. It provided clear and concise analysis as to the nations in the hemisphere and why America needed to keep them close at hand and on friendly terms. At the same time the plan detailed out what was needed from Congress in terms of budgets, types of expenditures, etc. Given the naval nature of the war and the long lead times to build ships, this kind of thinking was essential to the success of the plan and represents a new level of thinking on the part of the Joint Board. Going to war was not just something undertaken by the Army and Navy—it required the entire and full weight of the US Government in order to be successful.

Perhaps the most disturbing element of War Plan Red is that it was contemplated at all. With Hitler on the rise in Germany and openly defiant of treaty, the United States was maintaining a strange focus on Britain as a potential foe in a coming war. There was a prevalent thinking in the military at the time that Germany was not a threat to US interests. If he spawned a conflict, it would be an European war. The officers in command, having come out of the Great War, most likely envisioned a similar situation where American reaped the benefits of the war by selling arms and only had to send troops into battle when their interests became threatened.

This highlights the difference between military planning and the course of state in the US. There is not a shred of evidence that a copy of War Plan Red ever found its way to the White House or was presented to the President. US isolationism was a dominant political force in 1935. The views of the United States towards Britain have always been skewed, going back to the inception of the US as nation during the rebellion of the colonies. In 1935 the motivations for a conflict as presented in War Plan Red are the self-serving economic interests of the US, while ignoring a seemingly greater threat in Germany. With a sense of historical irony, the military, apparently on its own, was preparing for war against the one nation that would prove to be her greatest ally and the White House was seemingly oblivious to these efforts.

The US thinking in regards to the use of chemical weapons at the onset of the war is also highly disturbing. This is the only colored War Plan that specifically mentions the use of these weapons to achieve victory. America had introduced international treaties to restrict the use of such weapons. Why then was it considered so acceptable to utilize these weapons against Canada at the start of the war? Perhaps the overwhelming might of the British Empire was such that the US assumed that the use of such weapons was necessary to achieve victory. Or perhaps it was deemed necessary to achieve a quick decisive victory. It is conceivable that the US, as the victor, could justify this use of such weapons.

Epilogue

Until the late 1930s the Joint Board continued to construct plans. They never did complete plans for each of the countries that they had originally outlined; world events superseded that effort. The world was changing, and military planning had to change with it. As the storm clouds of war began to form and cast shadows on the planet, there was an evolution in the Joint Board in regards to military planning.

What began to emerge in the mid–1930s was the concept of wars against alliances of nations. This was not a new concept but it was clear that the Joint Board in its early years lacked the expertise to craft such plans. The first of these was the 1933 plan for Red–Orange. While hinted at in War Plan Red, there was a prevalent belief that the United States might be facing a two-ocean war at some point—in this case against an allied British and Japanese Empires. War Plan Red–Orange explored in-depth the logistical challenges of fighting a two-ocean war. It went so far as to say that alone, the United States would be drawn into a protracted fight which could go on for years and that victory would ultimately lie with the massive industrial production capacity of the United States and her burgeoning sea of manpower. In some respects, Red–Orange laid the foundation for how the United States might have to deal with World War II.

The next evolution of plans came in the late 1930s as to what is referred to as the Rainbow War Plans. These four sets of War Plans were test-cases for what was unfolding in Europe with the rise of Nazi Germany and Fascist Italy. The plans assumed that the enemies facing America were a united alliance of Germany, Japan, and Italy. These nations would, acting in concert, violate the letter or spirit of the Monroe Doctrine—forcing the United States to fight.

The basic set ups for the Joint Rainbow Plans (as they are also referred to) were as follows:

(1) The United States opposed to Germany, Italy, and Japan with the objective of the armed effort essentially confined to the Western Hemisphere north of 10 degrees South Latitude.

(2) The United States opposed to Germany, Italy, and Japan with the objective of armed effort in the Western Hemisphere restricted to that part of the Western Hemisphere north of 10 degrees South Latitude but also extended to protect vital United States interests in the Western Pacific.

(3) The United States opposed to Germany, Italy, and Japan with the objective of the armed forces directed toward the entire Western Hemisphere.

(4) The United States, England, and France opposed to Germany, Italy, and Japan, with the United States providing maximum participation, in particular as regards armies in Europe.

(5) The United States, England, and France opposed to Germany, Italy, and Japan, with the United States NOT providing maximum participation in continental Europe, but maintaining the Monroe Doctrine and carrying out allied Democratic Power tasks in the Pacific.[1]

These five set-up parameters eventually drove the creation of the Rainbow War Plans. This set of plans also assumed that the United States had friendly relations with the Democratic nations but that they would either be neutral or in a position to not provide support to the US. Rainbow War Plans one-through-four provided the foundation for the US to contemplate the coming war. The plans are broken down as follows:

Rainbow One

Prevent the violation of the letter or spirit of the Monroe Doctrine by protecting that territory of the Western Hemisphere from which the vital interest of the United States can be threatened, while protecting the United States, its possessions, and its sea borne trade. This territory is assumed to be any part of the Western Hemisphere north of the approximate latitude ten degrees south. This plan will not provide for projecting U.S. Army Forces farther south than the approximate latitude ten degrees south or outside of the Western Hemisphere.[2]

Rainbow Two

Carry out the missions of the Joint Army and Navy Basic War Plan—RAINBOW, No. 1. Protect the United States' vital interest in the Western Pacific by securing control in the Western Pacific, as rapidly as possible consisted with carrying out the missions....[3]

Rainbow Three

Prevent the violation of the letter or spirit of the Monroe Doctrine by protecting all territory and Governments of the Western Hemisphere against external aggression while protecting the United States, its possessions, and its sea borne trade. This plan will provide for projecting such U. S. Army Forces as necessary to the southern part of the South American continent or to the Eastern Atlantic.[4]

Rainbow Four

> Project the armed forces of the United States to the Eastern Atlantic and to either or both
> of the African or European Continents, as rapidly as possible consistent with carryout out
> the missions in 3 a. above (*Author's Notes: Rainbow One*) in order to effect the decisive
> defeat of Germany, or Italy, or both. This plan will assume concerted action between the
> United States, Great Britain, and France.[5]

It is clear that War Plan Rainbow Four eerily mirrors the US plans for the defeat for
Germany—and was drafted in 1939 in September, as Poland was crumbling under the
Nazi war machine.

There are some who discredit the value of exploring the colored war plans, pointing
out that none of them were ever fully implemented. They claim that these offer little
more than a glimpse into the staff work with the Army and Navy, and little more. But
in reality the plans show a gradual level of sophistication in US military planning and
strategy—as evidenced by the Rainbow War Plans. Gone was the era where the United
States rushed into wars with no plans, these colored plans marked an evolution in
military thinking.

And the argument that the colored war plans never were used simply does not hold
water. The best example of this was War Plan Orange which was the United States' plan
for fighting a war with the Japanese. Orange was utilized directly or indirectly to create
the US strategy for fighting against Japan in the Pacific in World War II. This plan, more
than any other, was drafted and re-drafted time after time, evolving it carefully and
slowly. War Plan Orange contemplated a world where Japan would be at war with the
United States—pressured into it by economic and political mismanagement. Various
iterations of the plan foresaw Japan striking devastating blows against the United
States, including an attack on the Pacific Fleet in Pearl Harbor. Orange offered eerie
premonitions about the fall of the Philippines and other islands of strategic interest.
War Plan Orange morphed over the years, playing with different strategies to deal with
a surging Empire of Japan.

Some of the plans, specifically the Rainbow Plans and early versions of War Plan
Black, themselves were teaching aides at the Navy and Army War Colleges too,
providing scenarios for fighting wars that might never happen. Several generations of
officers cut their proverbial teeth on the colored war plans. Their influence, with not
directly tangible, surely played some role in the many wars that followed.

Many plans however were deeply buried and kept secret, only to be dusted off if the
war erupted with a power. They represent a slice of military thinking at that time and
offer military perceptions of possible enemies.

In 1941, direction went out from the Joint Board that the old copies of the colored
War Plans were to be destroyed. In an era where America was joining or forming
alliances to fight a new war, it would be embarrassing if these old plans were to surface
showing the US planned to fight its now-allies. Many copies were completely purged
from existence. Fortunately some survived, either in whole or in parts. The beauty of

bureaucracies is that many times rules are not followed. Despite checklists demanding the destruction, some copies simply were tucked away in binders or in filing cabinets with their owners signing off that they had been burned.

Starting in 1974 large lots of military paperwork began to be declassified in bulk, including some of the earlier editions of the colored war plans. Many of these were filed away in boxes, barely catalogued, in the US National Archives. Some copies were retained by other institutions such as the Naval War College. Others would be declassified as materials moved through the slow methodical process at the National Archives. A few have been posted in whole or part on the internet.

In 2005 *The Washington Post* ran an article on War Plan Red and the proposed attack against Canada as part of that plan. It was one of the most public announcements ever regarding the colored war plans. *The Post* compared the plan to America's contemporary war with Iraq at the time. The War Plans had been declassified earlier (in some instances) but had been overlooked except for a handful of researchers and historians. *The Washington Post* article drew attention, with only vague context to the war in Iraq, to plans that were not described in terms of their true use and context. Members of the Canadian government were indignant and infuriated at the concept that their friendly neighbor to the south had been planning to wage war against them ... until it was revealed that Canada, in 1921, had drafted its own war plan for attacking the United States. The minor diplomatic rift was quickly mended.

Since that time only a few authors have dared to attempt to dust off the war plans for historical study. Steven T. Ross of the US Naval War College authored several books on how the planning process was implemented. Edward S. Miller wrote a groundbreaking book *War Plan Orange*, which covers every bit of material related to the creating and evolution of the plan to fight Japan. Avalanche Press, a game company in the United States, produced several naval war games attempting to simulate various colored War Plans—though their source material is never fully devised. D. M. Giangreco wrote *Hell to Pay*, which outlined Operation Downfall for the planned invasion of Japan. While not a colored war plan, it brought attention to the potential of such plans for historians.

The interest in these plans has slowly grown over time. There are destined to be authors that craft books that delve into the nuances and variations of these plans over time.

Endnotes

Chapter One

1 Stucky, Scott Joint Operations in the Civil War. Autumn/Winter 1994-95 issue of *Joint Force Quarterly*. http://usacac.army.mil/cac2/call/docs/10-63/ch_1.asp

2 Ross, Steven T. American War Plans 1890–1939 (Portland Oregon: Frank Cass, 2002) pp. 7-8.

3 *Ibid.*, pp. 8-10.

4 Chambers II, John Whiteclay. The Oxford Companion to American Military History (New York: Oxford University Press, 199) p. 166.

5 *Ibid.*, pp. 166-167.

6 Joint Board History Overview, US National Archives, Records Group 225, Entry NM-43.

7 *Ibid.*

8 Memo, Army War College, to Secretary of the Joint Board, 10 June 1904, Brigadier General Tasker Bliss (author) US National Archives, Records Group 225, Entry NM-43, pp. 1-2.

9 *Ibid.*, pp. 2-4.

10 *Ibid.*

11 *Ibid.*, pp. 3-6.

12 *Ibid.*, pp. 8-12.

13 *Ibid.*, pp. 12-15.

14 *Ibid.*, pp. 14-16.

15 *Ibid.*, pp. 12-17.

16 *Ibid.*, pp. 18-19.

17 *Ibid.*, pp. 19-21.

18 War Plan Coding, US National Archives, Record Group 165.

19 Louis Morton, Strategy and Command: The First Two Years (Washington: Department of the Army, 1962), p. 22.

20 Joint Board History Overview, US National Archives, Records Group 225, Entry NM-43.

21 War Planning Board History, US National Archives, Records Group 225.

22   Global Security—Rainbow War Plans http://www.globalsecurity.org/military/ops/war-plan-rainbow.htm

23   Joint Board History Overview, US National Archives, Records Group 225, Entry NM-43.

24   War Plan Indigo, US National Archives, Record Group 165.

Chapter Two

1   War has broken out with Great Britain, US National Archives, Records Group 165.

2   *Ibid.*, p. 1.

3   Crimson—Strategic Analysis Chief of Staff Memo 1904, US National Archives, Records Group 270, p. 1.

4   War has broken out with Great Britain, US National Archives, Records Group 165, p. 1.

5   *Ibid.*

6   *Ibid.*, pp. 1-2

7   *Ibid.*, p. 2.

8   *Ibid.*

9   *Ibid.*

10   *Ibid.*

11   *Ibid.*, p. 3.

12   *Ibid.*

13   Memorandum—Joint Board, Raid Details, Canada. 3 February 1905, US National Archives, Records Group 225, NM-43.

14   War has broken out with Great Britain, US National Archives, Records Group 165, p. 3.

15   *Ibid.*, p. 8.

16   *Ibid.*, p. 3.

17   *Ibid.*, p. 8.

18   *Ibid.*

19   *Ibid.*, p. 3.

20   *Ibid.*, p. 4.

21   *Ibid.*

22   *Ibid.*

23   *Ibid.*

24   *Ibid.*

25   *Ibid.*, p. 5.

26   *Ibid.*

27   *Ibid.*

28   *Ibid.*

29   *Ibid.*

30 *Ibid.*, pp. 5-6.

31 *Ibid.*, pp. 6-7. Not the draft for the vessels was a blank on the original plans that was not filled in.

32 *Ibid.*, p. 6

33 *Ibid.*, p. 7

34 *Ibid.*

35 *Ibid.*

36 *Ibid.*, p. 14.

37 Expeditionary Force, US National Archives, Canadian Operation, Records Group 165, p. 36.

38 *Ibid.*, pp. 35-36.

39 Memorandum—Joint Board, Raid Details, Canada. 3 February 1905, US National Archives, Records Group 225, NM-43.

40 Expeditionary Force, US National Archives, Canadian Operation, Records Group 165, pp. 36-40.

41 *Ibid.*, p. 45

42 *Ibid.*, p. 60.

43 *Ibid.*, p. 53.

44 *Ibid.*, pp. 40-59.

Chapter Three

1 War Plan Green—Purpose of Plan (Draft) May 1917, US National Archives, Records Group 225, NM-43.

2 Strategical Problem—War with Mexico, 1919, US National Archives, Records Group 225, NM-43, p. 1.

3 *Ibid.*, pp. 1-2.

4 War Plan Green—Basis of Plan, US National Archives, Records Group 225, NM-43, p. 1.

5 War Plan Green—General Assumption, US National Archives, Records Group 225, NM-43, p. 1.

6 War Plan Green—Special Situations Assumed, US National Archives, Records Group 225, NM-43, p. 2.

7 *Ibid.*, p. 2.

8 *Ibid.*

9 War Plan Green—Missions, US National Archives, Records Group 225, NM-43, p. 3.

10 Memo from the Joint Board—Revision of Joint Army and Navy Basic War Plan Green, To the Secretary of War from General Marlin Craig, 1930 Revision, US National Archives, Records Group 225, NM-43, p. 1.

11 War Plan Green—Task Assignments, US National Archives, Records Group 225, NM-43, p. 3.

12 War Plan Green—PLAN NO. 1, US National Archives, Records Group 225, NM-43, pp. 5-6.

13 War Plan Green—THEATERS OF OPERTIONS, COMMAND AND COOPERATION, US National Archives, Records Group 225, NM-43, p. 10.

14 War Plan Green—Missions, US National Archives, Records Group 225, NM-43, p. 3.

15 War Plan Green—Task Assignments, US National Archives, Records Group 225, NM-43, p. 4.

16 War Plan Green—PLAN NO. 1, US National Archives, Records Group 225, NM-43, pp. 7-8.

17 War Plan Green—ARMY FORCES, US National Archives, Records Group 225, NM-43, p. 7.

18 War Plan Green—TIME ORIGINS FOR EXECUTION OF THE PLANS, US National Archives, Records Group 225, NM-43, pp. 8-9.

19 War Plan Green—NAVAL FORCES, US National Archives, Records Group 225, NM-43, p. 8.

20 Forces necessary for the seizure and occupation for a period of two weeks of the Mexican Oil Region and the port of Vera Cruz. 29 July 1919, US National Archives, Records Group 225, NM-43, pp. 1-2.

21 Suggested Plan for the Landing and Occupation of Mazatlan, 1905 , US National Archives, Records Group 165, pp. 1-4.

22 War Plan Green—THEATERS OF OPERATIONS, COMMAND AND COOPERATION, US National Archives, Records Group 225, NM-43, p. 9.

23 *Ibid.*

24 *Ibid.*, p. 10.

25 *Ibid.*

26 War Plan Green—PASSAGE OF COMMAND, US National Archives, Records Group 225, NM-43, p.11.

27 War Plan Green—Missions, US National Archives, Records Group 225, NM-43, p. 3.

28 *Ibid.*

29 *Ibid.*

30 War Plan Green Plan #2 Assessment, US National Archives, Records Group 165, p. 1.

31 War Plan Green—Task Assignments, US National Archives, Records Group 225, NM-43, p. 5.

32 *Ibid.*

33 Army Strategical Plan Green, Memorandum of Information, US National Archives, Records Group 165, p. 1.

34 War Plan Green—Time Origins for the Execution of the Plans, US National Archives, Records Group 225, NM-43, p. 8.

35 War Plan Green—Task Assignments, US National Archives, Records Group 225, NM-43, p. 5.

36 *Ibid.*

37 Memorandum for the Chief of Staff—Current Estimate of the Situation Monograph—Green Plan #2. US National Archives, Records Group 165, p. 1.

38 War Plan Green—Concentration of Forces, US National Archives, Records Group 165, pp. 3-4.

39 Memorandum for the Chief of Staff, A Mexican War Plan, P.C. March, 14 July 1919. US National Archives, Records Group 225, NM-43, pp. 2-3.

40 Ibid., pp. 3-4.

41 War Plan Green—FORCES, US National Archives, Records Group 225, NM-43, p. 7.

42 *Ibid.*

43 War Plan Green—TIME ORIGINS FOR THE EXECUTION OF THE PLANS, US National Archives, Records Group 225, NM-43, p. 8.

44 Memorandum—War Plan Green #2, Adjutant General, 6 April 1929, US National Archives, Records Group 165, p. 1.

45 Code Radiogram—To War Department From Fort Sam Houston CO, 20 April 1929, US National Archives, Records Group 165, p. 1.

46 War Plan Green—THEATERS OF OPERTIONS, COMMAND AND COOPERATION, US National Archives, Records Group 225, NM-43, p. 9.

47 *Ibid.*, p. 10.

48 *Ibid.*, p. 11.

49 *Ibid.*

50 Joint Army and Navy Estimates of Conditions Governing the Preparation of Joint Army and Navy Basic War Plan—Green No. 3. US National Archives, Records Group 225, NM-43, p. 1.

51 *Ibid.*, p. 2.

52 War Plan Green—TASK ASSIGNMENTS, US National Archives, Records Group 225, NM-43, p. 4.

53 War Plan Green—Missions, US National Archives, Records Group 225, NM-43, p. 2.

54 Joint Army and Navy Estimates of Conditions Governing the Preparation of Joint Army and Navy Basic War Plan—Green No. 3. US National Archives, Records Group 225, NM-43, p. 2.

55 War Plan Green—FORCES, US National Archives, Records Group 225, NM-43, p. 7.

56 *Ibid.*

57 War Plan Green—TIME ORIGINS FOR EXECUTION OF THE PLANS, US National Archives, Records Group 225, NM-43, p. 8.

58 *Ibid.*

59 War Plan Green—THEATERS OF OPERATIONS, COMMAND AND COOPERATION, US National Archives, Records Group 225, NM-43, p. 10.

60 War Plan Green—PASSAGE OF COMMAND, US National Archives, Records Group 225, NM-43, p. 11.

61 Plan for the Occupation and Pacification of Northern Mexico, Memorandum for the Chief of Staff, 25 March, 1918, US National Archives, Records Group 225, NM-43, p. 1-2.

62 Ibid., pp. 2-3.

63 Action in the case of disorder on the Mexican Border, Commanding Officer Fort Ringgold Texas, 11 October 1927, US National Archives, Records Group 225, NM-43, p. 1.

64 War Game of War Plan—GREEN, 17 June 1927, US National Archives, Records Group 165, p. 2.

65 Army War College Session 1915–1916—Study of the Occupation of Tampico, Mexico and Vicinity, Major E. D. Anderson, 6th Cavalry. US National Archives, Records Group 165, p. 2.

66 *Ibid.*

67 *Ibid.*, p. 7.

68 *Ibid.*, pp. 2-3.

69 *Ibid.*, p. 7.

70 *Ibid.*, p. 3.

71 *Ibid.*, p. 7.

72 *Ibid.*, p. 19.

73 *Ibid.*, p. 30.

74 *Ibid.*, pp. 33-37.

75 Memorandum—Plan for the occupation and pacification of Mexico (Green), 25 March 1918, US National Archives, Records Group 165, p. 1.

Chapter Four

1 Trask, David, Library of Congress, The Spanish-American War http://www.loc.gov/rr/hispanic/1898/trask.html

2 Annual report of the Secretary of War, Part 3., United States War Department. United States Government Printing Office (1907), p. 2.

3 War Plan Tan, 1932. US National Archives, Records Group 407, Entry 365, pp. 1-2.

4 *Ibid.*, p. 2.

5 Ibid.

6 *Ibid.*, p. 3.

7 *Ibid.*

8 *Ibid.*, p. 4.

9 *Ibid.*

10 *Ibid.*, p. 5.

11 *Ibid.*

12 *Ibid.*, p. 6.

13 *Ibid.*, p. 7.

14 *Ibid.*, p. 16.

15 *Ibid.*, p. 5.

16 *Ibid.*

17 *Ibid.*, p. 6.

18 *Ibid.*

19 *Ibid.*

20 *Ibid.*, p. 7.

21 *Ibid.*, p. 25.

22 *Ibid.*, p. 7.

23 *Ibid.*, p. 9.

24 *Ibid.*, p. 10.

25 *Ibid.*

26 Basic Plan Tan, Part II, 1932. US National Archives, Records Group 407, Entry 365, p. 1.

27 Basic Plan Tan, Part II, Appendix B, 1932. US National Archives, Records Group 407, Entry 365, pp. 1-2.

28 War Plan Tan, 1932. US National Archives, Records Group 407, Entry 365, p. 16.

29 *Ibid.*

30 War Plan Tan—Appendix B, US National Archives, Records Group 407, Entry 365, p. 2.

31 War Plan Tan, 1932. US National Archives, Records Group 407, Entry 365, p.7.

32 *Ibid.* p. 2.

33 *Ibid.*

34 *Ibid.*, pp. 9-10.

35 *Ibid.*, p. 1.

36 *Ibid.*

Chapter Five

1 War Play Gray—Global Security. http://www.globalsecurity.org/military/ops/war-plan-gray.htm

2 Joint Army and Navy Basic Plan for the Capture and Occupation of the Azores, May 1941, US National Archives, Records Group 270, p. 1.

3 Memorandum for the Chief of Staff, Subject the Azores, 24 January 1941, War Plan Gray, US National Archives, Records Group 165, Entry 365. p. 1.

4 *Ibid.*, pp. 1-2.

5 *Ibid.*, p. 2.

6 *Ibid.*

7 *Ibid.*

8 *Ibid.*, p. 3.

9 Azores, War Plan Gray Files, US National Archives, Records Group 165, Entry 365, p. 1.

10 *Ibid.*

11 *Ibid.*, p. 2.

12 Advantages and Disadvantages of Attempting to Occupy the Azores, 1940. US National Archives, Records Group 165, Entry 365, p. 1.

13 *Ibid.*, p. 2.

14 Plan for the Seizure and Occupation of the Azores, War Plan Gray File, September 1941, US National Archives, Records Group 165, Entry 365, p. 1.

15 Recommended Task Force Organization—Gray. 1941. US National Archives, Records Group 165, Entry 365, p. 1.

16 Plan for the Seizure and Occupation of the Azores, War Plan Gray File, September 1941, US National Archives, Records Group 165, Entry 365, p. 2.

17 *Ibid.*, pp. 2-3.

18 *Ibid.*, p. 3.

19 *Ibid.*

20 *Ibid.*, p. 2.

21 *Ibid.*, p. 3.

22 *Ibid.*, p. 4.

23 *Ibid.*

24 *Ibid.*

25 *Ibid.*, p. 3.

26 Joint Army and Navy Basic Plan for the Capture and Occupation of the Azores, May 1941, US National Archives, Records Group 270, p. 6.

27 Plan for the Seizure and Occupation of the Azores, War Plan Gray File, September 1941, US National Archives, Records Group 165, Entry 365, pp. 4-5.

28 Joint Army and Navy Basic Plan for the Capture and Occupation of the Azores, May 1941, US National Archives, Records Group 270, p. 8.

Chapter Six

1 Memorandum for the A. C. of S., War Plans Division—Estimate of the Situation In China Today. 16 May 1924. US National Archives, Records Group 165, pp. 1-2.

2 *Ibid.*, p. 2.

3 *Ibid.*, pp. 2-3.

4 *Ibid.*, p. 3.

5 *Ibid.*, pp. 4-5.

6 *Ibid.*, p. 5.

7 *Ibid.*, pp. 7-8.

8 Memorandum for the Assistance Chief of Staff, War Plans Division—Considerations Affecting the Employment of United States Army forces in China as contemplated in the Yellow Plan. 14 November, 1929. US National Archives, Records Group 165, p. 1.

9 *Ibid.*

10 *Ibid.*, p. 2.

11 *Ibid.*

12 *Ibid.*

13 Memorandum for the Assistance Chief of Staff, War Plans Division Army Strategical Plan—Yellow, 2 March, 1931, US National Archives, Records Group 165, p. 1.

14 *Ibid.*

15 Land Transportation in China, 17 September 1931, US National Archives, Records Group 165, p. 1.

16 *Ibid.*, pp. 1-2.

17 *Ibid.*, p. 3.

18 War plans related to planned operations—War Plan Yellow, November 1929, US National Archives, Records Group 80, p. 3.

19 Report by Lieutenant Thomas Baxter, Corrections to the War Portfolio on the defenses of the Yangtze River, 12 May 1916, US National Archives, Records Group 80, pp. 1-5.

20 Memorandum for the Assistance Chief of Staff, War Plans Division—Considerations Affecting the Employment of United States Army forces in China as contemplated in the Yellow Plan. 14 November, 1929. US National Archives, Records Group 165, pp. 1-2.

21 *Ibid.*, p. 3.

Chapter Seven

1 Session 1914–1915 - Blue vs Black Series, Army War College Review, 1914. US National Archives, Records Group 165, Stack 370, p. 193.

2 *Ibid.*, pp. 194-195.

3 Hudson, James J. Hostile Skies, (Syracuse University Press: Syracuse New York, 1968), p. 3.

4 Army War College Session 1914–1915—Discussion on Map Problem 33., Lieutenant Colonel C. A. F. Flager, Corps of Engineers, Blue vs Black Series, Army War College Review, 1914. US National Archives, Records Group 165, Stack 370, p. 197.

5 *Ibid.*, pp. 197-200.

6 *Ibid.*, pp. 200-202.

7 *Ibid.*, p. 207.

8 Blue (US) Forces, Blue vs Black Series, Army War College Review, 1914. US National Archives, Records Group 165, Stack 370, p. 13.

9 Black (German) Forces, Blue vs Black Series, Army War College Review, 1914. US National Archives, Records Group 165, Stack 370, p. 194.

10 US Fortifications in Defense of Blue, Blue vs Black Series, Army War College Review, 1914. US National Archives, Records Group 165, Stack 370, pp. 195-196.

11   Army War College Session 1914–1915—Discussion on Map Problem 33., Lieutenant Colonel C. A. F. Flager, Corps of Engineers, Blue vs Black Series, Army War College Review, 1914. US National Archives, Records Group 165, Stack 370, pp. 201-202.

12   *Ibid.*, p. 206.

13   *Ibid.*, p. 202.

14   Army War College Session 1914–1915—Discussion on Map Problem 33., Lieutenant Colonel C. A. F. Flager, Corps of Engineers, Blue vs Black Series, Army War College Review, 1914. US National Archives, Records Group 165, Stack 370, p. 203.

15   *Ibid.*

16   *Ibid.*, pp. 203-204.

17   *Ibid.*, pp. 204-205.

18   *Ibid.*, p. 205.

19   *Ibid.*, p. 206.

20   *Ibid.*, p. 213

21   *Ibid.*, p. 219.

22   *Ibid.*, p. 220.

23   *Ibid.*, pp. 218-222.

24   *Ibid.*, pp. 222-225.

25   *Ibid.*, pp. 225-226.

26   *Ibid.*, p. 236.

27   *Ibid.*, p. 228.

28   *Ibid.*, pp. 228-229.

29   *Ibid.*, p. 210.

30   *Ibid.*, p. 212.

31   *Ibid.*, pp. 212-213.

32   *Ibid.*, p. 214.

33   *Ibid.*, p. 217.

34   *Ibid.*, p. 232.

35   Army War College Session 1914–1915—Discussion on Map Problem 34., Major Munroe McFarland, General Staff, Blue vs Black Series, Army War College Review, 1914. US National Archives, Records Group 165, Stack 370, pp. 236-238.

36   Army War College Session 1914–1915—Discussion on Map Problem 35., Major W. D. Conner, General Staff, Blue vs Black Series, Army War College Review, 1914. US National Archives, Records Group 165, Stack 370, p. 241.

37   *Ibid.*, pp. 241-242.

38   *Ibid.*, p. 242.

39   *Ibid.*

40   *Ibid.*, p. 243.

41   Ibid., pp. 247-252.

42 Army War College Session 1914–1915—Discussion on Map Problem 36., Major W. D. Conner, General Staff, Blue vs Black Series, Army War College Review, 1914. US National Archives, Records Group 165, Stack 370, pp. 256-260.

43 *Ibid.*, p. 264.

Chapter Eight

1 Joint Estimate of the Situation Red-Blue, Red Situation, US National Archives, Records Group 165, p. 1.

2 *Ibid.*, p. 1-4.

3 Joint Estimate of the Situation Red-Blue, Political, US National Archives, Records Group 165, pp. 4-6.

4 *Ibid.*, pp. 7-8.

5 Joint Army and Navy Basic War Plan—Red, US National Archives, Records Group 165, p. 79.

6 Joint Estimate of the Situation Red-Blue, Red War Aims, US National Archives, Records Group 165, p. 9.

7 Joint Army and Navy Basic War Plan—Red, US National Archives, Records Group 165, p. 80.

8 *Ibid.*

9 *Ibid.* pp. 80-81.

10 Joint Estimate of the Situation Red-Blue, Strength and Distribution (Red), US National Archives, Records Group 165, p. 14.

11 *Ibid.*

12 *Ibid.*, p. 19.

13 *Ibid.*, pp. 14-15.

14 *Ibid.*, p. 15.

15 *Ibid.*, pp. 15-16.

16 *Ibid.*, p. 16.

17 *Ibid.*, p. 17.

18 *Ibid.*

19 *Ibid.*

20 *Ibid.*, p. 19.

21 *Ibid.*, p. 18.

22 Joint Estimate of the Situation Red-Blue, Blue Situation Army, US National Archives, Records Group 165, p. 47.

23 *Ibid.*, p. 49.

24 *Ibid.*

25 Joint Estimate of the Situation Red-Blue, War Plan Red, Foreign Policy and External Condition, US National Archives, Records Group 165, p. 39.

26 Joint Estimate of the Situation Red-Blue, Courses of Action Open to Blue, US National Archives, Records Group 165, p. 58.

27 *Ibid.*

28 *Ibid.*

29 *Ibid.*

30 *Ibid.*

31 *Ibid.*, pp. 62-63.

32 *Ibid.*, pp. 64-65.

33 *Ibid.*, p. 82.

34 Joint Army and Navy Basic War Plan—Red, Operations Required, US National Archives, Records Group 165, p. 84.

35 *Ibid.*, p. 83.

36 *Ibid.*, p. 85.

37 Joint Estimate of the Situation Red-Blue, Probable Courses of Action By Red, US National Archives, Records Group 165, pp. 24-25.

38 Joint Estimate of the Situation Red-Blue, Probable Intentions (Red), US National Archives, Records Group 165, p. 28.

39 *Ibid.*

40 Joint Estimate of the Situation Red-Blue, General Conclusions, US National Archives, Records Group 165, p. 55.

Epilogue

1 Op-12-B-6-MaC Joint Rainbow War Plan Summary, US National Archives, Records Group 270, p. 2.

2 Draft of Joint Board Directives for Rainbow Nos., 1, 2, 3, 4, US National Archives, Records Group 270, p. 2.

3 *Ibid.*

4 *Ibid.*

5 *Ibid.*